Chaitanyology:

A Collection of Essays on Śrī Chaitanya

Second (Expanded) Edition

Steven J. Rosen
(Satyarāja Dāsa)

Bookwrights Press
Charlottesville, VA

Copyright © 2025 by Steven J. Rosen (Satyarāja dāsa)
All rights reserved.
No part of this book may be reproduced, stored in a retrieval system, or transmitted in any form by any means, electronic, mechanical, photocopying, recording, or otherwise, without the prior written permission of the publisher.

Published by

Bookwrights Press
Charlottesville, Virginia, USA
www.bookwrightspress.com
publisher@bookwrightspress.com

The translations of Sanskrit and Bengali texts found in this work, often slightly restructured for clarity and context, are primarily based on the work of His Divine Grace A. C. Bhaktivedanta Swami Prabhupāda, Bhānu Swami, Bhumipati dāsa, Kuśakratha dāsa, and Sarvabhāvana dāsa, unless otherwise indicated. Other friends with language skills gave their assistance as well.

ISBN paperback: 978-1-880404-59-1
Cover and text design by Māyāpriya devi dāsi

Bulk pricing available

Dedication

To my mom, Sylvia (1919–2023),

a golden personality,

who left her mortal frame on Gaura Pūrṇimā,

the auspicious appearance day of

Śrī Chaitanya Mahāprabhu

Contents

Introduction 1

1. The Glories of the *Śrī Caitanya-caritāmṛta* 7
2. Śrī Chaitanya's Holy Name 16
3. Śrī Chaitanya and the Six Gosvāmīs 32
4. "I am He": The Unique Secret of Mahāprabhu's Divinity 53
5. Mahāprabhu's Mantras: The primary sound vibrations Śrī Chaitanya 67
6. Śrī Caitanya in Gaya: More Than a Footnote 82
7. The Hare Krishna Mahā-mantra: Its Breadth and Meaning 94
8. Mahāprabhu Meets the Magistrate: A Spiritual Precursor to Gandhi's "Civil Disobedience" Movement 108
9. The Golden Sannyāsī: Śrī Caitanya in the *Mahābhārata* 136
10. Coming Home: Śrī Chaitanya's Journey to Vrindavan 149
11. The Mystery of the Pañca Tattva in Light of the Christian Trinity 168
12. The First Chaitanya Deities 182
13. Sanātana Gosvāmī in Benares: Focusing in on Deity Worship and the Ātmārāma Verse 192
14. Śrī Chaitanya and His Pillar of Ecstasy: The Garuḍa-stambha in the pastimes of the Lord 206

15. Books are the Basis: Śrī Caitanya's Discovery of *Śrī Brahma-saṁhitā* and *Śrī Kṛṣṇa-karṇāmṛta* 222

16. The *Gaura-ganoddeśa-dīpikā*: A Who's Who of Gauḍīya Vaishnavism 239

17. Rūpānuga Vaishnavism: An Inner Dimension of Krishna Consciousness 251

18. Prema-Vilāsa-Vivarta-Mūrti: Śrī Chaitanya as the Embodiment of the Highest Love 279

Afterword 328

Introduction

THIS BOOK IS INTENDED for seekers of all religions and denominations and even for those just curious about the nature of ultimate reality. That said, our guiding light and primary focus, to be sure, will be divine esoterica expressed in Vedic and post-Vedic texts, India's vast scriptural legacy, particularly as understood by proponents of the Gauḍīya Vaishnava tradition.

In fact, we begin our journey with an overview of the tradition's founder, Śrī Chaitanya Mahāprabhu (1486–1533), who is understood to be Krishna (God) himself in the role of his own devotee. We explore his life narrative in relation to the Six Gosvāmīs of Vrindavan, the primary theologians of his school of thought. Equipped with this much philosophical and historical background, the reader is then offered a series of essays elucidating both the more common aspects of the tradition along with its more confidential dimension.

Because Gauḍīya Vaishnavas are followers of Gaura, the Golden One, as we will see below, the tradition has sometimes been called the Golden Path.

In general, people like gold. It represents wealth and prosperity. A golden age refers to an era of goodness and plenty, and such a mythological time period has been acknowledged in Greek, Roman, and Indian cultures. If you have everything, you were born with "a golden spoon in your mouth." The Golden Rule is the epitome of cosmic justice, of fairness: "Do unto others as you would have others do unto you." As the saying goes, "As good as gold."

In India's ancient Krishna tradition, too, we are told of a Golden Avatāra, Gaurāṅga, Śrī Chaitanya Mahāprabhu, and he is considered the best of divine incarnations. In fact, he is said to be both Rādhā and Krishna—the female and male manifestations of divinity—combined, and it doesn't get any better than that. To be more specific, he is of golden hue because, as Krishna, he has taken on Śrī Rādhā's mood and complexion, which is golden. As the scriptures say: *rādhā-bhāva-dyuti suvalitaṁ*. Thus, Chaitanya is both female and male divinity in one, a particularly profound manifestation of the supreme. His golden complexion is emblematic of his intense beauty and esoteric nature.

What's more, he brings with him a snippet of the Golden Age. That is to say, within the darkness of Kali, the age of quarrel and hypocrisy in which we now find ourselves, there is a moment known as Prema-yuga, or the age of love. It is a facsimile of Satya-yuga, a time, millions of years ago, when all beings lived happy and prosperous lives. Mahāprabhu himself initiated this newer Satya age when he appeared in India, some 500 years ago, and all who partake of his process—the chanting of the holy name—can avoid being victimized by the horrors of Kali. Instead, they can bask in the glories of Prema.

Prema, or divine love, is itself compared to gold. The *Caitanya-caritāmṛta* (4.164) tells us, "Lust and love have different characteristics, just as iron and gold have different natures." The text elaborates (4.165): "The desire to gratify one's own senses is *kāma* [lust], but the desire to please the senses of Lord Krishna is *prema* [love].

One might compare lust to the misuse of gold. It can be seen as gold's "bad side," as it were. In the *Śrīmad Bhāgavatam* (1.17.39), we learn that gold can encourage falsity, intoxication, prostitution, envy, and enmity. How can something so pure lead to something so bad?

We might ask the same thing about "love" in the material world. How many countless books and songs have been written about the pains associated with love, about the horrors of being betrayed or deceived, as when one's beloved goes off with another?

The answer, of course, is that, in this world, when love leads to hardship and pain, it is usually not really love at all. It is, rather, lust, or love's grossly materialistic counterpart. As in the *Caitanya-caritāmṛta* verse already mentioned, we can understand the distinction between the two quite simply: when our love is egocentric, focused on our own gratification, it is merely lust—that is to say, it is iron, not gold. And when it is theocentric, focused on God and a spirit of selflessness, it is true love. Indeed, it is gold.

Even in the material sphere, we can see that when we are selfless and giving in our relationships, they bear sweeter fruit. But still we can be exploited. The highest kind of love, then, is love of God. This is the true gold standard, for it takes us out of the world of exploitation and into the realm of dedication, where true love becomes the very fabric of our being: it is expressed towards God directly, and through

Him, to all living entities, who are brothers and sisters under God's fatherhood.

Thus, the Golden Avatāra brings with him a golden process meant to help us distinguish between lust and love, to discern the difference between cheap iron and valuable gold. Simply by chanting the Hare Krishna *mahā-mantra*—Hare Krishna, Hare Krishna, Krishna Krishna, Hare Hare/ Hare Rāma, Hare Rāma, Rāma Rāma, Hare Hare—one can partake of this golden opportunity.

In fact, it is this chanting process that makes this age truly golden. As the *Bhāgavatam* (12.3.51) says: "My dear king, although Kali-yuga is full of faults, there is still one good quality about this age. It is that simply by chanting the holy name of Krishna, one can become free from material bondage and be promoted to the spiritual kingdom."

But chanting, like all other forms of meditation, must be executed in the proper way. The seed of the sacred sound, the tradition tells us, comes through a bona fide preceptor. Thus, His Divine Grace A. C. Bhaktivedanta Swami Prabhupāda (1896–1977), my guru, came to the United States in 1965 and shared the goldmine of the holy name by initiating people into Krishna Consciousness. Through this process, he made people shine like molten gold. Along these lines, the Vaishnava text *Hari-bhakti-vilāsa* (2.12) tells us: "As bell metal can be transformed into gold when treated with mercury, a disciple initiated by a bona fide guru immediately attains the position of a *brāhmaṇa*." But, further, devotees are said to be even more than *brāhmaṇa*—they are said to be God's own.

This identity is not embraced with arrogance. In fact, a true devotee does not think of himself as a devotee at all. Rather, he sees himself as a servant of the servant of the servant of Krishna. In other words, he is the servant of everyone, and this consciousness instills in him the greatest form of humility, wherein the devotee lives to serve others.

In conclusion, then, knowledge of Brahman, spiritual truth, descends into the heart of a sincere disciple through hearing from a self-realized spiritual master and committing to the process that he or she offers. This knowledge and commitment blossoms into divine love, making the disciple golden in every way. It is this that Śrī Chaitanya's movement seeks to share with the world.

A few words about the title: Christology, derived from the words "Christ," referring to Jesus, and "-ology," meaning "the study of," is a branch of Christian theology that explores the person, nature, and role of Jesus Christ, an enterprise that dates back to biblical times. Using this as a basis, Tamal Krishna Goswami (1946-2002), a well-known ISKCON leader, Vaishnava guru, and accomplished scholar, elaborated on the term "Krishnology" during his research at the University of Cambridge. A doctoral student under Julius J. Lipner, Goswami's dissertation, originally titled "High Krishnology," was eventually published posthumously as *A Living Theology of Krishna Bhakti: Essential Teachings of A. C. Bhaktivedanta Swami Prabhupāda* (New York: Oxford University Press, 2012). It is with the backdrop of both

Christology and Krishnology that I title the present work Chaitanyology, hoping to provide insights into the life and thought of the Golden Avatāra.

In fact, the volume you now hold in your hands is essentially a collection of in-depth essays on Śrī Chaitanya, and while some of these papers have been published elsewhere, such as in *Back to Godhead* magazine and the *Journal of Vaishnava Studies*—several readers have asked me to put these articles together in one volume, for easy access—others will be appearing in print form for the first time.

Nonetheless, these essays—whether previously published or not—are intended to help the reader dive deeply into the substance of *bhakti*, Krishna Consciousness, also known as the Gauḍīya Vaishnava tradition. Because some of these essays have appeared in various places, intended for various audiences, spelling may vary from article to article; pronouns for God may be capitalized or not; and certain rudimentary facts may be repeated several times over, depending on the audience I was trying to reach at the time. This repetition, in any case, will help drive certain points home.

But, overall, each article focuses on a different aspect of the Gauḍīya tradition, with the goal of helping readers understand what I have learned from my teachers after some fifty years of study and practice. May you all receive from this book far more than I have to offer. In other words, may the insights of my teachers engulf your soul.

One

The Glories of the *Śrī Caitanya-caritāmṛta*

Why this monumental work on Lord Caitanya's life and teachings is held in the highest esteem.

THE RELIGIOUS TEXTS of the world are said to be on different levels for people at various stages of spiritual progress. Śrīla Prabhupāda compared the native scriptures of India to an unabridged dictionary, and scriptures such as the Bible and the Koran to abridged dictionaries, being less comprehensive. This is not a mere value judgment but an objective assessment.

While the Bible and the Koran tell us that God is great and that His kingdom should be our desired destination, the Vedic texts tell us not only this but also just how great He is, with more details than the human mind can accommodate. The Vedic literature also describes the various levels of His kingdom with such graphic particularity that it all but takes you there. These ancient wisdom texts from India thus augment the information given in other religious traditions.

But even within this excellent literature, one finds gradation, with some texts overshadowing others. Spiritual authorities in the Gauḍīya Vaiṣṇava tradition, originating with

Śrī Caitanya Mahāprabhu, say that *Bhagavad-gītā*, *Śrīmad-Bhāgavatam* (*Bhāgavata Purāṇa*), and *Śrī Caitanya-caritāmṛta* are the best. And among these, *Caitanya-caritāmṛta* stands supreme.

This superlative text is known in the International Society for Krishna Consciousness (ISKCON) as the post-graduate study of spiritual learning. In other words, as one properly advances in Kṛṣṇa consciousness, this work offers detailed information, secrets, and transcendental joy not available anywhere else, facilitating further advancement on the spiritual path. As Śrīla Prabhupāda writes:

> Actually, the *Caitanya-caritāmṛta* is not intended for the novice, for it is the postgraduate study of spiritual knowledge. Ideally, one begins with the *Bhagavad-gītā* and advances through Śrīmad-*Bhāgavatam* to the *Caitanya-caritāmṛta*. Although all these great scriptures are on the same absolute level, for the sake of comparative study the *Caitanya-caritāmṛta* is considered to be on the highest platform. (Introduction to Śrī *Caitanya-caritāmṛta*).

Rich and Complex

The *Caitanya-caritāmṛta* (Cc) resists summarization. Its size is formidable, and its subjects the most complex and rich in the history of religion. Its central theme is the life and teachings of Śrī Caitanya Mahāprabhu (1486–1533), who is Lord Kṛṣṇa in the mood of His greatest devotee, Śrīmatī Rādhārāṇī. In explicating Śrī Caitanya's life, the text moves through various levels of spiritual knowledge, ranging from the most fundamental to the most exalted. We learn everything from the soul's essential nature to the soul's relationship with God; from basic concepts of divinity to the supreme forms of Rādhā and Kṛṣṇa and how to relate with Them in a mood of divine love (*prema*).

The text was completed in 1615 by Kṛṣṇadāsa Kavirāja Gosvāmī (1496–?), a senior disciple of Raghunātha Dāsa Gosvāmī and overall student of the highly revered Six Gosvāmīs of Vrindavan. Clearly, Kavirāja Gosvāmī was exceptionally learned and devoted, as is evident from his extant works: *Caitanya-caritāmṛta*, *Govinda-līlāmṛta*, and *Sāraṅga-raṅgada* (a commentary on *Śrī Kṛṣṇa-karṇāmṛta*). As opposed to his other two texts, written in Sanskrit, the Cc is primarily in Bengali, though a large number of quoted and original Sanskrit verses are included as well.

According to Vaiṣṇava scholar Brijbasi Dasa,

> In the *Caitanya-caritāmṛta* Śrīla Kṛṣṇadāsa Kavirāja Gosvāmī has quoted more than 90 different sources (among them he quoted *Śrīmad-Bhāgavatam* the most – 404 times). The book consists of 62 chapters ("*paricchedas*") divided into three parts ("*līlās*") and 11,555 verses, out of which 97 Sanskrit ślokas were composed by the author himself, 933 Sanskrit verses were quoted by him from many different sources, and the remaining 10,525 Bengali verses ("*payāras*") were, of course, composed by Śrīla Kavirāja Gosvāmī [himself].

In the 1970s Śrīla Prabhupāda gave the Cc to the western world by publishing a deluxe seventeen-volume English edition, complete with original text, word-for-word transliteration, translation, and commentary (based on the *Amṛta-pravāha-bhāṣya* and *Anubhāṣya* commentaries of Bhaktivinoda Ṭhākura and Śrīla Bhaktisiddhānta Sarasvatī, respectively). His edition included award-winning paintings, executed by his own disciples under his direction, in which various incidents from Lord Caitanya's biographical narrative virtually make the text come to life. This Bhaktivedanta Book Trust (BBT) edition, translated into numerous languages, has been distributed in mass quantities worldwide.

The Best of Books

When Śrīla Prabhupāda came West by ship in 1965, it was the Cc that gave him solace. His diary written during the voyage does not mention the *Gītā* or the *Bhāgavatam*. His preference was clear. As he records in the *Jaladuta Diary*,

> Till 4 o'clock afternoon we have crossed over the Atlantic Ocean for twenty-four hours. The whole day was clear and almost smooth. I am taking my food regularly and got some strength to struggle. There is slight lurching of the ship and I am feeling slight headache also. But I am struggling and the nectarine of life is *Sri Chaitanya Charitamrita* the source of my all vitality.

On the following day, there is a similar entry:

> Today the ship is plying very smoothly. I feel today better. But I am feeling separation from Sri Vrindaban and my Lords Sri Govinda, Gopinath, Radha Damodar. The only solace is *Sri Chaitanya Charitamrita* in which I am tasting the nectarine of Lord Chaitanya's Leela.

Prabhupāda's preference echoes that of his guru, Śrīla Bhaktisiddhānta Sarasvatī:

> *Śrī Caitanya-caritāmṛta* was Śrīla Bhaktisiddhānta Sarasvatī's favorite book. He regarded it as a matchless devotional work and the most important biography of Caitanya Mahāprabhu, because it succinctly yet definitively imparts His teachings and gives significantly more insights into the nature of the Lord's highest ecstasies than do *Śrī Caitanya-bhāgavata* or other narratives. Śrīla Bhaktisiddhānta Sarasvatī himself read both *Śrī Caitanya-caritāmṛta* and *Śrī Caitanya-bhāgavata* 108 times and told others to do likewise. Especially in his later life, whenever he got time he generally read *Śrī Caitanya-caritāmrta*. (Bhakti Vikāsa Swami, *Śrī Bhaktisiddhānta Vaibhava*, Vol. 1, pp. 277–278)

An interesting story in the life of Bhaktisiddhānta Sarasvatī Ṭhākura highlights his preference for the Cc, and even briefly explains why he viewed it as a superior text.

One day, while in the presence of Rājarṣi Śaradendu Nārāyaṇa Rāya, then Chairman of Philosophy at the University of Lahore in Agastya Villa, Darjeeling, Sarasvatī Ṭhākura turned to him and asked, "If you were forced to live without the association of devotees, but could keep just one spiritual text with you, which text would you choose?"

Without missing a beat, Rājarṣi Śaradendu replied, "*Śrīmad Bhagavad-gītā*." By way of explaining his verdict, he cited four verses from the *Gīta-māhātmya*, a text traditionally attributed to Śaṅkarācārya. Rājarṣi Śaradendu thought texts 4 and 7 were particularly persuasive:

> "One should attentively and regularly hear and read *Bhagavad-gītā*. What is the need to read any other Vedic

> literature? This one book is sufficient, since it contains the essence of the Vedic literature, having emanated from the lotus mouth of Śrī Kṛṣṇa." (text 4)
>
> "Śrī Kṛṣṇa's divine song (*Bhagavad-gītā*) is the topmost scripture among all holy scriptures." (text 7)

What more needed to be said? But Sarasvatī Ṭhākura wanted him to go deeper. In fact, using the same words that Caitanya Mahāprabhu uttered when discussing the goal of life with Rāmānanda Rāya – "speak further" (*āge kaha āra*) – the Ṭhākura expressed his dissatisfaction with Rājarṣi Śaradendu's answer.

Knowing full well that Sarasvatī Ṭhākura was pushing him forward for his own good, Rājarṣi Śaradendu now offered a more considered response: "*Śrīmad-Bhāgavatam*."

He then cited several verses to support his conclusion, including 1.1.2, 1.1.3, 1.7.7, 12.13.15, as well as a verse from the *Garuḍa Purāṇa* and one from the *Caitanya-bhāgavata*.

The quoted verses make clear that the *Bhāgavatam* is the most sublime scripture of all, revealing the highest knowledge of the Absolute Truth. Rājarṣi Śaradendu's carefully chosen texts indicate that "there is no need to hear or follow any scripture other than *Śrīmad-Bhāgavatam*," and that "simply by aural reception of this text, devotion, or *bhakti*, arises in one's heart, extinguishing the fire of lamentation, illusion, and fear."

Rājarṣi Śaradendu concluded by saying, "There are many other verses in various scriptures that similarly glorify *Śrīmad-Bhāgavatam*. One can therefore conclude that this text is the topmost among all Vedic scriptures. In my opinion, there is no scripture superior to *Śrīmad-Bhāgavatam*."

With a knowing smile, Sarasvatī Ṭhākura again said, "*āge kaha āra* –'speak further.'"

But Rājarṣi Śaradendu replied, "I am unqualified to say anything beyond this."

Sarasvatī Ṭhākura then spoke, offering conclusive words as a world *ācārya*:

> *Śrī Caitanya-caritāmṛta* is the most glorious scripture. If I were alive to witness the entire world being submerged in water at the time of its destruction (*mahā-pralaya*), I would preserve no other scripture than *Śrī Caitanya-caritāmṛta*; I would protect it by keeping it on my chest while swimming. The void left by the annihilation of all the Vedic literatures would be filled simply by the existence of *Śrī Caitanya-caritāmṛta.*
>
> In order to gloriously reveal the extraordinary and divine character of Śrīman Mahāprabhu, the author of *Śrī Caitanya-caritāmṛta*, Śrīla Kṛṣṇadāsa Kavirāja Gosvāmī, has described *nityānanda-tattva*, *śrī-guru-tattva*, *kṛṣṇa-tattva*, *rādhā-tattva*, and *advaita-tattva*, as well as Śrī Kṛṣṇa's special manifestation as *pañca-tattva.*
>
> In narrating the pastimes of Rathayātrā and the cleaning of the Guṇḍicā temple (*guṇḍicā-mandira-mārjana*), Śrīla Kavirāja Gosvāmī has established the glories of Vraja, the Vrajavāsīs, their surrender and service mood to Śrī Kṛṣṇa, and the superiority of the Vraja-gopīs among all the devotees of Śrī Kṛṣṇa.
>
> Through the narration of Rāya Rāmānanda Saṁvāda, he has presented the essence of all the Vedic literature by way of a comparative and progressive analysis of the significant instructions of all the various scriptures, and has established the most astonishing glories of *parakīya-rasa.*
>
> In Rūpa-śikṣā and Sanātana-śikṣā, he has provided analyses of the subtlest aspects of *sambandha-*, *abhidheya-*,

and *prayojana-tattvas* [i.e., the way, the means, and the goal]. Through his narration of the pastimes of Nāmācārya Śrīla Haridāsa Ṭhākura and others, he has established the splendid glories of Harināma [i.e., the importance of chanting the holy name of the Lord].

In describing Śrīman Mahāprabhu's discussions with Śrī Sārvabhauma Bhaṭṭācārya and Śrī Prakāśānanda Sarasvatī, he has recorded the Lord's thorough rejection of the principles of Advaitavāda (non-dualism) and His establishment of the doctrine of Acintya-bhedābheda-tattva (inconceivable, simultaneous oneness and difference) by citing references from *śāstra*.

Moreover, the way Śrīla Kavirāja Gosvāmī has described the multifarious pastimes of Śrīman Mahāprabhu, in which the Lord has imparted teachings through His exemplary behavior and conduct, is extremely beneficial for the living entities in this Kali-yuga.

Abiding by the *sūtra* "*mitaṁ ca sāraṁ ca vaco hi vāgmitā*–essential truth spoken concisely is true eloquence," Śrīla Kṛṣṇadāsa Kavirāja Gosvāmī has very concisely explained the essence of all the scriptures in *Śrī Caitanya-caritāmṛta*.

Qualifications to Study the Cc

Thus, both Śrīla Prabhupāda and his guru consider *Caitanya-caritāmṛta* the best of books, and although it contains extremely advanced subjects, one can approach it and enter its understanding as long as one observes an important caveat: One must study under the direction of a bona fide spiritual master.

Śrīla Prabhupāda's edition, with elaborate purports, or devotional explanations, allows readers – perhaps for the first time, especially in the western world – to absorb the mysteries of this esoteric text. Prabhupāda urged,

> So study this *Caitanya-caritāmṛta*. Now we have got this English edition, very elaborately described, following the footsteps of our Guru Mahārāja, Bhaktisiddhānta Sarasvatī Ṭhākura Prabhupāda. So there is no such edition of *Caitanya-caritamrta*, very elaborately described. But it can be understood by the advanced student. . . . Advanced means at least one should understand that Kṛṣṇa is the Supreme Personality of Godhead. If you simply understand these two words, that Krsna is the Supreme Personality of Godhead, then you are advanced. It is not very difficult. (Lecture on *Śrī Caitanya-caritāmṛta*, *Ādi-līlā* 1.1 – Mayapur, March 25, 1975)

In the concluding verse of *Śrī Caitanya-caritāmṛta*, Kavirāja Gosvāmī articulates his indebtedness to his readers: "*Śrī Caitanya-caritāmṛta* is filled with the activities of Śrī Caitanya Mahāprabhu, who is the Supreme Personality of Godhead Himself. It invokes all good fortune and destroys everything inauspicious. If one tastes the nectar of *Śrī Caitanya-caritāmṛta* with faith and love, I become like a bumblebee tasting the honey of transcendental love from his lotus feet."

Two

Śrī Chaitanya's Holy Name: The Open Secret of the Krishna Consciousness Movement

"The Western devotees are very sincerely chanting the holy names of Śrī Caitanya Mahāprabhu and His associates: *śrī-kṛṣṇa-caitanya prabhu-nityānanda śrī-advaita gadādhara śrīvāsādi-gaura-bhakta-vṛnda*. By the mercy of Śrī Caitanya Mahāprabhu and His associates, people are being purified and their consciousness directed from māyā [illusion] to Kṛṣṇa [reality]."

—Śrīla Prabhupāda, *Caitanya-caritāmṛta* Madhya 16.175, purport

PEOPLE IN GENERAL HAVE heard of the Hare Krishna movement, known more formally as the International Society for Krishna Consciousness (ISKCON). Some are even aware of Śrī Krishna, the Supreme Personality of Godhead, even if misconceptions about His nature and form run amok.[1] But few have even heard of Śrī Chaitanya Mahāprabhu (1486–1534), the form of Krishna who manifests in the mood of His own perfect devotee. This lacuna is especially concerning: Śrī Chaitanya is actually at the center of the Hare Krishna Movement, which arose in His wake some 500 years ago. The entire lineage is based on His personality, experience, and teaching, and on the efforts and scholarship of His immediate followers.[2]

Moreover, while devotees of the Krishna Consciousness Movement are known for the chanting of the Hare Krishna *mahā-mantra, Hare Krishna Hare Krishna, Krishna Krishna Hare Hare/Hare Rāma Hare Rāma, Rāma Rāma Hare Hare* — and while this chanting is indeed the cornerstone of our everyday practice — we chant Śrī Chaitanya's names as well, and that as a daily practice. In fact, an argument can be made that the name of Chaitanya is in some ways even more powerful than Krishna's, a point to which we will later return, and that unless one approaches Krishna through Chaitanya, evoking Chaitanya's holy name and the methods He lovingly bestowed on the world, the Supreme Lord will likely remain far, far away.[3] This article, then, will be about the primacy of Chaitanya and His name in the Krishna Consciousness movement.

"Krishna Consciousness"

The phrase "Krishna Consciousness," which is the name Śrīla Prabhupāda gave to his society in 1966, is derived from Śrī Chaitanya's *sannyāsa* name, "Krishna Chaitanya," which literally means "Krishna consciousness." There are, of course, alternate Sanskrit derivations for this phrase. For example, in his book *Journey to Self-Discovery*, Śrīla Prabhupāda tells us, "Rūpa Gosvāmī writes, *kṛṣṇa-bhakti-rasa-bhāvitā matiḥ krīyatāṁ yadi kuto 'pi labhyate.* I have translated the words Kṛṣṇa consciousness from *kṛṣṇa-bhakti-rasa-bhāvitā.* Here, Rūpa Gosvāmī advises, 'If Kṛṣṇa consciousness is available, please purchase it immediately. Don't delay.' It is a very nice thing."[4]

But tracing the term "Krishna consciousness" to "Śrī Krishna Chaitanya" is in a sense more immediate. That is to say, the word *chaitanya* means "consciousness," which is the symptom of the soul, and *krishna* refers to God, or "the all-attractive one."[5] In this way, the name Krishna Chaitanya directly points us toward Krishna Consciousness. Thus, chanting Śrī Chaitanya's name faithfully will grant the highest levels of spiritual realization.

For the followers of Chaitanya Mahāprabhu who were contemporaneous with Him, the power of Chaitanya's name became particularly evident immediately after His *sannyāsa* ceremony—His renunciation was a pivotal act in His earthly līlā, underlining the mood of what would become the Gauḍīya lineage. In *Chaitanya-bhāgavata*, Śrīla Vṛndāvaṇadāsa Ṭhākura, Śrī Chaitanya's first biographer, describes the pastime of the Lord's *sannyāsa* initiation along with His receiving the name, "Krishna Chaitanya," highlighting its translation as "Krishna consciousness":

> Madhya 28.169–176: The magnanimous Keśava Bhāratī then began to think of a name to give the Lord. "I cannot find such a Vaiṣṇava in the fourteen worlds. This is my conviction. Therefore I will give a name that is not found anywhere, then my desire will be fulfilled. Although the disciple of a Bhāratī should be named Bhāratī, that name is not appropriate for Him."
>
> As that fortunate, topmost *sannyāsī* was thinking like this, Śuddhā Sarasvatī, the transcendental goddess of learning, appeared on his tongue. The titles used by each class of person within a *sampradāya* (community) are accepted along with the person's name in that *sampradāya*, but in this case Śrī Gaurasundara [Chaitanya] did not receive the title of Bhāratī from Keśava Bhāratī.

By the influence of pure devotional service, the goddess of transcendental knowledge appeared on the tongue of Bhāratī during Mahāprabhu's name-giving ceremony. Selecting the suitable name, the pure-hearted Keśava Bhāratī placed his hand on the chest of the Lord and spoke.

"The goddess of material knowledge is known as Duṣṭā Sarasvatī. When statements that inspire service to the Supreme Lord are spoken, the goddess of learning remains engaged in the service of the Lord. You have induced the people of the world to chant the name of Kṛṣṇa, and by inaugurating the movement of *saṅkīrtana,* You have awakened people's consciousness."

Since the Lord made the arrangement for chanting the names of Kṛṣṇa while introducing the materially intoxicated people of the world to Kṛṣṇa, Keśava Bhāratī awarded Him the name "Śrī Kṛṣṇa Caitanya." The consciousness of people throughout the entire world of sense gratification was awakened. Previously they had been indifferent to the Supreme Lord. Śrī Kṛṣṇa Caitanya personally awarded all living entities the qualification to hear the fact that Śrī Kṛṣṇa Himself is Śrī Caitanya. "Therefore Your name will be Śrī Kṛṣṇa Caitanya. Because of You, everyone will become fortunate."[6]

The potency of Śrī Chaitanya's name, as given Him at this initiation ceremony, is again laid bare in *Bhakti-ratnākara*, Second Wave, texts 37-43:

Gaṅgādhara Bhaṭṭācārya, the father of Śrīnivāsācārya, was present at the time of Mahāprabhu's hair cutting [during the *sannyāsa* initiation]. He could not control himself and cried bitterly until he fainted on the ground. By the wish of Prabhu [Caitanya], he regained his senses after some time.

> Mahāprabhu was offered the name Śrī Kṛṣṇa Caitanya and when that name entered the ears of the brahmin Gaṅgādhara he began to utter it repeatedly while simultaneously crying. He could no longer stay at Kantakanagara [Katwa] and ran to the banks of the Ganges like a madman. He lost all interest in bathing or eating and simply repeated the name of Caitanya.[7]

When properly chanted under the guidance of a pure devotee, and with the benefit of one's inner spiritual evolution over many lifetimes, the name is intoxicating, as we see above in the example of Gaṅgādhara Bhaṭṭācārya, bringing practitioners to the stage of pure love of God. Śrīla Prabhupāda writes: "Krishna consciousness means the original consciousness; 'I am Krishna's. I am God's, part and parcel of God.' At the present moment, being illusioned by different material designations, we are thinking: 'I am American,' 'I am Indian,' 'I am a *brahmana* (teacher),' 'I am a *shudra* (laborer),' 'I am this,' 'I am that.' These are all designations. And Krishna consciousness means, 'I am Krishna's.' *'Aham brahmasmi* (I am spirit).' *'So 'ham.'*... 'I am an eternal servant of Krishna.'. This is the consciousness we need to awaken. That is the prime objective of human life."[8]

It is to be remembered that Krishna and Chaitanya are nondifferent, and that Chaitanya is a form of Krishna Himself in the highest throes of divine love. Their nondifference is stated throughout Gauḍīya scriptures but is especially highlighted by Śrīla Jīva Gosvāmī in his Sarva-samvādinī commentary on *Tattva-sandarbha* (1):

> *tad etad-āvirbhāvatvaṁ tasya svayam eva viśeṣaṇa-dvārā vyanakti, kṛṣṇa-varṇam, kṛṣṇety etau varṇau yatra yasmin śrī-kṛṣṇa-caitanya-deva-nāmni*

śrī-kṛṣṇatvābhivyañjakaṁ kṛṣṇeti varṇa-yugalaṁ prayuktam astīty arthaḥ.

"This very verse reveals that Śrī Gaura [Chaitanya] is in fact an appearance of Śrī Kṛṣṇa by using the descriptive phrase *kṛṣṇa-varṇam*. In this phrase the occurrence of the two syllables *kṛṣ-ṇa* in the name Śrī Kṛṣṇa Caitanya-deva suggests that He is Kṛṣṇa Himself." (translation by Gopīparaṇadhana dāsa)

This same explanation is found in the BBT's commentary on *Śrīmad Bhāgavatam* 11.5.32, which is based on Śrīla Prabhupāda's purport to *Caitanya-caritāmṛta* Ādi 5.32: "Śrīla Jīva Gosvāmī explains that *kṛṣṇa-varṇam* means Śrī Kṛṣṇa Caitanya. *Kṛṣṇa-varṇam* and Kṛṣṇa Caitanya are equivalent. The name Kṛṣṇa appears with both Lord Kṛṣṇa and Lord Caitanya Kṛṣṇa." That is to say, the divine name belongs to both Śrī Krishna and Śrī Krishna Chaitanya. As we will see, this becomes particularly significant with Mahāprabhu's profound prediction: "My name" will be chanted in every town and village of the world.

"Every Town and Village"

Śrī Chaitanya's famous prediction in the *Chaitanya-bhāgavata* (Antya 4.126) is known by all learned Gauḍīya Vaishnavas:

Pṛthivīte āche yata nagarādi grāma sarvatra pracāra haibe mora nāma

"In every town and village of the world, the chanting of My name will be heard."

In Śrīla Prabhupāda's translation, *mora nāma* clearly refers to "My name," which, on the face of it, would refer to the name of Śrī Chaitanya, since it is He who is speaking.[9]And yet, since Krishna and Chaitanya are one, the phrase "My name" can take on a double meaning, and the tradition indeed interprets it in that way: The verse can refer to the worldwide unfurling of the name "Krishna" as well.[10]

And Prabhupāda makes it clear: "Lord Chaitanya Mahāprabhu," Prabhupāda writes, "predicted that both His glorious names and the Hare Krishna *mahā-mantra* would be broadcast in all the towns and villages of the world. Śrīla Bhaktivinoda Ṭhākura and Śrīla Bhaktisiddhānta Sarasvatī Prabhupāda desired to fulfill this great prediction, and we are following in their footsteps." (*Srimad Bhagavatam* 4.22.42, purport) Or further, "*Prithivite ache yata nagaradi grama.* Chaitanya Mahaprabhu's prediction: 'In as many towns and villages are there on the surface of the globe, everywhere this Hare Krishna *mantra,* or Lord Chaitanya's name, will be celebrated.' That is being done." (Lecture, Hyderabad, November 23, 1972)

Thus, both readings are correct. For academic confirmation, I asked Professor Abhishek Ghosh, a Bengali Vaishnava scholar, to explain this double meaning in terms of the verse itself. He referred to it as a "playful simultaneous narration" and can thus mean either one: "Both meanings are correct," he added. "'My name' and 'the names I love and chant' (mora in this case is an endearing reference to the names he loves) — this gives way to purposeful dual meaning. It's a simpler Bengali version that resembles *śleṣa* poetry. In Sanskrit, *śleṣa* is a literary device by which two meanings are expressed by a single word or verse. That's the sort of implied meaning here."[11]

In conclusion, then, "My name" can be viewed in either way: One may understand the words "My name" to mean the name is His possession, i.e., the name belongs to Him as His property, as it were, because of His radical and loving attachment to it, His exceeding affection for it, and His constant chanting of it, and so on. Alternatively, one may understand "My name" to indicate one of the proper nouns that refers to Him as a unique individual. Both are correct interpretations, though the latter has pride of place, and this is why Śrīla Prabhupāda translates it in that way.

Pañca Tattva *Mahā-mantra*

As stated, devotees chant Mahāprabhu's name every day, largely in the form of the Pañca Tattva mantra, a traditional prayer revealed by Śrīla Prabhupāda shortly after establishing his movement in 1966.[12] The "Pañca Tattva" refers to the Lord in five features, as manifested 500 years ago: Krishna manifested Himself as a devotee (Śrī Chaitanya), an expansion of a devotee (Śrī Nityānanda), an incarnation of a devotee (Śrī Advaita Ācārya), a pure devotee (Śrī Śrīvāsa), and a devotional energy (Śrī Gadādhara), as expressed in the *Caitanya-caritāmṛta* (Ādi 7.6).

Of course, the notion of the Pañca Tattva predates the *Caitanya-caritāmṛta*. The concept of Śrī Chaitanya in five features is an eternal spiritual principle, but it appears in history in the following way: The earliest reference to it is said to be in Svarūpa Dāmodara Gosvāmī's no-longer-extant work, *Gaura-tattva-nirūpaṇa*, which was probably written during Śrī Caitanya's manifest pastimes or soon thereafter.

Although there is scholarly debate about the authenticity of this book, Kavi Karṇapūra's *Gaura-gaṇoddeśa-dīpikā* (9) does indeed credit Svarūpa Dāmodara for systematizing the doctrine in the earliest days of the Gauḍīya tradition.

Various Gauḍīya lineages articulate the *Caitanya-caritāmṛta*'s famous formulation of the mantra: *śrī-caitanya, nityānanda, advaita—tina jana, śrīvāsa-gadādhara-ādi yata bhakta-gaṇa:* "While chanting the Pañca Tattva *mahā-mantra*, one must chant the names of Śrī Caitanya, Nityānanda, Advaita, Gadādhara and Śrīvāsa with their many devotees. This is the process." (Cc. Ādi 7.169). ISKCON's version is a variation on this mantra. Although Śrīla Prabhupāda wanted the devotees to begin each *kīrtana* by chanting the Pañca Tattva mantra, he didn't want us to chant it many times, and to instead give emphasis to the Hare Krishna *mahā-mantra*. Prabhupāda's disciple Harikeśa writes:

> My personal experience with Prabhupada began when I was his servant for a while in July of 1971. At that time he had described to me in his room that the chanting of the Panca Tattva *maha-mantra* was much more powerful than the *hare krsna mantra*. I immediately asked him that since this is so, then why don't we chant some rounds of this *mantra* after finishing our 16 rounds of the *hare krsna mantra* each day? Prabhupada replied that we should not do so since Lord Caitanya came just to show us how to worship Lord Krsna and that the Lord wanted us to chant the *hare krsna mantra* and therefore we should follow His advice and example. Therefore he later restricted the chanting of this *mantra* in *kirtan* to only three times.[13]

In other words, though there is a certain logic to chanting the names of Mahāprabhu in abundance, since they are supremely powerful, Śrīla Prabhupāda advises that we instead follow the practices and methods of the ācāryas, for these are time-tested—shown to be reliable—and will work for all sincere practitioners. Regarding the power of the Pañca Tattva mantra, as well as that of the various names of Mahāprabhu and His associates in general, we may observe the following: "Whether he is offensive or inoffensive, anyone who even now chants *śrī-kṛṣṇa-caitanya prabhu-nityānanda* is immediately overwhelmed with ecstasy, and tears fill his eyes." (Cc Ādi 8.22) Or "If one only chants, with some slight faith, the holy names of Lord Caitanya and Nityānanda, very quickly he is cleansed of all offenses. Thus as soon as he chants the Hare Kṛṣṇa *mahā-mantra*, he feels the ecstasy of love for God." (Cc Ādi 8.31) It is to be understood that "His name, Krishna Chaitanya, is all-auspicious to the world. Everything about Him—His name, form, and qualities—is unparalleled." (Cc Madhya 17.113)

Even the greatest sinners can attain perfection by chanting the names of Mahāprabhu, even if they do so with undisguised malice: "Jagāi and Mādhāi had but one fault—they were addicted to sinful activity. However, volumes of sinful activity can be burned to ashes simply by a dim reflection of the chanting of Your holy name. Jagāi and Mādhāi uttered Your holy name by way of blaspheming You. Fortunately, that holy name became the cause of their deliverance." (Cc Madhya 1.194-195)

This should not be viewed as spectacular hyperbole. The greatest of *ācāryas* have told us about the nectar of Śrī Chaitanya's various names. Indeed, chanting the name "Gaurāṅga" is considered the equivalent of chanting the names of Rādhā and Krishna. Śrīla Prabhupāda writes in his purport to Caitanya-caritāmṛta Antya 2.31: "Śrīla Bhaktivinoda Ṭhākura explains the Gaura-gopāla mantra in his *Amṛta-pravāha-bhāṣya*. Worshipers of Śrī Gaurasundara [Chaitanya] accept the four syllables *gau-ra-aṅ-ga* as the Gaura mantra, but pure worshipers of Rādhā and Kṛṣṇa accept the four syllables rā-dhā kṛṣ-ṇa as the Gaura-gopāla mantra. However, Vaiṣṇavas consider Śrī Caitanya Mahāprabhu nondifferent from Rādhā-Kṛṣṇa *(śrī-kṛṣṇa-caitanya rādhā-kṛṣṇa nahe anya)*. Therefore, one who chants the mantra *'gaurāṅga'* and one who chants the names of Rādhā and Kṛṣṇa are on the same level."

Śrīla Prabhupāda emphasizes this point again and again. In his explanation of the Bengali song, "Gaurāṅga Bolite Habe" (Los Angeles, January 9, 1969), he says: "As soon as one will chant the name of Shri Krishna Chaitanya, there will be shivering. This is the first symptom that one is getting advanced in the perfectional stage of Krishna consciousness. So Narottama dasa Thakura says, *gaurāṅga bolite habe pulaka śarīre.* He's expecting [...] Although he was a great *acharya,* still, he was expecting, 'When that stage will come?'" We should all anticipate such a stage, and should fervently chant with feeling to Śrī Chaitanya and Śrī Śrī Rādhā-Krishna to attain it.

Conclusion

Earlier in this essay, the reader will have found a statement about Śrī Chaitanya's name as surpassing that of even Krishna. This may seem like an extreme position, given that Krishna is God Himself. Yet we have also shown that there is an interchangeability between the two, and that Śrī

Chaitanya is in fact Krishna in His most intense mood of divine love. Thus, among all the names of Krishna, which far surpass those of other manifestations of God, the names of Chaitanya stand supreme. Here is evidence from two of the greatest Vaishnava luminaries of all time:

> Jagannātha dāsa Bābājī Mahārāja spoke as follows: "Kṛṣṇa is the avatāra of Dvāpara-yuga. Gaura is the *avatāra* of Kali-yuga. We should chant the name and the *kīrtanas* of the *avatāra* in Whose age we live, just as we sing the praises of the king in whose kingdom we live. You should not forget Gaura for He is even more benevolent and merciful than Kṛṣṇa. Kṛṣṇa is just like a just ruler who takes into account your offenses in His administration of justice. Gaura does not take into account your offenses. While Kṛṣṇa is more interested in the dispensation of justice, Gaura is more interested in the dispensation of mercy. From this point of view, *Gaura-kīrtana* is also more useful than *Kṛṣṇa-kīrtana. Gaura-kīrtana* is, for example, *śrī kṛṣṇa caitanya prabhu nityānanda, śrī advaita gadādhara śrīvāsādī gaura bhaktavṛnda.*"[14]
>
> Śrīla Prabhupāda confirms: "Śrīla Bhaktisiddhānta Sarasvatī Ṭhākura remarks in this connection that if one takes shelter of Lord Śrī Caitanya Mahāprabhu and Nityānanda, follows Their instructions to become more tolerant than the tree and humbler than the grass, and in this way chants the holy name of the Lord, very soon he achieves the platform of transcendental loving service to the Lord, and tears appear in his eyes. There are offenses to be considered in chanting the Hare Kṛṣṇa *mahā-mantra*, but there are no such considerations in chanting the names of Gaura-Nityānanda. Therefore, if one chants the Hare Kṛṣṇa *mahā-mantra* but his life is still full of sinful activities, it will be very difficult for him

> to achieve the platform of loving service to the Lord. But if in spite of being an offender one chants the holy names of Gaura-Nityānanda, he is very quickly freed from the interactions of his offenses. Therefore, one should first approach Lord Caitanya and Nityānanda, or worship Guru-Gaurāṅga, and then come to the stage of worshiping Rādhā-Kṛṣṇa. ... It should be noted in this connection that the holy names of Lord Kṛṣṇa and Gaurasundara are both identical with the Supreme Personality of Godhead. Therefore one should not consider one name to be more potent than the other. Considering the position of the people of this age, however, the chanting of Śrī Caitanya Mahāprabhu's name is more essential than the chanting of the Hare Kṛṣṇa *mahā-mantra* because Śrī Caitanya Mahāprabhu is the most magnanimous incarnation and His mercy is very easily achieved. Therefore one must first take shelter of Śrī Caitanya Mahāprabhu by chanting *śrī-kṛṣṇa-caitanya prabhu nityānanda śrī-advaita gadādhara śrīvāsādi-gaura-bhakta-vṛnda.*[15]

How can anyone or anything surpass Lord Krishna? Indeed, only Krishna can surpass Krishna, for God, by definition, is supreme in all categories.[16] And when He surpasses even Himself, He is called Śrī Chaitanya Mahāprabhu.

Endnotes

1. In the modern world, both East and West, Krishna is often seen in sectarian terms, as one god among many, or as a "Hindu" manifestation of the Supreme, respectively. But this not how He is conceived in the Vaishnava tradition, both among practitioners throughout the ages and in the ancient Indic scriptures. Still, many modern encyclopedia entries, for example, perpetuate such misconceptions. In reality, however, He is the same one universal Lord who is revered in all the major world religions, and it is this latter view that is promoted in ISKCON.

2. Śrī Chaitanya's movement is an expression of *sanātana dharma*, "the eternal function of the soul," and it is therefore futile to try to trace its origins to any point in time. It is eternal. Still, its 500-year history, as mentioned above, might be understood as the movement's modern manifestation, arising with Śrī Chaitanya and His followers.

3. Śrīla Prabhupāda teaches that one must approach Krishna through Chaitanya. "And *Śrī Caitanya-caritāmṛta* is written for this purpose so that a person who is serious about Kṛṣṇa consciousness may understand Kṛṣṇa through the mercy of Śrī Caitanya Mahāprabhu. This is wanted. You cannot jump over Kṛṣṇa consciousness without going through the mercy of Śrī Caitanya Mahāprabhu." (See Śrīla Prabhupāda lecture, Māyāpur, March 28, 1975); "You have to approach through your spiritual master to the Gosvāmīs, and through the Gosvāmīs you will have to approach Śrī Caitanya Mahāprabhu, and through Śrī Caitanya Mahāprabhu you have to approach Kṛṣṇa. This is the way." (ibid.); "So Lord Caitanya is combined form of Rādhā-Kṛṣṇa. If Caitanya is pleased, Rādhā and Kṛṣṇa automatically become pleased. Now our mission, Kṛṣṇa consciousness mission, is to execute the will of Lord Caitanya." (See letter to Makhanlal, June 3, 1970).

4. Śrīla Prabhupāda attributes the English phrase "Krishna Consciousness" to that very same verse in several lectures, such as those in Vrindavan (March 13, 1974) and in Seattle, Washington (October 4, 1968), and he quotes it in the *Caitanya-caritāmṛta* 2.8.70. This attribution is based on Śrīla Rūpa Gosvāmī's *Padyāvalī* 14. However, Śrīla Prabhupāda offers other Sanskrit sources for the phrase as well: In *Śrīmad Bhāgavatam* 4.12.38, purport, for example, he writes, "The exact Sanskrit terminology for Kṛṣṇa consciousness is here mentioned: *kṛṣṇa-parāyaṇaḥ*. *Parāyaṇa* means 'going forward.' Anyone who is going forward to the goal of Kṛṣṇa is called *kṛṣṇa-parāyaṇa*, or fully Kṛṣṇa conscious." And also, "The phrase *man-manā bhava mad-bhakto* means 'just be always conscious of Me.' This then is Kṛṣṇa consciousness." (See *Elevation to Kṛṣṇa Consciousness*, Chapter Six) Finally, as Ravīndra Svarūpa Dāsa writes: "Śrīla Prabhupāda himself depicts his English coinage 'Krishna consciousness' as a translation of the Sanskrit compound *kṛṣṇabhāvanāmṛta*. He writes: 'Our Kṛṣṇa consciousness movement is therefore called *kṛṣṇa-bhāvanāmṛta-saṅgha*, the association of persons who are simply satisfied in thoughts of Kṛṣṇa' (SB 9.9.45, purport)." See Ravindra Svarupa Dasa, "Śrīla Prabhupāda:

The Founder-Ācārya of ISKCON - A GBC Foundational Document" (India: ISKCON-GBC Press, 2014). To be thorough, an early reference to the English phrase "Krishna Consciousness" comes from Baba Premananda Bharati (1858–1914) in his book, *Sree Krishna: The Lord of Love* (London: William Rider & Son, Ltd., 1904), 256, 292.

5. The Sanskrit word *caitanya* can be translated in various ways, and "living force," often used by Śrīla Prabhupāda (see Ref. VedaBase => TLC Introduction), is clearly one of them. Basically, the grammatical derivation runs as follows: *Caitanya* comes from *cetana* (conscious, cognizing), which arises from the verb, *cit* (cognize). Thus, it refers to living beings who are conscious entities, i.e., the living force. According to Hridayānanda Mahārāja, "The word *caitanya* means 'consciousness, soul, spirit, the Universal Spirit, etc.' and comes from *cetana*, which is an adjective meaning 'conscious, sentient, intelligent.' In the sense of 'soul,' it can indicate something like 'life force.'" (personal correspondence, August 22, 2024)

6. See Śrīla Vṛndāvana dāsa Ṭhākura, *Śrī Chaitanya-bhāgavata,* Madhya-khaṇḍa, with English Translation of the Gauḍīya-bhāṣya Commentary and Chapter Summaries of His Divine Grace Oṁ Viṣṇupāda Paramahaṁsa Parivrājakācārya Śrī Śrīmad Bhaktisiddhānta Sarasvatī Gosvāmī Mahārāja, translated by Bhumipati Dāsa (India: Vrajraj Press, 2008).

7. see Narahari Cakravarti, *Bhakti-ratnākara* (The Jewel-filled Ocean of Devotional Service), trans., Kuśakratha Dāsa (Vrindavan: Ras Bihari Lal & Sons, 2006).

8. Śrīla Prabhupāda, lecture, *Nectar of Devotion*, December 27, 1972, in Bombay, India.

9. Śrīla Prabhupāda is not alone in translating the verse in this way. For example, see Swami B.B. Bodhayan, *The Life of Chaitanya Mahaprabhu* (San Rafael: Mandala, 2023), viii.

10. See for example, Śrīdhara, Swami B. R., *The Golden Volcano of Divine Love* (Nadiya, West Bengal: Sri Chaitanya Saraswat Math, 1996, reprint), 143: "Śrī Chaitanya Mahāprabhu is the pioneer of Śrī Krishna *saṅkīrtana.* He said, "I have come to inaugurate the chanting of the Holy Name of Krishna, and that name will reach every nook and corner of the universe *(pṛthivīte āche yata nagarādi grāma sarvatra pracāra haibe mora nāma).*"

11. Personal correspondence, August 15, 2024. Professor Ghosh added, "What Mahāprabhu said can be construed in both ways—'my name will be heard' can even refer to the movement he was leading which one day would be known around the world, and "my name" or the "names that I love" (implied plural, which works in Bangla) would be heard across the world as well."

12. Śrīla Jagannātha dāsa Bābājī Mahārāja (1776–1894) is sometimes credited with introducing the *Pañca-tattva mahā-mantra,* though I have seen no evidence to suggest this is true. Bhakti Vikāsa Swami writes: "This chant is rendered as it appears in *Sarasvatī-jayaśrī*, p. 200. It is usually understood to have been introduced by Śrīla Jagannātha dāsa Bābājī, and there are several slightly varied versions extant. Similar to the above *(śrī-kṛṣṇa-caitanya prabhu-nityānanda jayādvaita śrī-gadadhara śrīvāsādi-gaura-bhakta-vṛnda)*, the *Gauḍīya* (10.324) gave the mantra as *jaya jaya śrī-kṛṣṇa-caitanya prabhu-nityānanda jayādvaita śrī-gadādhara śrīvāsādi-gaura-bhakta-vṛnda,* and in *Gauḍīya* 3.30.2 it appears in the same form sans the first jaya. The present standard form is *śrī-kṛṣṇa-caitanya prabhu nityānanda śrī-advaita gadādhara śrīvasa-di-gaura-bhakta-vṛnda.*" See Bhakti Vikāsa Swami, *Śrī Bhaktisiddhānta Vaibhava* (Surat: Bhakti Vikas Trust, 2009), Vol. II, 292.

13. See Jayādvaita Swami, *Śrīla Prabhupāda's Kīrtana Standards: A Handbook* (New York: Krishna Balarama Literary Trust, 2023), 65.

14. See O. B. L. Kapoor (Ādi-keśava dāsa), *The Saints of Bengal*, (South America: Sarasvatī Jayaśrī Classics, 1995), 13, 14.

15. *Śrī Caitanya-caritāmṛta* Ādi 8.31, purport.

16. Krishna describes Himself as being the first in all categories, such as the letter "A" and the generating seed of all existence. Interestingly, when Krishna manifests in this way, it is not His primary form or personality but rather an expansion. That is to say, in both Chapter 7 and Chapter 10 of the *Bhagavad-gītā*, Krishna frames all of such "identity verses" with repeated statements that He is describing His *vibhūti,* expansions, rather than plenary incarnations of Himself. In the case of Chaitanya, however, it is fully Krishna in His most confidential form.

Three

Śrī Chaitanya and the Six Gosvāmīs

NO DISCUSSION OF ŚRĪ CHAITANYA would be complete without an introduction to his primary and highly capable followers, the Six Gosvāmīs of Vrindavan—Rūpa Gosvāmī, Sanātana Gosvāmī, Raghunātha Bhaṭṭa Gosvāmī, Raghunātha Dāsa Gosvāmī, Gopāla Bhaṭṭa Goswami, and Jīva Gosvāmī. These six luminaries propounded a sensible doctrine of devotional practice that culminates in divine love and the highest levels of spiritual realization. Scientific, calculated procedure (*sādhana-bhakti*) and mystical spontaneity (*rāga-mārga*) both play a part in the Gosvāmīs' theology.

Theirs is not a concocted or sentimental philosophy propounded by conditioned souls who have imperfect senses and the tendencies to be illusioned, make mistakes, and cheat. Rather, it is an exhaustive theistic process that is deeply rooted in a time-honored scriptural tradition having as its source ancient India's divinely inspired Vedic texts. This immersion in bona-fide scriptural commentary, so characteristic of the Six Gosvāmīs, can spare one the otherwise inevitable burden of faulty mental speculation and gross misconception.

Thus, the Six Gosvāmīs sought not to invent some imaginative or novel interpretation of scripture, but rather to faithfully and clearly represent the original intent of the text itself. This was no easy task, for the Vedic scriptures represent a profoundly rich storehouse of spiritual knowledge, and the Gosvāmīs had the laborious if also loving task of thoroughly analyzing these scriptures for the benefit of all spiritual seekers—empowered, as they were, by Śrī Chaitanya himself.

Their endeavor was explained by Śrīnivāsa Āchārya, a great saint and scholar of the early seventeenth century. In the second stanza of his Śrī Śrī Ṣaḍ-gosvāmy-aṣṭaka, a song in praise of the Six Gosvāmīs, he makes clear that their most important contribution was to "scrutinizingly study all the revealed scriptures with the aim of establishing eternal religious principles for the benefit of all human beings." In other words, rather than contributing more speculative commentaries to an already confused religious world, they used logic and reason to scientifically analyze all existing religious scriptures. They passed down in disciplic succession the conclusions of the predecessor teachers and the compilers of the Vedic texts. In this way they sought to alleviate the suffering of mankind.

When properly applied, their philosophy of *yukta-vairāgya*, or "practical renunciation," solves the dichotomy between spiritual life and material pursuits, between tranquility and technology. Their method rejects the typical concept of renunciation, usually embraced by fledgling spiritualists, wherein one relinquishes any connection to material phenomenon—a relinquishing that is impractical, especially in the modern age. Rather, the Gosvāmīs taught the proper utilization of material phenomena. That is, everything is meant to be used in the service of the Absolute Truth. The confidential, detailed procedure of just how to do this was revealed by the Six Gosvāmīs in their massive literary output, now available to all, even to those who don't know Sanskrit (the language in which this literature originally appears).

I have addressed the specifics of their life and work, as well as their philosophical system, in a previous volume.[1] Here, I would like to briefly introduce them in connection to the life narrative of their major inspiration: Śrī Chaitanya Mahāprabhu, who appeared in West Bengal, India, in the late fifteenth century. Śrī Chaitanya was known by his followers as an esoteric descent of Lord Krishna in the role of his own devotee, particularly as Rādhā, the devotee par excellence. (Indeed, Rādhā is also viewed as the Female Godhead, a counterpart to Krishna, who is male.)

It was Śrī Chaitanya himself who gave the Six Gosvāmīs their mission, i.e., to recover the lost places of pilgrimage associated with the pastimes of Śrī Krishna, God himself, who is said to have walked the Earth in Vrindavan, India, some 5,000 years ago, and to compile scholarly literature on the subject of Krishna-bhakti—the path of devotional yoga, whereby one can reach perfection in one's own spiritual quest. In telling Śrī Chaitanya's story, I will highlight the situations in which he met each of the Gosvāmīs for the first time, for their connection with him is pivotal in the history of Gauḍīya Vaishnavism.

Introducing Śrī Chaitanya Mahāprabhu

During a lunar eclipse in the winter of A.D. 1486, the fortunate inhabitants of Navadvīpa (Māyāpura), a small village in West Bengal, India, saw the birth of Viśvambhar Miśra, later to be known as Śrī Chaitanya. His mother was known as Śacīdevī and his father was Jagannātha Miśra. Traditional commentators have remarked that this "winter" birth had great symbolic meaning. Śrī Chaitanya's system of yoga, which centered around chanting and dancing—the natural exuberance of the soul in communion with God—was especially recommended in the scriptures for the current age of Kali, the "winter" of the four cyclical ages that are enumerated in the Sanskrit Vedic literature of ancient India.

These scriptures predicted that an incarnation of the Absolute Truth would descend (*avatāra*) to teach the chanting of spiritual sound vibrations, mantra meditation, as a yogic science. When done congregationally, it is called Saṅkīrtana, and when done as a private meditation, quietly and on prayer beads, it is called *japa*. Both forms of chanting (*kīrtana*) were taught by Śrī Chaitanya Mahāprabhu and systematically detailed by the Six Gosvāmīs of Vrindavan.

Having fulfilled the prophesy of scripture, which not only predicted his Saṅkīrtana mission but also specifically mentioned his parentage and a number of his confidential activities, Śrī Chaitanya was gradually accepted as a dual manifestation of Rādhā and Krishna by his intimate followers. In fact, Śrī Chaitanya's most important biographers, such as Kavi Karṇapūra, Vrindavandāsa Ṭhākura, Murāri Gupta, Lochandāsa Ṭhākura, and especially Śrīla

Krishnadāsa Kavirāja Gosvāmī, have pointed out that both the female manifestation of God (Śrīmatī Rādhārāṇī) and the male manifestation (Śrī Krishna) dance together in the one body of Chaitanya Mahāprabhu. Through the agency of his Six Gosvāmīs, he taught the sweetness of this dancing to the rest of the world.

But before this was to occur, when still only a child, Śrī Chaitanya distinguished himself as a scholar of unprecedented caliber. This was important. He and his followers anticipated that the chanting and dancing process might be ridiculed as mere sentiment or even hysteria. Thus, Śrī Chaitanya's own example of rigorous scholarship, and that of the Gosvāmīs after him, was to eventually lay to rest all such unfounded speculation. Those who have taken the time to research the work of Śrī Chaitanya and his Six Gosvāmīs have seen that these exceptional personalities were not mere sentimentalists or utopian spiritual dreamers. For them, devotion was always counterbalanced by reason.

In fact, Śrī Chaitanya's fame as a scholar gradually took him to his ancestral village in East Bengal (now Bangladesh), where a major development took place in his fledgling Saṅkīrtana mission. It was here that he first disclosed his esoteric purpose in spreading his chanting movement as the divine dispensation for the present age. This mercy was bestowed upon Tapan Miśra (a scholar who had sincerely searched out Śrī Chaitanya to ask about the ultimate goal of life). Miśra was the first to hear directly from the Master's lips that the prescribed yoga for the current epoch in world history is the chanting of the holy name of Krishna. This process of chanting, said Śrī Chaitanya, is both the means and the end of spiritual life.[2]

Except for the benediction that he bestowed upon this scholar, Śrī Chaitanya kept his mission confidential, at least until some years later, after his initiation. Commentators have difficulty explaining why Śrī Chaitanya chose to make an exception in this one case by revealing his mission to Tapan Miśra. Critics have ridiculed this action as premature. Yet those who have faith in Śrī Chaitanya see a divine plan in all of his activities. In fact, there are scholars of Chaitanyite Vaishnavism who propose that Śrī Chaitanya instructed Tapan Miśra in this way because Miśra was the father of Raghunātha Bhaṭṭa Gosvāmī, who eventually became one of Śrī Chaitanya's most important followers, one of the Six Gosvāmīs of Vrindavan. For this reason, it is said, Śrī Chaitanya showed special mercy to Tapan Miśra, even if there is no textual evidence to suggest that Chaitanya met Raghunātha Bhaṭṭa at this time.

Rather, it is said that he met the Gosvāmī years later, when he visited Benares, an Indian city well-known as a center of impersonalistic and Māyāvādī philosophy.[3] These two traditional schools of thought, more monistic than theistic, were off-putting to Śrī Chaitanya. Yet he nonetheless asked Tapan Miśra to settle in Benares, where these unfortunate Vedic heterodoxies are often propounded. Śrī Chaitanya felt that Miśra would be an important representative there, especially after revealing to him the secrets of His Saṅkīrtana mission.

Although Tapan Miśra wanted desperately to return to Navadvīpa and in this way remain with Śrī Chaitanya, he sacrificed his own desire in order to carry out the will of the Lord. He did in fact go to Benares, eventually playing an important role in the spreading of the Saṅkīrtana movement. Thus, some say that Śrī Chaitanya revealed his mission to Miśra because of the latter's sense of total sacrifice. Whatever the reason, it is known for certain that Śrī Chaitanya revealed his Saṅkīrtana movement for the first time in East Bengal.

Soon after this interaction with Tapan Miśra, Śrī Chaitanya returned to his hometown, Navadvīpa. Upon returning, he found that his first wife had died prematurely (he married at a young age), and his mother, Śacīdevī, specifically requested that he marry a second time. This he did, and Śrīmatī Viṣṇupriyā proved to be an exemplary devotee and ideal wife. At this point, however, Śrī Chaitanya's life was more intellectual than familial, and he opened a school for the study of Sanskrit grammar, polemics, and philosophical hermeneutics. The chanting and dancing, for which he was soon to become so popular, had not yet manifested in his day-to-day narrative.

When he reached his sixteenth year, Śrī Chaitanya experienced a vital transformation. After a pilgrimage to Gayā, where he was initiated into the ten-syllable Gopāla mantra and the chanting of the holy name—Hare Krishna, Hare Krishna, Krishna Krishna, Hare Hare/ Hare Rāma, Hare Rāma, Rāma Rāma, Hare Hare—he returned to Navadvīpa in a "God-maddened" state. He was now like a live wire, his electrical devotion affecting everyone in proximity. One could feel his presence as he approached, and the contagious love he exuded had the peculiar effect of permeating the entire being of anyone who came into contact with him.

Both stuffy intellectuals and armchair philosophers would uncharacteristically sing and dance if Śrī Chaitanya crossed their path. Professional reciters of scripture, who were hardly faithful practitioners, would easily be transformed into serious devotees by something as simple as his glance. Businessmen and even kings would almost mystically cry in ecstasy by his mere presence. Śrī Chaitanya's contagion of divine love cut through all social stratifications and caste barriers. He and his followers, who by the time he returned to Navadvīpa were increasing by the hundreds, successfully established the Saṅkīrtana movement of chanting and dancing as the prescribed method of God realization for the current day and age.

Then, in February 1510, just prior to his twenty-fifth birthday, Śrī Chaitanya entered the monastic order of *sannyāsa*, shaving his head and donning the robes of a celibate mendicant. Just after accepting this renounced order of life, he intended to go on pilgrimage to Vrindavan, the transcendental village where Lord Krishna had advented some 4,500 years earlier. (His journey to Vrindavan had been thwarted on a prior occasion.) Nonetheless, his intense desire to go to Vrindavan would not be realized at this time. His associate Nityānanda Prabhu had conspired with the other devotees to bring him back to Shantipur, in West Bengal, in order to lovingly associate with him one last time before he assumed his role as a travelling mendicant.

It was here, in Shantipur, that Śrī Chaitanya met Raghunātha Dāsa Gosvāmī.[4] Chronologically, he was the first of the Six Gosvāmīs that Śrī Chaitanya would meet. The fifteen-year-old Raghunātha Dāsa had run away from an extremely wealthy family to pursue spiritual life. His father, Govardhan Majumdar, was in fact a multimillionaire. But the young boy had heard about Śrī Chaitanya from his earliest days and thus fervently wanted to adopt the life of a travelling mendicant, emulating Śrī Chaitanya by totally devoting himself to the service of the Lord. After ten blissful days in the company of Śrī Chaitanya's intimate followers, however, the Lord was ready to move on. And the young Raghunātha Dāsa returned home.

From Shantipur, Śrī Chaitanya went to Jagannātha Purī, for he had promised his mother that he would make Purī his headquarters—it was in close proximity to Navadvīpa, and she would thus regularly hear news of his activities. In Purī, He met Sārvabhauma Bhaṭṭācārya, a great scholar of the period. Śrī Chaitanya succeeded in impressing the Bhaṭṭācārya with his devotion and scholasticism, thus winning him as a disciple.

Soon after, however, Śrī Chaitanya decided to tour all of South India. Externally, he stated that his journey was primarily to search for his brother Viśvarūpa, who had taken *sannyāsa* some years earlier and had travelled into Maharashtra. But his inner purpose was to bring his method of divine love to all of India as an aromatic flower brings its delightful fragrance well beyond the area in which it is seeded.

Moving further south, Śrī Chaitanya met Rāmānanda Rāya on the banks of the Godāvarī River. The word *godāvarī* indicates "the summit or the fulfillment of the senses," and his dialogue with Śrī Rāmānanda unmistakably takes its listeners beyond that level of perfection. These conversations, in fact, are said to constitute the zenith of spiritual knowledge. Fortunately, they have been recorded for all time by Śrī Chaitanya's biographers, particularly Śrīla Krishnadāsa Kavirāja in his *Caitanya-caritāmṛta*.[5]

Śrī Chaitanya was so moved by this dialogue that he revealed to Rāmānanda his manifestation as Rādhā and Krishna. In the past, he had revealed to other devotees his form as Vishnu and his incarnations, the Universal Form, and even a highly esoteric six-armed form, but only to Rāmānanda Rāya did he reveal his complete ontological nature as a dual manifestation of Rādhā and Krishna, the original spiritual couple.

As Śrī Chaitanya progressed on his journey southward, he visited many holy places, further sanctifying them by bringing the divine name and teaching others how to chant with great devotion. Soon he reached Śrī Raṅgam, and there he stayed at the home of Vyeṅkata Bhaṭṭa, a South Indian priest (*brāhmaṇa*). Vyeṅkata and his two brothers, Tirumalla and Prabodhānanda Sarasvatī, frequently engaged in religious dialogue with Śrī Chaitanya. They would often discuss and compare the Supreme Lord's *aiśvarya* feature, the opulent Nārāyaṇa, as He is worshiped in Śrī Raṅgam, with the Lord's *mādhurya* aspect, the sweet, loving personality of Śrī Krishna, as envisioned by Śrī Chaitanya and his followers.

Both features of the Supreme are genuine and revealed in the Vedic literature, but Śrī Chaitanya's conception proved superior in the end, for love outshines opulence, intimacy trumps power. This truth is self-evident and is endorsed by the scriptures. Further, the scriptures are emphatic about Krishna's supreme position: *Kṛṣṇas tu bhagavān svayam*—that is, "Krishna is the original and Supreme Personality of Godhead." This is stated in *Śrīmad Bhāgavatam* (1.3.28), the cream of ancient India's scriptural legacy: After describing various manifestations of the Supreme, this most important

Indian wisdom text declares in no uncertain terms that the Krishna conception is complete, primeval, and the last word in transcendence.

These ideas were accepted by Vyeṅkata and his brothers, particularly Prabodhānanda Sarasvatī, who became a staunch follower of Śrī Chaitanya. Vyeṅkata's son, Gopāla Bhaṭṭa, at the time a young boy who was fortunate enough to hear his father and uncles converse with Śrī Chaitanya, was also moved to become a serious follower, and he eventually became the famous Gopāla Bhaṭṭa Gosvāmī, one of the Six. Thus, after meeting the second of the Six Gosvāmīs in Śrī Raṅgam, Śrī Chaitanya travelled further south.

Completing an exhaustive 4,000-mile walking pilgrimage throughout the Deccan, Śrī Chaitanya returned to Jagannātha Purī toward the end of 1512. Winning the heart of Mahārāja Pratāparudra, the king of Orissa, Śrī Chaitanya taught him the religion of chanting and dancing. As the yearly Ratha-yātrā, "The Festival of the Chariots," was underway, and as Śrī Chaitanya and Mahārāja Pratāparudra took part in it, the subcontinent seemed to be inundated with love of God. But after two years of relishing spiritual exchanges with his intimate followers in Purī, Śrī Chaitanya again decided to attempt a pilgrimage to Vrindavan. And so in 1513, with a retinue of enthusiastic followers, he started for the holy land of Lord Krishna.

Once again, however, he was detoured from his goal. As Nityānanda Prabhu and the residents of Navadvīpa had distracted him from going to Vrindavan just after his *sannyāsa* initiation, his plans again would be changed by divine providence. Commentators suggest that these diversions were meant to increase the sweetness of his eventual success of arriving in Vrindavan—but the time was not yet. Just as love of God in separation (*vipralambha-rasa*) is sometimes considered more intense than in union (*sambhoga*), the desire to go to Vrindavan became overwhelming because of his temporary inability to do so. The anticipation magnified the joy.

This was to be his third attempt, but while en route he passed through Rāmakeli, and there he met Dabir Khas and Sakara Malik, two brothers who were employed by the Islamic government in Bengal. These two gem-like personalities had corresponded with Śrī Chaitanya[6] and had lamented that although they were originally from a family of "priests" (*brāhmaṇas*) from Karnataka, they had now debased themselves by associating with outcaste political leaders who had no regard for the higher, spiritual values of life.

Initiating these two brothers into the Saṅkīrtana movement, Śrī Chaitanya revealed to them their eternal relationships with him. Then, he gave to the elder brother, Sakara Malik, the name "Sanātana Gosvāmī," and to Dabir Khas, he gave the name "Rūpa Gosvāmī." They were to become two of his most important followers. Being senior men, competent in many languages, such as Sanskrit, Persian, Arabic, and other local dialects, and being experienced in worldly affairs as well as in religious doctrine, they would become the natural leaders of the Six Gosvāmīs of Vrindavan.

Śrī Chaitanya instructed them to go to Vrindavan and unearth the then hidden holy places of Lord Krishna's advent. Due to the passage of time, these sites had become obscured, and due to Islamic fundamentalism, holy shrines had, in some cases, been destroyed. But now Rūpa and Sanātana Gosvāmīs would reestablish them. In addition, Śrī Chaitanya asked Rūpa and Sanātana to compile exhaustive treatises on the science of Saṅkīrtana. These texts would become widely known as the revered Bhakti-śāstras, or "scriptures that elucidate pure devotional service to Krishna."

After this historic meeting with the third and fourth of the Six Gosvāmīs, Śrī Chaitanya cancelled his trip to Vrindavan. In fact, tradition holds that the Lord in this particular case, did not really intend to go to Vrindavan at all. Rather, he merely used this as a pretext for meeting Rūpa and Sanātana. Geographically, this theory holds much weight, especially since Rāmakeli is hardly on the way to Vraja.

As the pastime unfolds, however, Rūpa and Sanātana Gosvāmīs, who were employed by the Sultan Hussein Shah, reminded Śrī Chaitanya of the tension between the sectarian Hindus and Muslims and insisted that he would not be safe traveling to Vrindavan at this time in any case. Further, they reminded him of the etiquette for *sannyāsīs*—that they should not travel with large retinues, like some worldly king or opulent politician, especially to a holy place such as Vrindavan. Śrī Chaitanya seriously considered their arguments and decided to return to Purī.

On his way back from Rāmakeli, however, he stopped at Shantipur to visit his mother and the other intimate followers living in the Navadvīpa area. There he met Raghunātha Dāsa Gosvāmī for the second time.[7] Now the boy was four years older (nineteen), and although he still wanted to renounce his riches and become an ascetic, Śrī Chaitanya instructed him to wait for the proper time, perhaps when he was even more mature. Submissive to Śrī Chaitanya's direction, the boy returned home after approximately six days. Having instructed Raghunātha Dāsa, Śrī Chaitanya completed his return trip to Purī.

But he could only remain there for a few months before he became anxious, once again, to go to Vrindavan. In this, his fourth endeavor, he was successful. Travelling with Balabhadra Bhaṭṭācārya and his assistant, Śrī Chaitanya passed through the dense Jhārikhaṇḍa forest in an attempt to avoid the Muslim soldiers about whom Śrī Rūpa and Sanātana had given warning.

Reaching Benares, Śrī Chaitanya stayed at the house of Tapan Miśra, who, as stated, had been instructed to reside there while in East Bengal and was now living with his family in a simple cottage. At this time Śrī Chaitanya met Raghunātha Bhaṭṭa, the fifth of the Six Gosvāmīs.[8] He was the young son of Tapan Miśra and would become well-known as a consummate chef, singer, and reciter of Śrīmad Bhāgavatam. After staying with Tapan Miśra's family for ten days, Śrī Chaitanya proceeded to Vrindavan.

Finally arriving in Mathurā, Krishna's birthplace, and then moving on to Vrindavan, Śrī Chaitanya was in his own element—for he was Krishna, and so Vrindavan was his natural habitat.

Now thirty years old, he at last succeeded in coming "home," back to the land of his Lord, although in this incarnation it was to be his first and last visit there. As he went to the various Vrindavan holy places associated with the Lord's pastimes, especially the twelve forests of Vraja, he was recognized even by the animals, who nuzzled him as if to welcome an old friend. Śrī Chaitanya's appreciation of Vrindavan was beyond words, and his already uncontrollable ecstasy increased by magnificent proportions.

In the winter of 1516, after an ecstatic pilgrimage throughout the Vrindavan area, Śrī Chaitanya proceeded back to Purī, passing through Prayag (now Allahabad), where he instructed Rūpa Gosvāmī for ten days, and then returned through Benares, where he instructed Sanātana Gosvāmī for a period of two months. While in Benares, it is said that Śrī Chaitanya converted Prakāśānanda Sarasvatī, then one of India's most famous impersonalistic philosophers. This won for Śrī Chaitanya great fame and tens of thousands of additional followers.

After returning to Purī, he spent the remaining eighteen years of his life in an exalted state of spiritual absorption, instructing followers, exhibiting mystical, ecstatic symptoms, and inspiring others to the level where they, too, would shed tears of divine love. Once, during these latter pastimes, he uttered the *Śikṣāṣṭakam*, eight prayers that are attributed to him as an original composition. These were written down by his intimate follower Svarūpa Dāmodara and compiled in Rūpa Gosvāmī's work, the *Padyāvalī*. They have additionally been preserved by Śrīla Krishnadāsa Kavirāja in his *Caitanya-caritāmṛta*.[9]

Other than these few stanzas, like Jesus and Buddha before him, Śrī Chaitanya committed nothing to writing. Rather, he instructed his intimate followers to codify and elaborate upon his already profound theological system. In this respect, Śrī Chaitanya has been compared to Socrates:

"Just as we know of Socrates and his teachings not from his own writings, but through the writings of his disciples, like Plato, so also we know of Śrī Chaitanya's philosophy principally through the writings of his spiritual disciples."[10]

This comment especially refers to the Six Gosvāmīs of Vrindavan. They, in particular, codified Śrī Chaitanya's teachings, elucidating every philosophical detail in complex Sanskrit jargon. For instance, Śrī Chaitanya's philosophy of the holy name was certainly demonstrated by the ecstasy he often displayed while chanting. But the understanding of just why such chanting should lead to rapturous spirituality was not given philosophical grounding until the works of the Gosvāmīs. They gave rational argument for Śrī Chaitanya's conclusion: the Lord and His name are one. Since God is absolute, the Gosvāmīs taught, there is no difference between Him and His name. Thus, when chanted purely, the name puts one in direct touch with the Supreme. This was experienced by Śrī Chaitanya, catapulting him into spiritual ecstasy. This was also experienced by the Gosvāmīs, and they put their conclusions into writing.

Norvin J. Hein, Professor Emeritus of Religion at Yale University, very nicely articulates the Gosvāmī conclusion of holy name theology:

> They [the Six Gosvāmīs] dared to say, not merely that the *power* of God is present in such recitation, but that, when the name is uttered in faith, God *Himself* is present. The Vṛndāvan Gosvāmins call this belief the doctrine of *nāmanāminoradvaita* or *nāmanāminorabheda*, the "non-difference between the Named One and the Name." Jīva Goswāmin in his *Bhagavat Sandarbha* states the main point bluntly: *bhagavat-svarūpam eva nām*,

> "The Name of the Supreme Lord is His very essence".... Jīva Goswāmin in one passage actualizes this possibility by remarking about the Name, "Speaking of *avatārs* [the descent of God], this is an *avatār* of the Supreme in the form of syllables: *varṇarūpenāvātaro 'yam*."[11]

In this way, Śrī Chaitanya's philosophy was given academic language and annotated for future generations. But, let it noted: in the task of origination the Gosvāmīs were not alone. Other important compilers, editors, and philosophers of the Chaitanyite school include dozens of notable personalities whose unique contributions should not be underestimated. Still, having been Śrī Chaitanya's direct disciples, the Six Gosvāmīs of Vrindavan are doubtless the most prominent of all.

It might be mentioned here that Jīva Goswāmī, youngest if also the most prolific of the Six, was not a direct disciple of Śrī Chaitanya but was, rather, a disciple of his uncle, Rūpa Gosvāmī. Consequently, some scholars opine that Śrī Jīva never came into direct personal contact with Śrī Chaitanya, or never even saw him, and they consequently compare him to Luke, or even Paul, who never came into contact with Jesus.[12]

But the great teachers of Chaitanyite Vaishnavism do indeed describe a meeting between the two. For example, in the 17th-century text, *Bhakti-ratnākara*, Narahari Chakravartī tells us that when Śrī Jīva was a mere child he saw Chaitanya Mahāprabhu at Rāmakeli.[13] The story runs as follows: Since Śrī Rūpa and Sanātana were important officials in the Muslim government, they had to meet Śrī Chaitanya secretly, and therefore they did not bring Śrī Jīva, who, at the time, was a small child. Nonetheless, the boy hid nearby and watched his uncles and father (Vallabha, Rūpa and Sanātana's younger brother) lovingly converse with Śrī Chaitanya. This same clandestine meeting, with special attention to Jīva Gosvāmī, is mentioned by Bhaktivinoda Ṭhākura in his *Navadvīpa-dhāma Māhātmya*, affirming that the boy saw Mahāprabhu "in the flesh."[14]

In one sense, it may be questioned why such a meeting should be considered relevant. If Śrī Jīva was just a child when he saw Śrī Chaitanya, it may be said that the meeting was devoid of any real substance. But Śrī Jīva, like Gopāla Bhaṭṭa, Raghunātha Dāsa, and Raghunātha Bhaṭṭa, who were also very young when they met Śrī Chaitanya for the first time, eventually decided to devote his life to the Saṅkīrtana mission. This was the effect that Śrī Chaitanya had on people. By merely catching sight of Him, people's hearts were touched, and (regardless of age, caste, or creed) they became inundated with genuine spiritual insight and divine love. Thus, Jīva Goswāmī's early meeting with Śrī Chaitanya must be considered a significant occurrence—and in fact, the net result was that Śrī Jīva became the most prolific of the Six as well as the indisputable head of the Vrindavan Vaishnavas of his generation.

To summarize, although Śrī Chaitanya's pastimes are replete with mystical occurrences and profound theological revelations, upon which we have barely touched, his respective meetings with the Six Gosvāmīs of Vrindavan constitute the most monumental developments in the early history of his movement. This is so because it was they who initially gave academic shape to Śrī Chaitanya's incomparably profound teachings. We conclude with an appreciation from the late Chicago University professor Edward C. Dimock, a respected academic authority on Chaitanya Vaishnavism: "The Six Gosvāmins among them produced over 219 different works in Sanskrit—it is most significant that they wrote in Sanskrit—tying every teaching of the Bengal school into the orthodox traditions of Indian religion."[15]

Endnotes

1. See Steven J. Rosen, *The Six Gosvamis of Vrindavan* (New York: Folk Books, 1991).

2. The Hare Krishna *mahā-mantra*—Hare Krishna, Hare Krishna, Krishna Krishna, Hare Hare/ Hare Rāma, Hare Rāma, Rāma Rāma, Hare Hare—was revealed to Tapan Miśra before the Śrī Chaitanya's mission took formal shape. See Vrindavandāsa Ṭhākura, *Chaitanya-bhāgavata*, Ādi 14, text 145.

3. Impersonalism is the philosophy that God is not, in an ultimate sense, a person. Impersonalists claim that personal traits are limiting and thus the Absolute Truth must be devoid of all such qualities. Advaita-vedānta, the natural extension of this philosophy, teaches that all living beings are one with God, and that both God and man are ultimately formless. This view is now considered characteristic of Indian philosophy as a whole. Nonetheless, Vaishnavism represents a different thread of Indic thought, in which we see a monotheistic component of the Vedic tradition. According to the four genuine *sampradāyas*, or the recognized lineages of disciplic descent, the Vaishnavas' personalistic, theistic view, propounded by Śrī Chaitanya and his followers, is the original Vedic understanding of reality. Indeed, Vaishnavas claim that both personal and impersonal understandings have a place, though they hold the personal view as prior and more complete. Parenthetically, Māyāvādīs represent yet another strain of impersonalism. They claim that the Lord's form, as when He descends (*avatāra*), is ultimately an illusion. There are two types of Māyāvādīs: Kāśīra

Māyāvādīs—followers of Śaṅkarācārya (popular in Kashi, also known as Benares); and Saranātha Māyāvādīs, or Buddhists.

4. His Divine Grace A. C. Bhaktivedanta Swami Prabhupāda (trans.), *Caitanya-caritāmṛta*, 17 volumes (Los Angeles, Bhaktivedanta Book Trust, 1975), Antya-līlā 2, ch. 6, p. 203. In addition, see Madhya-līlā 6, 16.223. Also see Bhaktipradip Tirtha, *Sri Chaitanya Mahaprabhu* (Calcutta, Gaudiya Mission, 1947), 279. Taken together, these texts indicate that Raghunātha Dāsa, also known as Dāsa Gosvāmī, was the first of the Six to meet Śrī Chaitanya. If this is true, then the chronology would run as follows: First Śrī Chaitanya met Raghunātha Dāsa at Shantipur; then he met Gopāla Bhaṭṭa in South India; Rūpa, Sanātana, and Jīva at Rāmakeli; and, finally, Raghunātha Bhaṭṭa in Benares.

5. For more information see Steven. J. Rosen, *India's Spiritual Renaissance: The Life and Times of Lord Chaitanya* (New York, FOLK Books, 1988), Chapter 9. Also see the more recent, *Śrī Chaitanya's Life and Teachings The Golden Avatāra of Divine Love* (Lanham, Maryland: Lexington Books, 2017), Chapter 9.

6. See *Caitanya-caritāmṛta*, op. cit., Madhya 1.209. Also see Bhaktivinoda Ṭhākura, *Shri Chaitanya Mahaprabhu: His Life and Precepts* (1896), published as a prologue in His Divine Grace A. C. Bhaktivedanta Swami Prabhupada, *The Teachings of Lord Chaitanya* (Los Angeles, Bhaktivedanta Book Trust, 1974, reprint), p. xx.

7. *Caitanya-caritāmṛta*, op. cit., Madhya 6.16.

8. Ibid., Madhya 17. 90.

9. For detailed accounts of the eight prayers and their meaning, see Steven J. Rosen, *Śrī Chaitanya's Life and Teachings The Golden Avatāra of Divine Love*, op. cit., Chapter Six, *Śikṣāṣṭakam*: Eight Beautiful Prayers, 105-122; Satyarāja Dāsa, "Thus Spake Śrī Caitanya," *Back to Godhead*, March/April 2017, 24-29; Tripurāri, Swami B. V., *Śikṣāṣṭakam of Śrī Caitanya* (San Rafael, California: Mandala Publishing, 2005); and Jan K. Brzezinski, "Śrī Chaitanya's *Śikṣāṣṭakam*." in *Journal of Vaishnava Studies*, vol. 12, issue 1 (Fall 2003), 87–111.

10. See O. B. L. Kapoor, *The Philosophy and Religion of* Śrī *Chaitanya* (Delhi, Munshiram Manoharlal, 1977), 57.

11. Norvin Hein, "Caitanya's Ecstasies And The Theology of the Name" in Bardwell L. Smith (ed.), *Hinduism* (Leiden, E.J. Brill, 1976), 28-9.

12. Sushil Kumar De, *Early History of the Vaishnava Faith and Movement in Bengal* (Calcutta, Firma KLM, reprint, 1961), 86.

13. Narahari Chakravarti, *Bhakti-ratnakara* (Bengali edition), First Wave (Calcutta, Gaudiya Math, 1960), text 638, p. 30. Also see Jadunatha Sinha, *Jiva Goswami's Religion of Devotion and Love* (Varanasi, Chowkhamba Vidyabawan, 1983), 5.

14. See Bhaktivinoda Ṭhākura, *Navadvīpa-dhāma Māhātmya*, verses 38-42.

15. Edward C. Dimock Jr., *The Place of the Hidden Moon* (Chicago, The University of Chicago Press, 1966), 77.

Four

"I am He": The Unique Secret of Mahāprabhu's Divinity

ŚRĪ CHAITANYA MAHĀPRABHU is Krishna, God, in the form of his own devotee, appearing in 15th-century Bengal, India, as a divinity who walked the Earth. When I was first introduced to this idea, as someone who came of age in the West, I naturally thought of Jesus, who in the Christian tradition is similarly viewed as God in human form. Also like Jesus, Mahāprabhu insisted on a certain secrecy regarding his divine nature, though this aspect of his behavior is not usually emphasized by those who write about him.

In terms of Jesus, we first encounter this notion of reticence in the book of Mark (1.24-25): "What have you to do with us, Jesus of Nazareth? Have you come to destroy us? I know who you are—the Holy One of God. But Jesus rebuked him, saying, 'Be silent…!'"Jesus tells others to keep quiet about his identity as well, as we see in Mark 1.34, 3.12, 8.30 and 9.9, and also in Luke 8.56 and 9.21.

Why the secrecy? For the most part, it seems clear that he wanted his mission known: God himself openly declared that Jesus was his "Son" (1.9–11), even if exactly what is meant by "Son" is interpreted variously, and Jesus also proclaims his divine gospel and mission outwardly in Galilee (1.14–15). He even tells a healed man to widely disseminate the news of his mission (5.19–20), as he eventually does many others.

Yet biblical scholars make much of the "Messianic Secret." Indeed, both political leaders and the religious orthodoxy of first-century Palestine expected a Messiah to appear in their time, as per Old Testament prophecy. They envisioned him as a political revolutionary, a "king" who would emerge among his people and release them from Roman sovereignty. They lived in anticipation of a political savior as much as a spiritual one.

Jesus wanted his identity as Messiah kept secret because the Jewish people of the time expected a warrior Messiah to overthrow the Romans—and the Romans knew this as well. For this reason, his safety was always in question. Additionally, Jesus knew his identity was beyond human comprehension, perceivable only by believers who receive God's grace. In other words, Jesus's reasons for divine secrecy had to do with the political climate of the time as well as the inability of those around him to understand who he was.

There are elements of this in Mahāprabhu's secrecy as well. It is certainly true that the Muslim government of his time would have looked askance at any claim of divinity that would compromise their regime, creating danger for all involved.[1] Their fears seemed all but justified in the Chand Kazi episode, when chanting of the Holy Name resounded through the streets of Navadvīpa, threatening the Kazi's rule.[2] Similarly, in Śrī Chaitanya's time, many Hindus (*māyāvādīs, smārta-brāhmaṇas*, etc.) misunderstood who he actually was (also immortalized in the Chand Kazi episode),[3] and this, too, creates a parallel with Jesus's reasons for secrecy. But Mahāprabhu's primary reason was different—it was first and foremost based on his internal reason for incarnation, a statement on who he was as a special, intimate and esoteric manifestation of the Supreme.

Śrī Chaitanya's Secrecy

Śrī Chaitanya's incarnation is the methodology by which God experiences the depth and richness of a perfect devotee's love. After all, by definition, love of God is the prerogative of the devotee. God is always the object (*viṣaya*) and a devotee is always its vessel or shelter (*āśraya*)—God is the beloved, while the devotee is the lover.[4] That said, God is enamored by his devotees' love, for when perfect in its intensity, such love attracts him like a magnet.

Thus, Krishna wants to be the lover and not just the beloved, as we read in the *Caitanya-caritāmṛta*: "If I can sometimes be the abode of that love (*āśraya*), only then may I taste its joy." Śrīla Prabhupāda, the commentator, elaborates on Krishna's words: "I am Krishna, and I experience pleasure as the *viṣaya*. [However,] the pleasure enjoyed by Rādhārāṇī, the *āśraya*, is many times greater than the pleasure I feel." (Ādi 4.135, verse and purport) Therefore, Krishna descends as Śrī Chaitanya to feel what his devotee feels, specifically to tangibly and viscerally realize what Rādhikā—the devotee par excellence—experiences in her heart of hearts.

Accordingly, the *Caitanya-caritāmṛta* (Ādi 4.15–16) informs us that, "Krishna's desire to appear in this world can be traced to two primary reasons: He wanted to taste the sweet essence of love of God (*prema-rasa*), and he wanted to propagate that devotion to the world at large through the path of spontaneous attraction (*rāga-mārga bhakti loke karite pracāraṇa*). Thus he is known as the super-excellent taster of all spiritual relationships and as the most merciful of all."

In this way, Chaitanya was the beloved wanting to know what it felt like to be the lover, and he knew well not to conflate the two. Such commingling, he thought, would defeat his confidential purpose.

Consequently, when he descended to Earth some 500 years ago, he was careful not to upset the *bhāva*, or the emotional component, associated with his secret mission, often expressing an aversion to being called God in any form whatsoever, as we will show below. Again, his goal was to experience the mood of a devotee, which runs counter to being glorified as Supreme. For this reason, he keeps his identity as God a secret, only to be shared with his most intimate associates.[5]

Examples are numerous: When the impersonalist philosopher Sārvabhauma Bhaṭṭācārya claims that seeing Mahāprabhu is tantamount to seeing Krishna himself, Mahāprabhu rebukes him, calling out the name of Vishnu for protection. He insists that such glorification is in reality just another form of blasphemy.[6]

Similarly, when asking the townspeople of Vrindavan where they go to get direct audience of Krishna, they courageously point out that seeing him is in fact seeing Krishna. His response was unequivocal: "Vishnu! Vishnu! Do not refer to me as the Supreme Godhead. An ordinary soul cannot become Krishna at any time. Do not say such a thing!"[7]

Another example is when the Māyāvādī philosopher Prakāśānanda Sarasvatī recognized Mahāprabhu's divine status. At that time, the Lord again called out the name of Vishnu, protesting that an ordinary living being should never be identified with God.[8]

And then there is the incident where Rāmānanda Rāya attempts to unite Mahāprabhu with the King for a much-anticipated audience, telling him, "My Lord, you are the supreme independent personality. You have nothing to fear from anyone because you are not dependent on anyone." His implication was that Mahāprabhu was God. To this, the Lord adamantly objects, saying, "I am not the Supreme Personality of Godhead, but an ordinary human being."[9]

Perhaps the most famous example of Mahāprabhu's aversion to being viewed as divine is found in his response to Rūpa Gosvāmī's two verses of glorification. Although the *Vidagdha-mādhava* and the *Lalita-mādhava*, where the two verses in question originally appear, are otherwise solely about the pastimes of Rādhā and Krishna, Śrī Rūpa includes in each an introductory verse about Mahāprabhu's divinity. These verses are not only beautiful poetry, but also glorify Mahāprabhu as the Supreme Lord. Consequently, upon having them read to him, Śrī Chaitanya is clearly not pleased, referring to the verse in the *Vidagdha-mādhava* as mere exaggeration (*ati stuti*), and the one in *Lalita-mādhava* as being like alkali, i.e., a type of salt often used in industrial cleaning settings and soap-making.[10]

Śrīla Prabhupāda clarifies:

> Śrī Caitanya Mahāprabhu was God Himself according to the indication of the revealed scriptures, but He

played the part of a devotee. People who knew Him to be God addressed Him as God, but He used to block His ears with His hands and chant the name of Lord Viṣṇu. He strongly protested against being called God, although undoubtedly He was God Himself. The Lord behaves so to warn us against unscrupulous men who take pleasure in being addressed as God.[11]

And again:

> The most astonishing fact is that Lord Caitanya, although the Supreme Personality of Godhead, Kṛṣṇa, never displayed Himself as Kṛṣṇa. Rather, whenever He was detected by intelligent devotees as Lord Kṛṣṇa and was addressed as Lord Kṛṣṇa, He denied it. Indeed, He sometimes placed His hands over His ears, protesting that one should not be addressed as the Supreme Lord. Indirectly, He was teaching the Māyāvādī philosophers that one should not falsely pose himself as the Supreme Lord and thereby misguide people. Nor should followers be foolish enough to accept anyone and everyone as the Supreme Personality of Godhead.[12]

Thus, not only did Śrī Chaitanya accomplish his goal of experiencing how a devotee loves God, but his mission also embodied an instructive dimension: By being a devotee who denied his own Godhood, Mahāprabhu was showing the world how a real devotee behaves, eschewing any personal glorification or artificial posturing, particularly in terms of divinity. Indeed, in the India of his day, there were many "godmen," or people who claimed to be God, as there are even today, and he wanted to be perfectly clear that such a perspective is not part of the Vaishnava mentality.

Mahāprabhu shows through his own example that a

devotee never tolerates such blasphemy and forcefully speaks out at the mere suggestion that he may in some sense be God.

But there were certainly exceptions. While a thorough investigation of the scriptures lays bare Śrī Chaitanya's actual divinity, as do the teachings of legitimate *ācāryas* throughout history,[13] below we document some of the prooftexts from Mahāprabhu's own lips (as well as several pastimes that underline the point), wherein he suspended his mission of being a devotee to let his intimate followers know that he was in fact God. Such instances are as plentiful as his denials. Indeed, they are more so.

"I am He!"

As Tony K. Stewart notes, "The sequence of events described by Vṛndāvana Dāsa in Caitanya's early life is reminiscent of the messianic secret in the Gospel of Mark. ... The parallel [between Jesus and Chaitanya] is much closer in detail than the above information might suggest. For instance, both performed miracles or extraordinary feats, then forbade the witnesses to reveal what they saw. Jesus finally acknowledged the title 'Son of the Blessed' and responds to the accusations by answering in the first person 'I am,' an act which formally abandoned the messianic secret (Mark 14.61-62). Similarly, when Caitanya publicly manifested his full divinity for the first time in Śrīvāsa's courtyard, he mounted the throne of Viṣṇu and proclaimed 'I am He! I am He!' whereupon he showed Śrīvāsa his four-armed form, ending all speculation and waiting for the *avatāra* of the age."[14]

There are at least three instances of Mahāprabhu voicing his identity as "I am He" in the *Caitanya-bhāgavata*. Studying these texts closely, we watch as Krishna-bhāva engulfs his soul: "Some of the cows raised their tails and ran about, some of them fought each other, some laid down, and some drank water. On seeing this, the Lord repeatedly thundered, 'I am He, I am He.'"[15] According to the commentary of Bhaktisiddhānta Sarasvatī, the phrase *muñi sei*, translated as "I am He," means, in this context, "I am that son of Nanda, the King of the cowherd men." We find the phrase again at Madhya 19.119, where Śrī Chaitanya is depicted as being in a state of ecstasy, repeatedly shouting, "I am He! I am He!" And yet again, in Madhya 2.86, where he reacts to the mistreatment of his devotees, repeatedly exclaiming these same words again and again.

Truth be told, however, Śrī Chaitanya had been revealing his divinity from his earliest earthly pastimes.

For example, there is the story of the determined *brāhmaṇa*, the basic narrative of which runs as follows. When Mahāprabhu's parents, Jagannātha Miśra and Śacī, received at their home a visit from a *brāhmaṇa* pilgrim, they stocked their entire kitchen and placed it at his disposal. The *brāhmaṇa* prepared an offering of food to be placed before his worshipable deity, Śrī Bāla-gopāla, the infant form of Śrī Krishna. As the story goes, the child Nimāī (Śrī Chaitanya) came along and devoured the entire offering that was meant for Krishna. The *brāhmaṇa* complained and Nimāī's parents apologized, asking the *brāhmaṇa* to cook once more, excusing their little boy. This he did, but Nimāī again appeared and usurped the offering, causing the *brāhmaṇa* great vexation. Nonetheless, with great persistence, he cooked and offered food to his deity for a third time, even as baby Nimāī was kept away in a neighbor's house. Yet somehow, in the midst of the offering, the divine child mysteriously appeared again, relishing the *brāhmaṇa's* food preparations. This time, however, before the *brāhmaṇa* could react, Nimāī suddenly revealed his four-armed form, with conch, disc, club and lotus. After that, he also showed his hauntingly beautiful, two-handed form as child Krishna, Śrī Bāla-gopāla, the *brāhmaṇa's* worshipful deity, holding butter in one hand and eating it with the other.[16] Thus, for the devoted *brāhmaṇa,* Śrī Chaitanya suspended his secrecy.

Significantly, too, there is an episode called Mahābhāva-prakāśa, where, for twenty-one hours, he showed his many divine forms to all his intimate devotees in Śrīvāsa Ṭhākura's courtyard. This is detailed in Vrindāvandāsa's *Caitanya-bhāgavata,* Madhya 9 and 10. Some other examples may be cited as follows: He showed Śrīvāsa his form as Vishnu (*Caitanya-bhāgavata*, Madhya 2.256–258); Murāri Gupta saw both his Varāha Avatāra (*Caitanya-bhāgavata,* Madhya 2.3) and Rāma Avatāra (*Caitanya-bhāgavata*, Madhya 2.10); Advaita Ācārya, Śrīdhara, and Śacī saw his form as Krishna (*Caitanya-bhāgavata*, Madhya 2.6, 2.9, and 2.8, respectively); Nityānanda, Sārvabhauma, and Pratāparudra viewed his six-armed form (*Caitanya-bhāgavata*, Madhya 2.5, *Caitanya-caritāmṛta,* Ādi 17.13, and Murāri's *Kaḍacā* 3.16.13, respectively); Advaita saw his universal form (*Caitanya-bhāgavata*, Madhya 24.32–55); and Rāmānanda Rāya saw his combined manifestation as Śrī-Śrī Rādhā and Krishna (*Caitanya-caritāmṛta,* Madhya 8.282–284).

As he says in the *Chaitanya-bhāgavata* (1.8.76-77): "I am Īśvara, the Lord of all the worlds. My name is thus Viśvambhara, for I maintain the entire universe. I am He, but no one recognizes it."

Conclusion

What is one to make of Śrī Chaitanya's dichotomous behavior? His reasoning behind concealing his identity is clearly established in the tradition, as is his reason for revealing who he is. Let it not be forgotten, too, that God is inconceivable and that he need not be subject to our laws of logic, which he himself created. Because he is their source, he is beyond them. Indeed, if his transcendental activity were not in some sense paradoxical, he would not be God. By definition he must be beyond human understanding.

We encounter a particularly poignant example of the Lord's paradoxical nature in the *Śrī Īśopaniṣad* (Mantra 5): "The Supreme Lord walks and does not walk. He is far away, but he is very near as well. He is within everything, and yet he is outside of everything." Śrīla Prabhupāda offers explanation in his commentary:

> The contradictions given here prove the inconceivable potencies of the Lord. "He walks, and He does not walk." Ordinarily, if someone can walk, it is illogical to say he cannot walk. But in reference to God, such a contradiction simply serves to indicate His inconceivable power. With our limited fund of knowledge we cannot accommodate such contradictions, and therefore we conceive of the Lord in terms of our limited powers of

> understanding. For example, the impersonalist philosophers of the Māyāvāda school accept only the Lord's impersonal activities and reject His personal feature. But the members of the Bhāgavata [Vaishnava] school, adopting the perfect conception of the Lord, accept His inconceivable potencies and thus understand that He is both personal and impersonal. The Bhāgavatas know that without inconceivable potencies there can be no meaning to the words "Supreme Lord."

Let us also remember Lord Krishna's words from *Bhagavad-gītā*: "By me, in my unmanifested form, this entire universe is pervaded. All beings are in me, but I am not in them." (9.4) "And yet everything that is created does not rest in me. Behold My mystic opulence! Although I am the maintainer of all living entities and although I am everywhere, I am not a part of this cosmic manifestation, for my Self is the very source of creation." (9.5) Indeed, if he were not both paradoxical and transcendental to paradox, he would not be God.

Perhaps the Lord's intimate associate Śrīvāsa Paṇḍita said it best, "O my Lord, what will you do now? The whole world is singing your glories. Where will You hide? ... O Lord, the entire world chants your glories in this way. O Lord, although you are unseen and unmanifest, you have now mercifully manifest yourself before the people of this world. You hide yourself, and you manifest yourself. Only one who receives your favor can know You." (*Chaitanya Bhāgavata*, 9.220-223)

Endnotes

1. Rāmachandra Khan advised Śrī Chaitanya about dangers on the road from Odisha to Bengal (in *Caitanya-bhāgavata* Antya 2.96-97): "But, Lord, the situation is very tense right now. There is no travel between the two states." (*sabe prabhu, haiyāche viṣama samaya*) "The King's men have booby-trapped the road with sharp spears. If they happen to find a traveler, they accuse him of being a spy and execute him." (*se deśe e deśe keha patha nāhi vaya, rājārā triśūla puṅtiyāche sthāne sthāne, pathika pāile 'jāśu' bali' laya prāṇe*). Also see *Caitanya-caritāmṛta*, Madhya 16.156-159.

2. See the Chand Kazi episode in *Caitanya-caritāmṛta* Ādi 17.

3. Bhaktivinoda Ṭhākura writes, "The *devotees* were highly pleased. But the *Smārta Brāhmaṇas* became jealous of Nimāi Pandit's success and complained to Chand Kazi, deprecating the character of Śrī Chaitanya as un-Hindu. (https://bhaktivinodainstitute.org/chaitanya-mahaprabhu-life-precepts-the-life-of-sri-chaitanya-mahaprabhu/) While the Muslim population remained tolerant, at least to some degree, it was the caste-conscious Hindus—*smārta brāhmaṇas*—who complained and created difficulty for Mahāprabhu's mission, their conventional understanding of Hinduism virtually forcing them to deprecate the Lord's ever-growing religion of love.

4. Of course, while the particular Sanskrit terminology used here—*āśraya* and *viṣaya*—indicate that the devotee is always the lover and God is always the beloved, this truth adheres only within a specific context, in terms of understanding carefully delineated categories for living beings and God found in the Vedic literature. In truth, Krishna, too, is a lover—the Ultimate Lover—and the devotee is, of course, always the beloved of Krishna, under all circumstances. Love eternally flows from the lover to the beloved and from the beloved back again to its source.

5. As a side note, Śrī Chaitanya was "secretive" in another if also related way: Because he descends as a devotee, he is not properly counted among the incarnations: "You appear in various incarnations as a human being, an animal, a great saint, a demigod, a fish or a tortoise, thus maintaining the entire creation in different planetary systems and killing the demoniac principles. According to the age, O my Lord,

You protect the principles of religion. In the Age of Kali, however, You do not assert Yourself as the Supreme Personality of Godhead, and therefore You are known as Triyuga, or the Lord who appears in three *yugas*." (*Śrīmad-Bhāgavatam* 7.9.38) Based on this verse, we learn that the Lord appears as *channaḥ kalau*, the Divinity of Kali-yuga in hidden form. The word *channaḥ* comes from the verbal root *chad* and means "concealed." This signifies that in Kali-yuga, Svayam Bhagavān Śrī Krishna comes disguised under the golden complexion of Śrīmatī Rādhikā to relish the *rasa* of a devotee. Prabhupāda concurs, "Unlike other incarnations, Lord Śrī Caitanya Mahāprabhu appears in this age of Kali as a devotee of the Lord. Therefore He is called a concealed incarnation" (*channāvatāra*)." See *Śrīmad Bhāgavatam* 5.18.35, purport. That concealed form of the Supreme Lord is *svayaṁ-avātarī*, or the source of all incarnations. *Śrīmad-Bhāgavatam* 11.5.32 brings the point home: "In the Age of Kali, intelligent persons perform congregational chanting to worship the incarnation of Godhead who constantly sings the names of Krishna. Although his complexion is not blackish, he is Krishna himself. He is accompanied by his associates, servants, weapons and confidential companions."

6. See *Caitanya-caritāmṛta* Madhya 10.182.

7. See *Caitanya-caritāmṛta* Madhya 18.109-112.

8. See *Caitanya-caritāmṛta* Madhya 25.78-81.

9. See *Caitanya-caritāmṛta* Madhya 12.49–50.

10. See *Caitanya-caritāmṛta* Antya 1.31 and Antya 1.179. The verses that Mahāprabhu is responding to, originally found in *Vidagdha-mādhava* 1.2 and *Lalita-mādhava* 1.3, respectively, may be rendered as follows: "May the Supreme Lord who is known as the son of Śrīmatī Śacī-devī be transcendentally situated in the innermost core of your heart. Resplendent with the radiance of molten gold, He has descended in the Age of Kali by His causeless mercy to bestow what no incarnation has ever offered before: the most elevated mellow of devotional service, the mellow of conjugal love." And "The moonlike Supreme Personality of Godhead, who is known as the son of mother Śacī, has now appeared on Earth to spread devotional love of Himself. He is the emperor of the *brāhmaṇa* community. He can drive away all the darkness of ignorance and control the mind of everyone in the world. May that rising moon bestow upon us all good fortune."

11. See *Śrīmad Bhāgavatam* 1.2.16, purport.

12. See *Teachings of Lord Chaitanya*, Chapter Seventeen (https://prabhupadabooks.com/tlc/17).

13. I have presented extensive evidence regarding Mahāprabhu's divinity in my book, *Śrī Chaitanya's Life and Teachings The Golden Avatāra of Divine Love* (Lanham, Maryland: Lexington Books, 2017).

14. See Stewart, Tony K., "The Biographical Images of Kṛṣṇa-Caitanya: A Study in the Perception of Divinity," Ph.D. thesis (Department of South Asian Languages and Civilizations, The University of Chicago, 1985). Stewart observes these parallels at footnote 1 on p. 116 of his thesis. Indeed, Mahāprabhu's consistent repetition of "I am He" is reminiscent of Jesus, with his famous biblical utterance of "I AM": This was Jesus's response to the Pharisees' question "Who do you think you are?" Jesus answered, "... before Abraham was born, I AM!" The claim of divinity was clear to them—Jesus was equating himself with the "I AM" title that God gave himself in Exodus 3:14—and consequently they endeavored to stone him. But Jesus hid himself, slipping away from the temple grounds." (John 8:56–59)

15. See *Caitanya-bhāgavata*, Madhya 2.253-255.

16. See *Caitanya-bhāgavata,* Ādi 3; also see *Caitanya-caritāmṛta,* Ādi 14.37, translation and purport.

Five

Mahāprabhu's Mantras:
The primary sound vibrations Śrī Chaitanya received from His guru

WHILE THE LIFE AND teachings of Śrī Chaitanya Mahaprabhu, Krishna himself in the role of his own devotee, are often associated with the Hare Krishna *mahā-mantra* (Hare Krishna Hare Krishna Krishna Krishna Hare Hare Hare Rāma Hare Rāma Rāma Rāma Hare Hare)—and rightly so—there are other mantras that were central in his manifested earthly pastimes. Indeed, among his various reasons for appearing in our world, his mission involved establishing the *yuga-dharma*, or the prescribed method of self-realization for the current epoch in world history, i.e., the congregational chanting of the holy name of the Lord. Thus, numerous mantras and other holy sound vibrations are associated with his life and mission.

But if one studies his life carefully according to the standard Sanskrit and Bengali biographies, there are four mantras that stand out as having special potency, and these were either given to him directly by his guru, Īśvara Purī, or otherwise embraced by him around the time of his initiation. This article focuses on these four mantras, briefly outlining how they played a role in his pastimes as described in Gauḍīya literature. Below, we will translate them and briefly discuss their significance.

The four mantras may be enunciated as follows: (1) *Hare Krishna Hare Krishna Krishna Krishna Hare Hare Hare Rāma Hare Rāma Rāma Rāma Hare Hare*; (2) *Haraye namaḥ, Krishna Yādavāya namaḥ Gopāla Govinda Rāma śrī-Madhusūdana*; (3) the Gopāla mantra, i.e., *Gopījana-vallabhāya svāhā*; and (4) *harer nāma harer nāma harer nāmaiva kevalam kalau nāsty eva nāsty eva nāsty eva gatir anyathā.*

1. Hare Krishna Mahā-mantra

The most famous of Mahāprabhu's mantras has been called "the great chant for deliverance" (*mahā-mantra*), though it is technically referred to as *kṛṣṇa-nāma*. According to Śrīla Prabhupāda, this mantra consists solely of Rādhā and Krishna's names and are presented in the vocative, calling out to Them to be engaged in Their loving service. He translates it as follows: "O Lord! O energy of the Lord! Please engage me in Your service!"

Originally a *śruti* text, i.e., derived from the Vedic literature, we find it first cited in the *Kali-santaraṇa Upaniṣad*, part of the Krishna-yajur-veda.[1] The original verse should be known to all:

hare kṛṣṇa hare kṛṣṇa kṛṣṇa kṛṣṇa hare hare
hare rāma hare rāma rāma rāma hare hare
iti ṣoḍaśakaṁ nāmnāṁ kali-kalmaṣa-nāśanaṁ
nātaḥ parataropāyaḥ sarva-vedeṣu dṛśyate

"These sixteen names counteract the evil effects of the Kali-yuga. After searching through the gamut of Vedic texts, one cannot find a method so sublime as the chanting of these names."[2]

The *Ananta-saṁhitā,* another ancient text, echoes the words of the *Kali-santaraṇa* Upanishad, making clear exactly which *mahā-mantra* it refers to (the texts mention several) by spelling out the entire chant and the exact number of words and syllables it contains:

> Hare Krishna, Hare Krishna, Krishna Krishna, Hare Hare/ Hare Rāma, Hare Rāma, Rāma Rāma, Hare Hare. This sixteen-name, thirty-two syllable mantra is the *mahā-mantra* in the age of Kali, and it is by this mantra that all living beings can attain salvation. One should never abandon this mantra, adopting other religious processes practiced by less qualified souls. Nor should one chant contrived combinations of Krishna's names that contradict the pure conclusions of the scriptures or are filled with illegitimate emotions. Regarding this entirely spiritual *mahā-mantra,* which frees one from material existence, the original teacher, Lord Brahmā, has said, "The Kali-santaraṇa Upanishad has declared this mantra to be the best means of deliverance in the age of Kali."

We see a similar occurrence in the *Sanat-kumāra-saṁhitā*:

> The words "Hare Krishna" are to be repeated twice, then "Krishna" and "Hare" are repeated separately twice. Similarly, "Hare Rāma," "Rāma," and "Hare" are also to be repeated in the same way. The mantra will thus be chanted as follows—Hare Krishna, Hare Krishna, Krishna Krishna, Hare Hare/ Hare Rāma, Hare Rāma, Rāma Rāma, Hare Hare.

There are many Puranic texts confirming the *mantra* as well. For example, in the *Brahmāṇḍa Purāṇa* (6.59–60), we find: "By engaging in *nāma-saṅkīrtana* (congregational chanting), specifically with the Hare Krishna Mahā-mantra, one situates oneself in complete spiritual reality." And another from the *Padma Purāṇa* (Svarga-khaṇḍa 50.6): "If one worships Śrī Hari, the Lord of all lords, by chanting the *mahā-mantra*, all sinful reactions are automatically removed." There are numerous scriptural quotes along similar lines, and even more if one considers the many verses composed by Gauḍīya sages throughout the centuries.

As far as Mahāprabhu's use of the mantra, it can be traced to his earliest pastimes, even before his formal initiation. Indeed, although he chanted the *mahā-mantra* from childhood, as did those around him, his initiation into the mantra marked a turning point in his life. That said, he was already offering the mantra to others prior to meeting his guru. The prominent example is Tapan Miśra, father of Raghunātha Bhaṭṭa Gosvāmī, one of the Six Gosvāmīs of Vrindavan.

As the *Chaitanya-bhāgavata* conveys the story, Tapan Miśra was undergoing spiritual crisis, and when he happened upon Nimāi, who would soon be known as Śrī Chaitanya, the Lord addressed Miśra's concerns in the following way: "Chanting the holy name of the Lord is the real object and goal of spiritual life." And with that, he gave him the *mahā-mantra*: "Hare Krishna, Hare Krishna, Krishna Krishna, Hare Hare/ Hare Rāma, Hare Rāma, Rāma Rāma, Hare Hare."[3] This is the first time in Mahāprabhu's manifest *līlā* that he recites the full *mahā-mantra*, showing deep appreciation for the chanting process he will soon champion.

Soon after, he repeats it again to the inhabitants of Navadvīpa, assuring them, too, of its unique efficacy.[4] After reciting the mantra in full, he says, "Everyone will attain all perfection by it. At every moment chant it; there is no other rule." (*ihā haite sarva-siddhi haibe sabāra sarva-kṣaṇa bala' ithe vidhi nāhi āra*).

Although Śrī Chaitanya had been chanting the mantra from early on, he officially received this mantra from his guru, too, as is clear from the *Caitanya-caritāmṛta* (Ādi 7, verses 71-77).[5] Here we learn that Śrī Īśvara Purī told him the value of the mantra in no uncertain terms: "You must always chant the holy name of Kṛṣṇa. This is the essence of all mantras, or Vedic hymns. ... Simply by chanting the holy name of Kṛṣṇa one can obtain freedom from material existence. Indeed, simply by chanting the Hare Kṛṣṇa mantra one will be able to see the lotus feet of the Lord."

After describing the potency of the mantra, Śrī Chaitanya tells us this: "My spiritual master taught me another verse, advising me to always keep it within my throat: 'For spiritual progress in this Age of Kali, there is no alternative, there is no alternative, there is no alternative to the holy name, the holy name, the holy name of the Lord.'" This is the "Harer Nāma" verse, which we will explore more fully below. Śrī Chaitanya concludes: "Since I received this order from my spiritual master, I always chant the holy name ..."

2. Haraye namaḥ, Kṛṣṇa Yādavāya namaḥ

This is a popular chant closely related to the *mahā-mantra*, and it is clear from the texts that Mahāprabhu engaged with this mantra from early on. In fact, the tradition teaches that the *mahā-mantra* can be expressed in two distinct ways. The most significant and well-known version is Hare Krishna, Hare Krishna, Krishna Krishna, Hare Hare/ Hare Rāma, Hare Rāma, Rāma Rāma, Hare Hare. The *Caitanya-caritāmṛta* (Madhya 25.64), however, provides another version: *Haraye namaḥ kṛṣṇa yādavāya namaḥ, gopāla govinda rāma śrī-madhusūdana*—"I offer my respectful obeisances unto the Supreme Personality of Godhead, Krishna. He is the descendant of the Yadu dynasty. Let me offer my respectful obeisances unto Gopāla, Govinda, Rāma, and Śrī Madhusūdana, for these are all names of the same Supreme Lord."

Śrīla Prabhupāda, in his commentary to the above verse, is unequivocal: "This is another way of chanting the Hare Kṛṣṇa *mahā-mantra*."

And sure enough, when Mahāprabhu's early students asked, "How shall we perform *saṅkīrtana*?" he personally taught them to chant as follows: "*(hare) haraye namaḥ kṛṣṇa yādavāya namaḥgopāla govinda rāma śrī-madhusūdana*."[6] The *Caitanya-caritāmṛta* further tells us that all the devotees sang this popular song along with the well known Hare Krishna *mahā-mantra*.[7]

The initial lines of the mantra were eventually developed into a full song by noted Gauḍīya poet and theologian Narottama Dāsa Ṭhākura (c 16th century). It is now called "Hari Haraye Namaḥ (Śrī Nāma Saṅkīrtana)," and its extension glorifies all prominent personalities in the tradition from Krishna to the Six Gosvāmīs of Vrindavan: (1) *hari haraye namaḥ kṛṣṇa yādavāya namaḥ yādavāya mādhavāya keśavāya namaḥ*; (2) *gopāla govinda rāma śrī-madhusūdana, giridhārī gopīnātha madana-mohana;* (3) *śrī-caitanya-nityānanda śrī-advaita-sītā, hari guru vaiṣṇaba bhāgavata gītā;* (4) *śrī-rūpa sanātana bhaṭṭa-raghunātha śrī-jīva gopāla-bhaṭṭa dāsa-raghunātha.* There are several more stanzas as well, and the song is a favorite among Gauḍīya Vaishnavas to this day. But in its original seed-like form, it was chanted by the Lord himself.

3. The Gopāla mantra, i.e., *Gopījana-vallabhāya svāhā*

This chant is pivotal as the ubiquitous *dīkṣā* (initiation) mantra in the Gauḍīya tradition. As Prabhupāda writes, "Those who are initiated by a bona fide spiritual master and who chant the Gāyatrī mantra three times a day know this *aṣṭādaśākṣara* (eighteen-syllable) mantra."[8] Like the *mahā-mantra*, it is part of the Vedas, thoroughly explicated in the *Gopāla Tāpanī Upaniṣad*, an important proof text for Vaishnavas of various lineages.[9]

Originally, as Prabhupāda says, the mantra comes to us in 18-syllables—*klīṃ kṛṣṇāya govindāya gopījana-vallabhāya svāhā*—though there are important variants with fewer syllables as well, and we will see how this is particularly relevant in the pastimes of Śrī Chaitanya. The mantra itself cannot be translated as a flowing sentence, since it is solely composed of Krishna's most intimate names, each meant for a specific kind of meditation. But in general it refers to the offering of oblations to Krishna, Govinda, the lover of the *gopīs*. Thus, as the tradition teaches, one needs sufficient background in Krishna consciousness to meditate on each of these names properly. Among other things, they represent *sambandha, abhidheya*, and *prayojana*, i.e., the establishing of one's relationship with God, the process for developing that relationship, and the culmination of that relationship in pure love, respectively.

Although confidential, the mantra is revealed to devotees in general in the *Brahma-saṁhitā*, both in Text 5.24 and in Śrīla Bhaktisiddhānta Sarasvatī Ṭhākura's purport to Text 3, where the Ṭhākura breaks down its syllables and then comments: "This is a hexagonal mantra consisting of six transcendental words, viz., (1) *kṛṣṇāya*, (2) *govindāya*, (3) *gopījana*, (4) *vallabhāya*, (5) *svā*, (6) *hā*."[10] Thus, the chanting of this esoteric sound vibration is available for all who are ready for it, though the tradition, again, asserts that true readiness comes with initiation by a bona fide guru.

Its reference in the *Brahma-saṁhitā* is particularly significant, for it was Lord Brahmā, the first created being and the original preceptor of the Brahma-Mādhva-Gauḍīya Sampradāya, who was initiated into its chanting at the dawn of time.[11] As Prabhupāda writes, "The inhabitants of Brahmaloka and the planets below Brahmaloka worship Lord Govinda by meditating with this mantra. There is no difference between meditating and chanting, but in the present age meditation is not possible on this planet. Therefore loud chanting of a mantra like the *mahā-mantra*, Hare Kṛṣṇa, with soft chanting of the *aṣṭādaśākṣara*, the mantra of eighteen syllables, is recommended."[12]

Consequently, numerous Vaishnava texts elaborate on the mantra's secrets and glories. The *Sādhana-dīpikā* and *Hari-bhakti-vilāsa*, two of the most important in terms of the Gauḍīya tradition, reference numerous texts in support of the mantra's primacy, including those found in the *Gautamīya* and *Sammohana Tantras*, the *Krama-dīpikā*, and the already mentioned *Gopāla Tāpanī Upaniṣad* and the *Brahma-saṁhitā*.

The mantra also plays a key role in Śrīla Sanātana Gosvāmī's *Bṛhad-bhāgavatāmṛta*, beginning in Text 37-38 of Volume 2, where the protagonist Gopa-kumāra "receives the ten-syllable mantra for worshiping the lotus feet of Madana-gopāla" and thereby attains spiritual perfection.[13] The 10-syllable version of the mantra is concentrated love for God, evoking Krishna in his highest feature as the lover of the *gopīs*. It is comprised of the last 10 syllables of the 18-syllable mantra, and is described in the *Gautamīya Tantra* (2.1) as the *mantra-rājaṁ daśākṣaraṁ*, "the king of all mantras," used specifically for those who are in *rāga-mārga*, or the path of passionate devotion.[14]

This abbreviated, more concentrated form of the Gopāla mantra plays a major role in Chaitanya-līlā.

For example, in his introductory remarks to *Chaitanya-bhāgavata*, Ādi 17, Śrīla Bhaktisiddhānta Sarasvatī writes that Mahāprabhu was initiated with the mantra:

> The Lord personally served all the foodstuffs that He cooked for Himself to Śrī Īśvara Purīpāda, and by directly serving His spiritual master, Purīpāda, with His own hands, He displayed the ideal example of serving the spiritual master. On another day, in a solitary place, Mahāprabhu offered obeisances to Īśvara Purī and requested him for mantra initiation. Then the Lord received the ten-syllable mantra from His spiritual master and surrendered everything unto his lotus feet.

We find this initiation confirmed in the text itself (*Chaitanya-bhāgavata*, Ādi 17.107): "Then in order to instruct everyone, the Lord accepted the ten-syllable mantra from Īśvara Purī." (*tabe tāna sthāne śikṣā-guru nārāyaṇa/ karilena daśākṣara-mantrera grahaṇa//*)[15]

This lesson is important, particularly the phrase "in order to instruct everyone." Indeed, one may ask why Śrī Chaitanya, God himself, would have to serve a spiritual master and accept mantra *dīkṣā* from him. The tradition responds by saying that Mahāprabhu was God in the form of a devotee, and he was showing by example how a devotee should act: By rendering loving service to his guru and taking initiation from him.

The great *ācārya* Śrīla Bhaktivinoda Ṭhākura (1838–1914) confirms this as follows: "Thereafter He went to Gayā and accepted spiritual initiation in the ten-syllable Gopāla mantra from Śrīpad Īśvara Purī, a great servant of the Lord and torch-bearer of the disciplic succession coming down from Lord Brahmā to Madhvācārya. *The Lord's wish was to teach the living entities their duty of taking shelter of a self-realized spiritual master, as instructed by the scriptures.*"[16]

4. Harer Nāma Harer Nāma Harer Nāmaiva Kevalam ...

Finally, the fourth mantra—one that the *Caitanya-caritāmṛta* clearly says was given to Mahāprabhu by his guru, as mentioned above—is originally found in the *Bṛhan-nāradīya Purāṇa* (38.127). The full mantra runs as follows:

harer nāma harer nāma harer nāmaiva kevalam
kalau nāsty eva nāsty eva nāsty eva gatir anyathā

"In this Age of Kali there is no other means, no other means, no other means for self-realization than chanting the holy name, chanting the holy name, chanting the holy name of Lord Hari."[17]

In many ways, this verse encapsulates all the other mantras in Mahāprabhu's life, and it is likely for this reason that his guru asked him to keep this mantra with him always.[18] It articulates the essence of all spiritual instructions, particularly for the age of Kali. As we learn from Bhaktivinoda Ṭhākura's *Śrī Bhajana-rahasya*:

> In Kali-yuga, Svayam Bhagavān Śrī Kṛṣṇa has appeared in the form of His name. Through *harināma* the whole world can be delivered. The words *harer nāma* in this Text are used three times to make people with mundane intelligence become fixed in chanting *harināma*. The word *kevala* (meaning "only") is used to make it extremely clear that *jñāna, yoga, tapasya* and other activities are to be renounced. Salvation is never possible for one who disregards this instruction of the scriptures. To emphasize this, the words *nāsty eva* (meaning "no other way") are repeated three times at the end of the verse.[19]

In conclusion, Mahāprabhu's method centers on chanting the holy name of the Lord, and this is reflected in all the above mantras—in fact, this is the main overriding principle that they share in common. And it is nicely summed up in the "Harer Nāma" verse.

With this as a focus, there is yet another mantra, not

necessarily associated with Īśvara Purī, but definitely sung by Mahāprabhu in his earthly pastimes and which epitomizes his focus on the holy name:

> kṛṣṇa! kṛṣṇa! kṛṣṇa! kṛṣṇa! kṛṣṇa! kṛṣṇa! kṛṣṇa! he
> kṛṣṇa! kṛṣṇa! kṛṣṇa! kṛṣṇa! kṛṣṇa! kṛṣṇa! kṛṣṇa! he
> kṛṣṇa! kṛṣṇa! kṛṣṇa! kṛṣṇa! kṛṣṇa! kṛṣṇa! rakṣa mām
> kṛṣṇa! kṛṣṇa! kṛṣṇa! kṛṣṇa! kṛṣṇa! kṛṣṇa! pāhi mām
> rāma! rāghava! rāma! rāghava! rāma! rāghava! rakṣa mām
> kṛṣṇa! keśava! kṛṣṇa! keśava! kṛṣṇa! keśava! pāhi mām

> "O Lord Kṛṣṇa, please protect Me and maintain Me.
>
> O Lord Rāma, descendant of King Raghu, please protect Me.
>
> O Kṛṣṇa, O Keśava, killer of the Keśī demon, please maintain Me."[20]

This prayer is featured in the introduction to Śrīla Prabhupāda's book "Kṛṣṇa: The Supreme Personality of Godhead"—as the opener for the entire book—and again shows the primacy or centrality of Krishna's name. In his commentary to *Caitanya-caritāmṛta* Ādi 8.26, Prabhupāda writes about Śrī Chaitanya's chanting of this mantra, "While passing on the road, He used to chant ..." This suggests that it may have been the Lord's usual practice.

And why not? Mahāprabhu's intimate associate, Murāri Gupta, tells us in his diary that when the Lord sang these names, "tears of divine love fell from his eyes. Those tears formed an ocean, and upon the billows of that ocean he floated about, lost to the external world of men. In this intoxicated state, he rolled on the ground, his body trembled greatly, and he would run senselessly, here and there."[21] In the teachings of Chaitanya Mahāprabhu, this is the divinely blissful state awaiting those who truly embrace the name of Krishna.

Endnotes

1. The *Muktikā Upaniṣad* includes a list of the authorized, standard 108 *upaniṣads* that are traditionally considered a genuine part of the Vedic literature. The *Kali-santaraṇa Upaniṣad* is listed as number 103.

2. In certain manuscripts of the *Kali-santaraṇa Upaniṣad*, the *mahā-mantra* appears with the "Hare Rāma" part first. While it is true that in later versions published by Venkateśa Press, Mumbai, the mantra is presented in this way, earlier manuscripts, still preserved in research libraries of Kolkata and Jaipur, clearly show it as beginning with "Hare Krishna" instead. The version commencing with "Hare Krishna" is also corroborated by its presentation in early Saṁhitās and Purāṇas. This subject has been thoroughly addressed in Śrīla Bhaktisiddhānta Sarasvatī, the *Gauḍīya*, Volume 11, No. 7 (October 22, 1932), 101, and also in Kostyantyn Perun (Brijbasi das), "Hare Kṛṣṇa Mahā-Mantra From the Caitanya-Vaiṣṇava Perspective" in *Journal of Vaishnava Studies*, Volume 24, No. 2 (Spring 2016), 179–222. See also Śrīmad Bhaktivedānta Nārāyaṇa Mahārāja, trans., *Sri Hari-Nāma Mahā-mantra* (Mathura, U.P.: Gauḍīya Vedānta Publications, 2001, 2nd Edition), 3–15. Significantly, in terms of sequence, Chaitanya Mahāprabhu, too, always uttered it with the Hare Krishna part first, as we will see in the *Chaitanya-bhāgavata* verses cited below.

3. See *Caitanya-bhāgavata*, Ādi 14.143–47.

4. See *Caitanya-bhāgavata* 23.74-78, 82. These instructions to the residents of Navadvīpa are also related in Narahari Cakravartī's *Bhakti-ratnākara* (12.2047-2054) where the Hare Krishna *mahā-mantra* is again recorded in its entirety (12.2049).

5. In regard to Śrī Chaitanya receiving the *mahā-mantra* from his guru, modern Vaishnava leader Nārāyaṇa Mahārāja (1921–2010) offers the following: "Sri Caitanya Mahaprabhu took initiation from Sri Isvara Puripada, who first gave Him harinama,

and [then] gave Him Gopal-mantra." (See "The Absolute Necessity Of Second Initiation," January 13, 2003 (https://www.purebhakti.com/teachers/bhakti-discourses/22-discourses-2003/290-the-absolute-necessity-of-second-initiation) Also, "Sri Caitanya Mahaprabhu took harinama initiation and diksa (brahminical initiation) from Sri Isvara Puripada." (See "Don't Worry About What Others are Doing," April 29, 2005 (https://www.purebhakti.com/teachers/bhakti-discourses/24-discourses-2005/447-dont-worry-about-others)

6. See *Caitanya-bhāgavata*, Madhya 1.406-407. See also Madhya 23.80-81 and Madhya 23.222.

7. See Ādi 17.122. That they sang both is endorsed by Śrīla Prabhupāda's translation.

8. See *Caitanya-caritāmṛta* Ādi 5.221, translation and purport.

9. The *Muktikā Upaniṣad* counts this as Number 95 in its list of 108 authorized *upaniṣads*.

10. Śrīla Prabhupāda also shares with the world the Gopāla mantra in his own *Caitanya-caritāmṛta* commentary (Ādi 5.221 and Madhya 8.139).

11. See Śrīla Prabhupāda, *Śrīmad Bhāgavatam* (2.9.6), purport: "It is stated in the *Brahma-saṁhitā* that Lord Brahmā was initiated into the eighteen-letter Kṛṣṇa mantra, which is generally accepted by all the devotees of Lord Kṛṣṇa. We follow the same principle because we belong to the Brahmā sampradāya, directly in the disciplic chain from Brahmā to Nārada, from Nārada to Vyāsa, from Vyāsa to Madhva Muni, from Madhva Muni to Mādhavendra Purī, from Mādhavendra Purī to Īśvara Purī, from Īśvara Purī to Lord Caitanya and gradually to His Divine Grace Bhaktisiddhānta Sarasvatī, our divine master." *Brahma-saṁhitā* 5.24 suggests that Brahmā was initiated via Sarasvatī, the goddess of learning.

12. See *Caitanya-caritāmṛta* Ādi 5.221, translation and purport.

13. The text also tells us that the goddess Kāmākhya gave the 10-syllable mantra to a *brāhmaṇa* from Prāgjyotiṣapur.

14. This is also confirmed in Dhyānachandra Goswāmī's *Śrī Gaura-govindārcana-smaraṇa-paddhati* (137-141).

15. In Kavi Karnapura's *Caitanya-candrodaya-nataka* (1.36), it is also said that the Lord received the "10-syllable" mantra (*daśa-varṇa-vidyā*),

and in the same author's *Caitanya-caritāmṛta-mahā-kāvya* (4.60) the mantra is described as "the mantra of the Lord of the women of Vraja" (*manum vraja-bhāvinī-jana-pateḥ*).

16. Commentary on *Śikṣāṣṭaka*, Text 8, *Śrī Sanmodana Bhāṣyam* (https://nbsarticles.blogspot.com/2017/03/sri-sanmodana-Ò bhasyam-on-sri-siksastaka.html?view=classic). Italics added for emphasis.

17. The verse in *Bṛhan-nāradīya Purāṇa* has the same meaning but slightly different Sanskrit wording: *harer nāmaiva nāmaiva nāmaiva mama jīvanam / kalau nāsty eva nāsty eva nāsty eva gatir anyathā.*

18. The verse in question, as stated earlier, is *Caitanya-caritāmṛta* Ādi 7.75-76, but it also appears in Ādi 17.21, Madhya 6.242, and elsewhere as well.

19. See Bhaktivinoda Ṭhākura's *Śrī Bhajana-rahasya: The Deep Secrets of Bhajana*, with Nārāyaṇa Mahārāja's *Bhajana-rahasya-vṛtti*, 55-56 (https://www.purebhakti.com/resources/ebooks-magazines/bhakti-books/english/3-bhajana-rahasya/file).

20. See *Caitanya-caritāmṛta* Madhya 7.96. A shorter version is found in Madhya 9.13. The mantra is found throughout the gamut of Gauḍīya literature with numerous variants, the earliest likely belonging to Murāri Gupta as found in his *Kaḍaca* (3.14.9). Mahāprabhu famously sang some version of this mantra at the commencement of His South Indian tour shortly after taking *sannyāsa*.

21. See Murāri Gupta *Kaḍaca* (3.14.10): *iti paṭhati sa mantraṁ prema-viplāvitāśrur/ luṭhati dharaṇī-madhye dhāvati ca prakampaiḥ// iha harir iti vākyair bāṣpa-ruddhāvakaṇṭho/ rudati taru-latāyāṁ prema-dṛṣṭiṁ karoti//.* This verse occurs directly after enunciating the mantra mentioned here.

Six

Śrī Caitanya in Gaya:
More Than a Footnote

Lord Caitanya's visit to the holy site of Lord Viṣṇu's footprint marks a significant transition during His divine descent.

"I offer my respects to the sacred dhāma of Gaya, which is decorated with the lotus feet of Lord Viṣṇu, the visit of the great saint Īśvara Purī, the first teardrop of Śrī Rādhā Bhāva Gaurāṅga, and the Lord Himself [Śrī Caitanya Mahāprabhu], who took His new birth, dīkṣā, in the lineage of prema."

– *Lalitā Kiśora Dāsa, sixteenth-century poet*

GAYA, IN NORTHEASTERN India, sits peacefully along the Falgu River, a tributary of the Ganges. The second largest city in Bihar, it is home to a rich history of both Buddhist and Hindu lore, but its place in the Gauḍīya Vaiṣṇava tradition is dominated by the pastimes of Śrī Caitanya Mahāprabhu, Kṛṣṇa Himself in the role of His own devotee.

When studying the life of Śrī Caitanya, however, we find that most of His biographers give very little attention to His time in Gaya. Indeed, in Śrīla Kṛṣṇadāsa Kavirāja Gosvāmī's *Caitanya-caritāmṛta*, the most prominent of the Lord's biographies, we learn only that Mahāprabhu (as Viśvambhara Miśra, a householder) went to Gaya to perform *śrāddha* (funeral rites) for His father, happened to meet

Īśvara Purī there,[1] and took Vaiṣṇava initiation from him there – all consequential events, but all told rather abruptly. Almost like a footnote.

Still, one thing is clear: something mysterious occurred in Gaya. Mahāprabhu returned to His hometown of Nabadwip completely God-intoxicated.[2] To be absorbed in thought of Kṛṣṇa with a mood of ecstatic love (*prema*) is the very substance of Śrī Caitanya's *avatāra*. But He chose to exhibit such love for the first time in Gaya, and it is therefore worth exploring what happened there, and why.

Four "Footnotes"

There are four incidents that immediately precipitate Mahāprabhu's vital transformation. I call them "footnotes," not only because some of His biographers treat them rather cursorily, but also because these incidents share one thing in common: a reference to holy feet, a common trope in Vaiṣṇava literature.[3]

The first of our footnotes comes from Śrīla Bhaktisiddhānta Sarasvatī, who informs us that Śrī Caitanya desired to make specific holy places even holier than they already are. To accomplish this, He places *His* footprints on such holy ground by visiting the places Himself.[4] Gaya is but one example.

Commenting on Vṛndāvana Dāsa Ṭhākura's *Caitanya-bhāgavata* (Ādi-khaṇḍa 17.13), Bhaktisiddhānta Sarasvatī writes, "The second line of this verse indicates that the Lord's lotus feet came to Gaya; in other words, Lord Śrī Gaurasundara [Caitanya], whose sanctified feet are the source of all holy places, came here in order to purify the holy place of Gaya. In the Lord's journey to Gaya, all those villages and places that were marked by His lotus feet, which purify the entire universe, became famous as most sanctified holy places."

It is after this initial act of purification that Mahāprabhu would show the external world His internal mood, exhibiting the intense love for Kṛṣṇa that only Rādhā possesses. As Bhaktisiddhānta Sarasvatī writes in his introduction to chapter seventeen of the Ādi-khaṇḍa of *Caitanya-bhāgavata*: "It was then that the Lord saw fit to manifest His true nature." And Vṛndāvana Dāsa Ṭhākura is even more specific (Ādi-khaṇḍa 17.120): "The Master who was extremely grave (*parama-gambhīra*) now became extremely restless (*parama-asthira*) under the impact of love (*prema*)."

The next footnote can be delineated as follows. According to the *Caitanya-bhāgavata*: On the way to Gaya, Viśvambhara performs the pastime of catching a fever. (Ādi 17.16) In order to instruct people, the Lord of Vaikuṇṭha displays illness like an ordinary person. (Ādi 17.17) Thus He temporarily interrupts His journey, as His companions try to remedy His physical ailment. (Ādi 17.18–19) At this point, He prescribes Himself the water used to clean *brāhmaṇas'* feet, which He says can remove all suffering; so He drinks the holy water, and His fever subsides. (Ādi 17.20–22) In this way He shows the importance of revering the feet of those dedicated to God. His teaching here is both symbolic and literal – it is not just their feet, but service to such holy people in general that is the prescribed method for overcoming the scourge of material existence.

With this as a backdrop, the Lord entered Gaya proper, where the footprint of Viṣṇu has its very own temple, the Viṣṇupāda Mandira. Mahāprabhu had ostensibly come to this sacred place to execute His father's obsequies, and He indeed performed the prescribed rituals in due course.[5] But why Gaya? The ceremony can be performed at any number of holy places. With this question in mind, we should briefly look at the history of this temple and why it is important to the Gauḍīya Vaiṣṇava tradition.

Mahāprabhu approached the Viṣṇupāda temple with great anticipation. Echoing the words of Vrindavana Dāsa Ṭhākura's *Caitanya-bhāgavata,* as we will soon see, Locana Dāsa Ṭhākura writes in his *Caitanya-maṅgala*:

> [Mahāprabhu] set off quickly to see the Viṣṇupāda, His heart full of joy. "I will see with My own eyes the impressions of Viṣṇu's feet." Happily He kept telling Himself this as He went along. Saying this, and arriving at His destination, Mahāprabhu washed the Viṣṇupāda, performing *abhiṣeka* to His heart's content. Revealing His devotion, Lord Viśvambhara Hari showed the world that He was indeed a possessor of *prema.* He began to tremble, and horripilation spread over His body as *prema* commenced. Streams poured forth from His eyes and He suddenly became stunned and motionless. The Lord became overwhelmed upon seeing those lotus feet and He started dancing, initiating a grand festival of *prema.* While at Gaya, He thus performed *piṇḍa-dāna* to those lotus feet, fulfilling His ancestral obligations and being delighted within.[6]

That Śrī Caitanya experienced ecstatic symptoms upon viewing the Viṣṇupāda imprint in Gaya should come as no surprise. Seeing the distinct marks of the Lord's feet is called an *uddīpana,* something that kindles devotional sentiment, as stated in the *Bhakti-rasāmṛta-sindhu* (2.1.302): "Kṛṣṇa's smile, the fragrance of His transcendental body, His flute, bugle, ankle bells and conchshell, the marks on His feet, His place of residence, His favorite plant (*tulasī*), His devotees, and the observance of fasts and vows connected to His devotion all awaken the symptoms of ecstatic love."

The Viṣṇupāda temple is traced to a demon known as Gayāsura, who terrorized the earth in the Tretā-yuga, millions of years ago. The story is retold in the *Vāyu Purāṇa*, the *Garuḍa Purāṇa,* and other Vaiṣṇava literature. To give the essence of a very long story, Lord Viṣṇu killed Gayāsura at this spot by stamping His foot on the demon's chest. After Lord Viṣṇu pushed him into the earth with His foot, the Lord's footprint – with its unique markings of *śaṅkha-cakra-gadā-padma* (conch shell, disc, club, and lotus) – was retained in what is now a sixteen-inch-long imprint in basalt rock. (Although there is only one footprint, the *Caitanya-bhāgavata* and other sources commonly refer to it as "footprints" or "feet.") A temple was subsequently built around it.

Again, why did Mahāprabhu come to this particular place? In general, Hindus of the time, and still to this day, believe that the mourning ceremonies of *śrāddha* achieve a two-fold purpose, propitiating the ancestors and facilitating their approach to heavenly planets. It is important to note that in Vaiṣṇava theology there is a vast difference between heavenly planets and Vaikuṇṭha, or the kingdom of God. This is where the Viṣṇupāda temple comes in. When one performs the *śrāddha* ceremony at this site, one guarantees that the departed ancestor will return to Viṣṇu/Kṛṣṇa and not merely be promoted to heaven. Jagannātha Miśra, the Lord's father, was an eternally liberated soul, but to show the world that a Vaiṣṇava desires the supreme abode and not merely higher planetary systems, Mahāprabhu made the pilgrimage to Gaya.

A. C. Bhaktivedanta Śrīla Prabhupāda explains the difference between going to heaven and going to the kingdom of God:

> So what is the difference between going to the higher planetary system and going back home, back to [Godhead]? Everything is explained. If you go to the higher planetary systems, suppose to the planets of the demigods, Kṛṣṇa says, "Then you will have to again come back." *Ābrahma-bhuvanāl lokāḥ punar āvartino 'rjuna* [*Gītā* 8.16]. Even if you go to the topmost planet, then from there also, after . . . *Kṣīṇe puṇye martya-lokaṁ viśanti* [*Gītā* 9.21]. After your resultant action of pious activities is finished, then you have to come back again here. *Yad gatvā na nivartante tad dhāma paramaṁ mama* [*Gītā* 15.6]. But there is another planet, which is called Goloka Vṛndāvana. If you go there, then you'll haven't to come back again in this material world, which is described by Kṛṣṇa Himself: *duḥkhālayam aśāśvatam. Mām upetya tu kaunteya duḥkhālayam aśāśvatam nāpnuvanti mahātmānaḥ.* [*Gītā* 8.15] No ordinary person can go to Kṛṣṇa's *loka*, back to home. Who can go? *Mahātmānaḥ*, those who are great souls. And who are great soul? They are called *mahātmās.* Who are *mahātmās*? *Mahātmānas tu māṁ pārtha daivīṁ prakṛtim āśritāḥ, bhajanty ananya-manasaḥ.* [*Gītā* 9.13] This is *mahātmā*. Those who are fully engaged in Kṛṣṇa consciousness, absorbed in the service of Kṛṣṇa, they are called *mahātmā*.[7]

The rituals for the deceased are part of the *karma-kāṇḍa* section of the *Vedas*, which prescribes the performance of rituals and sacrificial rites for material benefits or for liberation. As Śrīla Prabhupāda writes: "In the *Vedas* there are three *kāṇḍas*, or divisions: *karma-kāṇḍa, jñāna-kāṇḍa,* and *upāsanā-kāṇḍa*. The *karma-kāṇḍa* portion stresses the execution of fruitive activities. But ultimately it is advised that one abandon both *karma-kāṇḍa* and *jñāna-kāṇḍa* (speculative knowledge) and accept only *upāsanā-kāṇḍa*, or *bhakti-kāṇḍa*." (*Caitanya-caritāmṛta*, *Madhya-līlā* 9.263, Purport) The *Nārada Paṇcarātra* states: "The essence of all Vedic knowledge – comprehending the three kinds of Vedic activity [*karma-kāṇḍa, jñāna-kāṇḍa,* and *upāsanā-kāṇḍa*], the *chandas*, or Vedic hymns, and the processes for satisfying the demigods – is included in the eight syllables Hare Kṛṣṇa, Hare Kṛṣṇa. This is the reality of all Vedānta. The chanting of the holy name is the only means to cross the ocean of nescience." (quoted in *Caitanya-caritāmṛta*, Ādi-līlā 7.76, Purport)

To be sure, Vaiṣṇavas need not perform *śrāddha* at all. As Kṛṣṇa says in the *Bhagavad-gītā* (8.28): "A person who accepts the path of devotional service is not bereft of the results derived from studying the Vedas, performing sacrifices, undergoing austerities, giving charity or pursuing philosophical and fruitive activities. Simply by performing devotional service, he attains all these, and at the end he reaches the supreme eternal abode." This is the teaching of Śrī Caitanya Mahāprabhu. If one intends to perform the *śrāddha* ceremony, it should be done in the tradition of the Viṣṇupāda temple, where the ritual performed is called

"Vaikuṇṭha-samārādhanā," meaning that it focuses on the Supreme Lord and entering His abode.

So it should be clear: Mahāprabhu's reason for being in Gaya, at least in terms of His father's funeral services, was to show that such ceremonies are valuable only if they are directed toward Viṣṇu/Kṛṣṇa and the ultimate goal of life. Thus, as He approached the transcendental footprint enshrined in that temple, He experienced divine love in full. The *Caitanya-bhāgavata* tells us: "As the Lord looked at those lotus feet, tears flowed from His lotus eyes, His hairs stood on end, and He began shivering." (Ādi-khaṇḍa 17.43) "Lord Gauracandra then began to manifest ecstatic devotional service for the benefit of the entire world." (17.44) "The *brāhmaṇas* were all startled to see tears flow from the Lord's eyes like the unbroken flow of the Ganges." (17.45)

Nonetheless, soon thereafter, Mahāprabhu would encounter the fourth and ultimate footnote, surpassing even His profound experience in the Viṣṇupāda temple: "By the divine will of the Supreme Lord, at that moment [while Mahāprabhu was conducting funeral services at the Viṣṇupāda temple] Śrī Īśvara Purī arrived at that same place." (17.46) Śrīla Bhaktisiddhānta Sarasvatī comments on this verse: "When Lord Śrī Gaurasundara's hair stood on end due to love of God while seeing His own lotus feet, by the will of the Lord and by providence, Śrī Īśvara Purīpāda arrived there as a *mahānta-guru* in order to serve the Lord by assisting Him in His pastimes."

The Ultimate Footnote

The nonpareil Gaya experience occurs soon after seeing Viṣṇupāda: Mahāprabhu surrenders to the feet of his guru, Īśvara Purī: "The Lord said, 'My journey to Gaya became successful the moment I was able to see your lotus feet.'" (*Caitanya-bhāgavata,* Ādi-khaṇḍa 17.50) And as the *Caitanya-caritāmṛta* (Ādi 17.9) tells us: "In Gaya, Śrī Caitanya Mahāprabhu was initiated by Īśvara Purī, and immediately afterwards He exhibited signs of love of Godhead. He again displayed such symptoms after returning home [i.e., to Nabadwip]."

Mahāprabhu explains why meeting His guru outshines even His intense experience at Viṣṇupāda: "If one offers oblations to the forefathers in a holy place, then the forefathers are delivered. But one delivers only him to whom the oblation was offered. If one sees you, however, millions of forefathers are immediately freed from material bondage." (*Caitanya-bhāgavata,* Ādi 17.51–52)

In his introductory remarks to *Caitanya-bhāgavata,* Ādi, chapter 17, Śrīla Bhaktisiddhānta Sarasvatī writes that Īśvara Purī initiated Mahāprabhu with the Kṛṣṇa mantra, the attainment of which is itself among the highest goals of human life.

> The Lord personally served all the foodstuffs that He cooked for Himself to Śrī Īśvara Purīpāda, and by directly serving His spiritual master, Purīpāda, with His own hands, He displayed the ideal example of serving the spiritual master. On another day, in a solitary place, Mahāprabhu offered obeisances to Īśvara Purī

and requested him for mantra initiation. Then the Lord received the ten-syllable mantra from His spiritual master and surrendered everything unto his lotus feet.

We find this initiation confirmed in the text itself (*Caitanya-bhāgavata*, Ādi 17.107): "Then in order to instruct everyone, the Lord accepted the ten-syllable mantra from Īśvara Purī."[8]

This lesson is important, particularly the phrase "in order to instruct everyone." Indeed, one may ask why Śrī Caitanya, God Himself, would have to serve a spiritual master and accept mantra *dīkṣā* from him. The tradition responds by saying that Mahāprabhu was God in the form of a devotee and was showing by example how a devotee should act: the disciple should render loving service to the guru and take initiation from him.

The great *ācārya* Śrīla Bhaktivinoda Ṭhākura confirms this: "Thereafter, He went to Gaya and accepted spiritual initiation in the ten-syllable Gopāla mantra from Śrīpāda Īśvara Purī, a great servant of the Lord and torch-bearer of the disciplic succession coming down from Lord Brahmā to Madhvācārya. *The Lord's wish was to teach the living entities their duty of taking shelter of a self-realized spiritual master, as instructed by the scriptures.*"[9]

We conclude with a well-known prayer of Śrīla Narottama Dāsa Ṭhākura: "The lotus feet of our spiritual master are the only way by which we can attain pure devotional service. I bow to his lotus feet with great awe and reverence. By his grace one can cross the ocean of material suffering and obtain the mercy of Kṛṣṇa."

As should by now be clear, none of the above incidents or teachings can be relegated to mere footnotes. Rather, they speak to the essence of Vaiṣṇava philosophy.[10]

Endnotes

1. Among Mahāprabhu's various authorized biographies, only the *Caitanya-bhāgavata* says that He had once met Īśvara Purī earlier, while Śrīla Purīpāda traveled through Nabadwip as a wandering mendicant. Thus, when Mahāprabhu saw him in Gaya, they already knew each other. See especially *Caitanya-bhāgavata,* Ādi-khaṇḍa, chapter eleven.

2. It was at this point that He was overcome with ecstatic love (*prema*), absorbed in Kṛṣṇa's holy name and unable to divert His mind for even a moment.

3. In Vaiṣṇava traditions, bowing to the feet of devotees and to those stationed highly in spiritual life, such as *brāhmaṇas* and *sannyāsīs*, is considered an act of humility. The feet represent the lowest part of the body, and thus bowing to another person's feet is a statement of subservience and submission. Indeed, meditation on the deity form of the Lord begins by focusing on the feet, which is considered a humble and much desired way to approach God.

4. To commemorate this phenomenon, Bhaktisiddhānta Sarasvatī and his disciples installed numerous *pāda-pīṭhas*, replicas of Śrī Caitanya's footprints, at sacred locations He visited.

5. The complex ritual known as the *śrāddha* ceremony is essentially an offering of *prasādam* to one's forefathers to make sure they arrive at a better place in the next life. The ceremony involves balls of cooked rice mixed with ghee and black sesame seeds (a preparation called *piṇḍa*, and so the ceremony is also known as *piṇḍa-dāna*). According to the *Garuḍa Purāṇa*, offering a *piṇḍa* to a recently departed soul helps that soul to unite with its ancestors and guarantees a gradual promotion to heaven.

6. See Locanadāsa Ṭhākura, *Śrī Śrī Caitanya-maṅgala*, edited by Mahānta Śrī Bhagavān Dāsa (Navadvīpa, Nadiyā: Śrī Ānanda-gopāla Śāstrī, 1981), Ādi-khaṇḍa, Chapter 7, *Payārs* 487–493. Special thanks to Śrīvāsa Prabhu for his help with translation.

7. See *Bhagavad-gītā* 7.3, lecture – London, March 11, 1975 (https://vedabase.io/en/library/transcripts/750311bglon/).

8. In the Gauḍīya tradition, the eighteen-syllable Gopāla mantra is sometimes shortened to its last ten syllables – *gopījana-vallabhāya svāhā* – when given to disciples during mantra *dīkṣā*.

9. Commentary on *Śikṣāṣṭaka*, Text 8, *Śrī Sanmodana Bhāṣyam* (https://nbsarticles.blogspot.com/2017/03/sri-sanmodana-bhasyam-on-sri-siksastaka.html?view=classic). Italics added.

10. It should be mentioned here that the Lord's ecstasy increased steadily for the duration of His manifest pastimes. This is the principle known as *sadā-vardhamānānandam,* or "ever-increasing bliss." In fact, after His visit to Gaya, on His return journey to Nabadwip, He passed through Kanai Natshala. While there, He is said to have experienced a mystical vision of Śrī Kṛṣṇa, thus attaining a level of spiritual ecstasy that few ever achieve. His outpouring of beatific glorification upon seeing that form has been preserved in *Caitanya-bhāgavata, Madhya-khaṇḍa*, chapter two, and *Prema-vilāsa*, chapter eight.

Seven

The Hare Krishna Mahā-mantra: Its Breadth and Meaning

ŚRĪ CHAITANYA'S TRADITION focuses on chanting as a yogic science. Consequently, to understand his personality and tradition, one must understand the holy name and its potency. Although I have touched on the *mahā-mantra* elsewhere, I will elaborate on it here.

Throughout history, a plethora of scriptures and sages have enriched the world with innumerable prayers, incantations, and mantras (purificatory sound vibrations), meant for the betterment of all living beings. But there is one chant that stands out in the Gauḍīya Vaishnava tradition, and it is called the Hare Krishna *mahā-mantra*, or "the great chant for deliverance": Hare Krishna, Hare Krishna, Krishna Krishna, Hare Hare/ Hare Rāma, Hare Rāma, Rāma Rāma, Hare Hare.

The Sanskrit word *mantra* is composed of the root *man*, which refers to the mind, and the suffix *tra*, the root of *trayate*, literally meaning "delivers" or "releases." A *mantra* is thus a word or combination of words that delivers the mind from material afflictions, bringing peace, satisfaction, and, ultimately, situating practitioners on the spiritual platform. But the *mahā-mantra*, in particular, goes even further—again showing its pride of place among *mantras*. For practitioners its recitations takes them far beyond mere pacification of the mind and even beyond enhanced spiritual awareness: The *mahā-mantra* has the capacity to catapult sincere chanters into the realm of complete transcendental consciousness, situating them, when perfected, in love of God.

Scripturally, the mantra is chiefly traced to Puranic texts, Vaiṣṇava-āgamas, and Sātvata-tantras.[1] However, the most important scriptural reference, especially for Vedic scholars, is found in the *Kali-santaraṇa Upaniṣad*, part of the Krishna-yajur-veda—this is because, like most Upaniṣads, this is a śruti text, which Vedic scholars deem the most authoritative part of the Vedic literature. Says the *Kali-santaraṇa Upaniṣad*:

hare kṛṣṇa hare kṛṣṇa kṛṣṇa kṛṣṇa hare hare
hare rāma hare rāma rāma rāma hare hare
iti ṣoḍaśakaṁ nāmnāṁ kali-kalmaṣa-nāśanaṁ
nātaḥ paratаropāyaḥ sarva-vedeṣu dṛśyate

"These sixteen names counteract the evil effects of Kali-yuga [our current age of quarrel and hypocrisy]. After searching through the gamut of Vedic texts, one cannot find a method so sublime as the chanting of these names."[2]

Thus, the mantra has Vedic backing and sanction. But, perhaps even more importantly, it is the preferred mantra of Gauḍīya Vaishnava masters, who advocate the daily chanting of Hare Krishna as a central spiritual practice.

In terms of literal composition, the mantra consists of three names of God—Hari, Krishna, and Rāma. Thus, it is made up of specific nouns, or personalities, in a form that directly calls out to them in a mood of exhortation. "This is in the seventh case ending," says contemporary Vaishnava scholar Shrivatsa Goswami, "what you call in English the 'vocative case'—when you are addressing or calling someone. In Sanskrit this is called *sambodhana,* 'addressing.'"[3]

If we break down the mantra in terms of word meaning, we see that Hari, the first word in the mantra, means "he who takes away." Its root stems from the Sanskrit *hṛ-*, i.e., "to take away or remove evil or sin." Accordingly, Hari [Krishna] takes away all unwanted things, from undesirable conditioning and bad habits to our overarching material consciousness. In the Vaishnava tradition, Hari is a generic name for God, indicating the presence of Vishnu or Krishna.[4]

But the word Hari has a deeper dimension as well. For Gauḍīyas, it is also identified with Mother Harā, the female Absolute, Śrīmatī Rādhārāṇī, and when it appears in the vocative, as it does in the *mahā-mantra*, it calls out to her to kindly engage one in the process of *bhakti*, devotional service. This is because she is the highest exemplar of unalloyed service to Krishna.[5] Apropos of this, hers is the first and last name in the mantra and overall comprises eight of its sixteen words. The tradition further views her as Krishna's transcendental female counterpart and his pleasure-giving potency (*hlādinī-śakti*)—she alone is able to "steal" Krishna's mind and heart, making her the true embodiment of the word Hari.

In this way, the "Hare" in the *mahā-mantra* can be seen as either Krishna or Rādhā. It should be noted, however, that the Rādhā version is more representative of Gauḍīya *siddhānta*, and has a history that goes back to the beginning of the tradition, making its way into the commentaries of both Gopāla Guru Gosvāmī and Jīva Goswāmī, among others.[6] We will elavorate on the importance of Rādhā's place in the *mahā-mantra* later.

Krishna literally means "blackish," referring to the color in general and, in the current context, to the Lord's beautiful dark complexion. Among Vaishnavas, though, Krishna is more commonly defined as "the all-attractive one," which is also a legitimate reading of the word. This rendering derives from the word *karṣati* ("attracts"), indicating his all-attractive form and character, attributes unique to him. Thus, it connotes the Supreme Personality of Godhead—the source of all incarnations and manifestations of God, to Whom Rādhā (Hare) is intimately connected.

In Lakṣmīdhara's *Nāma Kaumudī*, a Vaishnava text that Śrīla Prabhupāda quotes repeatedly, the word *krishna* is defined as, "the supreme spiritual substance." This harkens to *Gopāla-tāpanī Upaniṣad*, which explains (in *pūrva*.1.1) that *kṛṣ-* means "existence," and *-ṇa* means "carefree." The word *krishna* therefore indicates an entity whose existence is effortless, causeless, without defects, and blissful—the Lord of *līlā*, or divine sport. he is *brahman*, i.e., the supreme spiritual substance—consciousness itself in its pure, original, and wholesome form, the source of all.

Śrīla Prabhupāda elaborates, "If we analyze the *nirukti*, or semantic derivation, of the word 'Kṛṣṇa,' we find that *na* signifies that He stops the repetition of birth and death, and *kṛṣ* means *sattārtha*, or 'existence.' (Kṛṣṇa is the whole of existence.)"[7] Prabhupāda offers an alternate version of this explanation from the *Mahābhārata* as well: "The word '*kṛṣ*' is the attractive feature of the Lord's existence, and '*ṇa*' means 'spiritual pleasure.' When the verb '*kṛṣ*' is added to the affix '*ṇa*,' it becomes 'Kṛṣṇa,' which indicates the Absolute Truth."[8] Thus, the name Krishna points to total existential reality, the ultimate spiritual substance, and indicates, too, that the Lord extricates us from material life, ultimately situating us within his loving embrace.

Rāma, the name that accompanies Hare and Krishna in the mantra, refers to "the pleasing one" (*ramaṇa*, literally, "one who pleases, delights in, charms") and generally indicates either Krishna's brother Balarāma or Rāmachandra, the incarnation of Krishna who is the hero of India's ancient epic, the *Rāmāyaṇa*.[9] For Gauḍīyas, however, Rāma primarily refers to "Krishna as the lover of Rādhā."[10]

In Shrivatsa Goswami's explanation of the *mahā-mantra*, he writes, "In the second line, the new word is 'Rāma.' *Ramayati rādhikayā sa iti rāmaḥ*: 'The one who sports with Rādhā is Rāma.' This 'Rāma' is Krishna. This is the meaning given by Jīva Gosvāmī."[11] Regarding the distinct Gauḍīya reading of the *mantra*—with Rādhā and Krishna as its main focus—this is perhaps best summed up by Prabhupāda's guru, Bhaktisiddhānta Sarasvatī (1874–1937). He clarifies that the *mantra* is embraced by each person according to his or her own preponderant internal proclivity—for those inclined toward awe and reverence, they will read it in one way, but for those given to the sweetness of *mādhurya*, or intimate love as found in the Gauḍīya tradition, they will read it in quite another:

> . . . when the words "Hare Rāma" are pronounced in a mood of reverential service to God, they indicate

> Śrī Rāma, the son of Daśaratha in Ayodhyā. However, devotees who worship in the mood of conjugal service understand Krishna, the son of Nanda in Vrindavan, as the lover of the cowherd girls (*gopī-rāmana*), and thus Rāma. When the word "Rāma" indicates service to Krishna, the lover of Rādhā (Rādhā-rāmaṇa), the term of address or "Harā" (Hare is the vocative form) indicates Rādhā, understood as the metaphysical or internal energy (*parā-śakti*) of God. In accordance with this understanding, the names Hare, Krishna, and Rāma refer to Rādhā and Krishna alone.[12]

Accordingly, the entire gamut of Gauḍīya Vaishnava spirituality is found in the Hare Krishna *mahā-mantra*, prompting devotee-scholars, like Garuḍa Prabhu (Graham Schweig), to write as follows:

> This mantra is virtually a sonic reenactment of the Rāsa Maṇḍala, consisting of a series of alternating names of God in the vocative case, both calling out for and praising the presence of the divine. When the mantra is recited repeatedly in meditation or song, it worshipfully enthrones the Soul of the soul within the heart of the devotee, forming a sonic *maṇḍala*. ...The circuitous arrangement of the words of this *mahā-mantra* consists of an alternating pattern between an equal number of feminine (as *hare*) and masculine (as *kṛṣṇa* ...and as *rāma*) names of the divine. The sacred thirty-two-syllable mantra appears as follows: *hare kṛṣṇa / hare kṛṣṇa / kṛṣṇa kṛṣṇa / hare hare / hare rāma / hare rāma / rāma rāma / hare hare.* The patterned movement of eight pairs of feminine and masculine names of the divine can be observed in the mantra. Within four of the pairs (the first, second, fifth, and sixth) the feminine and masculine names appear alternately. In the other four pairs (the

> third, fourth, seventh, and eighth) two masculine names appear together in one pair, followed by two feminine names in the next pair. Thus the dancelike movement can be observed both within and between pairs. Additionally, the mantra begins and ends with feminine names, enclosing the masculine names, just as the *Gopīs* engulf Krishna when they encircle him during the commencement of the Rāsa dance. When practitioners recite the mantra over and over, the divine names form a circular pattern imitative of the exchange between the feminine and masculine partners in the Rāsa dance. It can be seen, then, that the presence of the Rāsa Maṇḍala is archetypal in Vaishnava practices.[13]

Comparing the *mahā-mantra* to the Rāsa-līlā is high praise. Viśvanātha Chakravartī refers to the Rāsa-līlā as "the crown jewel of all līlās" (*sarva-līlā-cūḍa-maṇi*), for it expresses the purest love, focusing, as it does, on the heartfelt exchange of Krishna and His highest devotees, the *gopīs*, in the mood of romantic spirituality (*mādhurya-rasa*).[14] This is significant for all living beings. "The reason the Lord displays the rāsa-līlā" writes Śrīla Prabhupāda, "is essentially to induce all the fallen souls to give up their diseased morality and religiosity, and to attract them to the kingdom of God ..."[15] This is accomplished through the pure chanting of the Hare Krishna *mahā-mantra*.

While all of these nuances can play an important role in understanding the full import of the mantra, Śrīla Prabhupāda encouraged us to enter into the chanting in the simplest of ways, mainly by sincerely intoning and hearing the sound vibration itself, with a basic understanding of its overall meaning.

When I was a young devotee, I was especially taken by Śrīla Prabhupāda's simple and direct translation: "O Lord. O energy of the Lord. Please engage me in Your pure devotional service." I appreciated the prayer's selflessness. In a world where people tend to not approach God at all, or, if they do, it is mainly to get something for themselves—"Please give us our daily bread"—it was refreshing and heartening to find a prayer that focuses only on serving the Lord, purely, without asking anything in return.

Additionally, the breadth and meaning of the mantra's inner dimensions are, in fact, encoded in these simple words, "Please engage me in Your service." Still, one might question how Śrīla Prabhupāda derives this translation, particularly since the mantra, as we have discussed, is only made up of three names in the vocative. How can it be interpreted so as to ask the Lord for engagement in his service? Here's how: As mentioned above, Śrī Rādhā is the very emblem of devotional service (*bhakti-seva*). In other words, beseeching her is beseeching service. The presence of her name, then, is what gives the mantra its real connection to *bhakti*. It is the inner secret of the *mahā-mantra*.

And there is precedent for Prabhupāda's translation. Prabhupāda always said that he was presenting the tradition "as it is," without change or addition, and, sure enough, this holds true even in his explication of the *mahā-mantra*.

In one of the tradition's earliest explanations, Gopal Guru Gosvāmī offers a similar reading, including the urgent request for engagement in devotional service: "Hare! O Hari! Make me worthy to engage in Your service." (*hare—he hare, nija-sevā-yogyaṁ māṁ kuru*) And "Rāma! O Rāma! As

I enter into those pastimes by the path of meditation, make me worthy to engage in Your service." (*rāma—he rāma, tatra māṁ nija-sevā-yogyaṁ kuru*) It is to be noted that he refers to *sevā*, the specific Sanskrit word for devotional service.

The same is found in Bhaktivinoda Ṭhākura's commentary on the mantra, "With the seventh pair, one takes shelter of Rādhā's lotus feet, with attachment for the sentiment of divine romance. Here one chants "Rāma Rāma" in the mood of separation. With the eighth pair, one is fixed in the identity of a *gopī* in Vrindavan, attaining the ultimate goal of *service to the Divine Couple*, Rādhā and Krishna.[16] [emphasis added] So it is a deeply established part of the tradition.

Still, Prabhupāda's fundamental explanation gives us all we need to actually realize the esoteric truths at the heart of the mantra:

> The transcendental vibration established by the chanting of Hare Kṛṣṇa, Hare Kṛṣṇa, Kṛṣṇa Kṛṣṇa, Hare Hare/ Hare Rāma, Hare Rāma, Rāma Rāma, Hare Hare is the sublime method of reviving our Kṛṣṇa consciousness. As living spiritual souls we are all originally Kṛṣṇa conscious entities, but due to our association with matter from time immemorial, our consciousness is now polluted by the material atmosphere. The material atmosphere, in which we are now living, is called *māyā*, or illusion. *Māyā* means "that which is not." And what is this illusion? The illusion is that we are all trying to be lords of material nature, while actually we are under the grip of her stringent laws. When a servant artificially tries to imitate the all-powerful master, this is called illusion. In this polluted concept of life, we are all trying to exploit the resources of material nature, but actually we are becoming more and more entangled in her complexities. Therefore, although

> we are engaged in a hard struggle to conquer nature, we are ever more dependent on her. This illusory struggle against material nature can be stopped at once by revival of our Kṛṣṇa consciousness.[17]

Śrīla Prabhupāda's conclusion is clear: "By vibrating this transcendental sound, the meaning of everything, both material and spiritual, is revealed."[18]

So, in the end, the *mahā-mantra*'s meaning ranges from a simple calling out to the Lord in earnest supplication, asking to be engaged in his exclusive loving service, to a reenactment of the Rāsa-līlā, the most intimate and esoteric pastime of Rādhā and Krishna in the spiritual world. But to begin, the practitioner can start by simply chanting and listening attentively to the sound vibration. And, through practice, with sincerity and devotion, one can gradually reach the pinnacle of the spiritual pursuit.

Endnotes

1. For specific Puranic references, see Kostyantyn Perun (Brijbasi das), "Hare Kṛṣṇa Mahā-Mantra From the Caitanya-Vaiṣṇava Perspective" in *Journal of Vaishnava Studies*, Volume 24, No. 2 (Spring 2016), 179–222.

2. In certain manuscripts of the *Kali-santaraṇa Upaniṣad*, the *mahā-mantra* appears with the "Hare Rāma" part first, leading to a controversy on the order in which the names are said to originally appear in the mantra. Vaishnava scholars have proven, however, that the version with the "Hare Krishna" part first is most authoritative. This is a complex subject and has been thoroughly addressed in Brijbasi das, op. cit., 185–187, and also in Bhaktisiddhānta Sarasvatī, the *Gauḍīya*, Volume 11, No. 7 (October 22, 1932), 101. See also Śrīmad Bhaktivedānta Nārāyaṇa Mahārāja, trans., *Sri Hari-Nāma Mahā-mantra*, op. cit., 3–15.

3. Steven J. Gelberg, ed., *Hare Krishna, Hare Krishna: Five Distinguished Scholars on the Krishna Movement in the West* (New York: Grove Press, 1983), 222.

4. One way to understand the word "Hare" is that it refers to Krishna, or "Harati," indicating one who "unties the knot of material existence." See *Chaitanya Upanishad*, Mantra 12 (*The Glories of Śrī Chaitanya Mahāprabhu*, trans., Kuśakratha Dāsa, New York: Bala Books, 1984).

5. The word "Radha" literally means "the one who worships Krishna best." Śrīla Prabhupāda repeatedly lauds Her as greatest among devotees: "In this way Śrīla Rūpa Gosvāmī gradually concludes that Śrīmatī Rādhārāṇī is the most exalted devotee of Kṛṣṇa..." (*Nectar of Instruction* 10, Purport). "Śrīmatī Rādhārāṇī, She is the topmost servitor of Kṛṣṇa." (Lecture on Śrīmad Bhāgavatam 3.25.7—Bombay, November 7, 1974). "Rādhārāṇī is the servitor, serving. Rādhārāṇī is so expert that She always attracts Kṛṣṇa by Her service. This is Rādhārāṇī's position." (Lecture on Śrīmad Bhāgavatam 6.1.62—Vrndavana, August 29, 1975)

6. See *Śrīmad Bhaktivedānta* Nārāyaṇa Mahārāja, trans., *Śrī Hari-Nāma Mahā-mantra* (Mathura, U.P.: Gauḍīya Vedānta Publications, 2001, 2nd Edition), 27–30. Interpreting Hare as Rādhā can also be found in Narahari Chakravartī's *Bhakti-ratnākara* 5.2,214 to 2,218.

7. *Śrīmad-Bhāgavatam* 10.8.15, purport. Prabhupāda's source for this is the *Gautamīya-tantra* as quoted in in Śrīla Jīva Gosvāmī's commentary to the *Brahma-saṁhitā* 5.1: "*Kṛi* means 'existence' and *ṇa* means 'having a form of bliss.' He is the very form of happiness, because He is composed of the bliss that arises from *prema*." (*kṛṣi-śabdaś ca sattārtho | ṇaś cānanda-svarūpakaḥ || sukha-rūpo bhaved ātmā | bhāvānanda-mayatvataḥ ||*) See translation by Bhanu Swami, Śrī Brahma-saṁhitā: with the commentary Dig-darśanī-ṭīkā of Śrī Jīva Gosvāmī (Sri Vaikuntha Enterprises, 2008).

8. See *Caitanya-caritāmṛta,* Madhya 9.30.

9. See *Śrīmad Bhāgavatam* 10.2.13, purport, and *Caitanya-caritāmṛta* 1.5.132, purport.

10. From the *Rāma Tāpinīya Upaniṣad* (1.6): "Krishna is also known as 'Rāma' because the bliss of the conjugal mellow of pure love is the very essence of His being, because He is the titular Deity of loving sports incarnate, and because He brings pleasure to His eternal

consort Śrīmatī Rādhārāṇī." (http://sriradhakrishnabhakti.blogspot.com/2015/08/ maha-mantra-meaning.html) Quoted in Śrīla Gopāla Guru Gosvāmī's *Svarūpa-siddhānta-vākyam*, which is his commentary on the *mahā-mantra*. As Prabhupāda confirms, "You can say Rādhā-Rāma, the same meaning. sssRādhā-Ramaṇa or Rādhā-Rāma." (audio/ transcripts/1972/721101R1.VRN.mp3) Or, "*Ramante yoginaḥ anante. Ramante,* this very word, one who is engaged, he is called *iti rāma-padenāsau paraṁ brahmābhidhīyate* (See *Caitanya-caritāmṛta,* Madhya 9.29). This is the meaning of Rāma—Rāma, Kṛṣṇa, Rādhā-Rāmaṇa…" (audio/transcripts/1973/730110ND.BOM.mp3)

11. See Steven J. Gelberg, ed., *Hare Krishna, Hare Krishna, op. cit.*, 222.

12. Originally found in the correspondence of Bhaktisiddhānta Sarasvatī. See letter dated October 10, 1928 (*Prabhupādera Patravali*, Volume 1, 57). Quoted in Ferdinando Sardella, *Modern Hindu Personalism* (Oxford University Press, 2013), 81, footnote 82.

13. Graham M. Schweig, *Dance of Divine Love: the Rāsa Līlā of Krishna from the Bhāgavata Purāṇa, India's Classic Sacred Love Story* (Princeton, N.J.: Princeton University Press, 2005), 179. In their commentaries on the *mahā-mantra*, both Gopāla Guru Gosvāmī and Jīva Gosvāmī refer to the Rāsa-līlā, but only peripherally. It might also be mentioned that Lord Krishna calls the *gopīs* to the Rāsa Dance with the sound of his flute, and that flute playing, the tradition tells us, has some correlation with the *mahā-mantra*. As Prabhupāda says, "This vibration of Krishna's flute is represented by the Hare Krishna *mahā-mantra*." (*Caitanya-caritāmṛta*, Madhya 21.144, purport)

14. See Viśvanātha's commentary on the *Bhāgavatam* 10.29.1.

15. See *Caitanya-caritāmṛta* 1.4.30.

16. See "Explanation of the Hare Krishna Mantra" by Śrīla Bhaktivinoda Ṭhākura, from his Book *Bhajan Rahasya: saptame madhurāsakti rādhā-padāśraya, vipralambhe rāma rāma nāmera udaya, aṣṭame vrajete aṣṭa-kāla gopī-bhāva, rādhā-kṛṣṇa-prema-sevā prayojana lābha* (https://iskcondesiretree.com/forum/topics/explanation-of-the-hare-krishna-mantra-by-srila-bhaktivinod)

17. https://prabhupadabooks.com/tys/6

18. See *Śrīmad Bhāgavatam* 4.24.40, purport.

The Offenses to the Holy Name

The tradition offers various methods by which one can assure pure chanting. There is a list of ten "don'ts" that are said to aid the serious practitioner in chanting the holy name of Krishna. We find this list, first and foremost, in the *Padma Purāṇa* and the *Hari-bhakti-vilāsa*. These two texts are then elaborated upon by Jīva Gosvāmī (c. 16th century), both in his commentary on Rūpa Gosvāmī's *Bhakti-rasāmṛta-sindhu* (1.2.120) and in his *Bhakti Sandarbha* (Anuccheda 265). After Jīva, Viśvanātha Cakravartī highlights this same list in his *Bhakti-rasāmṛta-sindhu-bindhu* (Pūrva-vibhāga, First Wave, text 7).

In the modern era, Bhaktivinoda Ṭhākura offers a discussion on these offenses in *Jaiva Dharma*, Chapter 24, and *Hari-nāma-cintāmaṇi*, Chapter 4. Prabhupada, too, highlights the importance of this list: See especially his commentary on *Śrīmad Bhāgavatam* 2.1.11, and the first chapter of *The Teaching of Lord Chaitanya*, pp. 29-30. The basic list appears as follows:

It is an offense:

1. To blaspheme the devotees of the Lord.
2. To consider the names of Shiva and similar entities to be equal to that of Vishnu.
3. To disobey the order of the spiritual master.
4. To minimize the importance of scripture.
5. To interpret the the name outside of traditional exegesis.

6. To consider the name's glories as mere imagination.
7. To commit sinful acts with the idea that the name will absolve one of necessary reaction (karma).
8. To enumerate the glories of the name to those who have no faith.
9. To consider the chanting to be mere pious activity.
10. To not have complete faith in the name.

As an addendum, it is often said that the most egregious offense is to be inattentive while chanting.

Eight

Mahāprabhu Meets the Magistrate: A Spiritual Precursor to Gandhi's "Civil Disobedience" Movement

Introduction

IN ALL OF HUMAN HISTORY, there are no greater icons of nonviolent protest than Mahatma Gandhi (1869–1948) and Dr. Martin Luther King (1929–1968). Their teachings of understanding and compassion—rooted in both Hindu and Christian traditions, as well as in common sense—have served to underline their considerable wisdom, highlighting the power of love. Predating both these peaceful warriors, however, stands an original pioneer of non-aggressive civil disobedience, someone unknown to most students of civil rights. I refer here to Śrī Chaitanya Mahāprabhu, who, in the Gauḍīya Vaishnava tradition, is said to be Krishna himself in the guise of his own devotee. Five hundred years ago he orchestrated a nonviolent demonstration unlike the world had ever seen, before or since.

The name Chaitanya Mahāprabhu is certainly less familiar than those of Gandhi or King. In fact, a more common triptych regarding the fathers of the civil rights movement would be Thoreau, Gandhi, and King, with the latter two deriving inspiration from Henry David Thoreau's book, *Civil Disobedience* (1849). It was in that text that Thoreau famously asked, "Must the citizen ever for a moment, or in the least degree, resign his conscience to the legislator? Why has every man a conscience then? I think that we should be men first, and subjects afterward."[1]

Thoreau taught that individuals could effectively oppose unscrupulous government action by very simply refusing to cooperate. When faced with unjust laws, he wrote, there are three possible ways to react: "Obey them, amend them, or transgress them."[2]

Various kinds of people are inclined to various means. Without being overly simplistic, people in darkness (*tamo-guṇa*) tend to blindly follow, accepting authority even when unjust; those in passion (*raja-guṇa*) will work for change, often compulsively, sometimes even when said change is not necessarily warranted; and those in goodness (*sattva-guṇa*) will generally subsist outside of unjust laws, following them when they must, but answering, whenever possible, to a higher power. Nonviolent resistance is generally a merger of the latter two, changing an existing regime by protesting and rising beyond it—but always through peaceful means.

Make no mistake: Gandhi and King's commitment to nonviolence was not a commitment to passivity. In fact, they were committed to action—to the direct confrontation of violent oppression. What distinguished them was that their combative spirit was always peaceful, at least as far as possible. We will see much the same in Mahāprabhu's "forceful" uprising in premodern Bengal, which is at the heart of our story.[3] The then Muslim administration largely lived in harmony with the Vaishnavas of the time, some of whom even held positions of power in the governing state.[4] But tension would periodically flare up, and when it did, the Vaishnavas would defend their rights, as they did in the episode under discussion, but always with a sense of love, compassion, and higher purpose.

The best among nonviolent activists rarely intend to undermine the rule of law, but only to repeal those laws and customs that are patently unjust. Gandhi and King's focus, for example, revolved around laws that supported colonial rule and prejudicial discrimination, such as racism, which they attempted to abolish. Realizing that most people are not equipped to win a violent battle, nor was it right to take a life for personal reasons, they adopted many of Thoreau's fundamental ideas of peaceful resistance, adapting these principles in their own way.

For instance, Gandhi, in developing his concept of Satyagraha (literally "holding firmly to truth" but now identified with non-cooperation in general), was insistent on avoiding violence, overcoming brute force with placid determination. This method, he admitted, would not always work. But it was clearly "the higher road" and often more advantageous for the greatest number of people.[5] In fact, it was Gandhi's non-cooperation philosophy that informed King's approach to civil rights; he merely adapted the Mahatma's idea to the specific circumstances then prevalent in America, particularly the systemic racism directed toward the African-American community. King always acknowledged Gandhi as one of his central influences, and in 1959 even made the pilgrimage to India in his honor.[6]

Abdul Ghaffar Khan should be mentioned in this context, too, since he was a Gandhian freedom fighter and founder of the Khudai Khidmatgar resistance movement against British colonial rule in India—a devout Muslim and an advocate for Hindu–Muslim unity in the Indian subcontinent. Following Gandhi, he was a major proponent of civil disobedience.[7]

It can be said, then, that India is in some ways the home of the modern nonviolent resistance movement.

Taking this notion further, in the narrative of Śrī Chaitanya and the Chand Kazi (*qāzī, kājī*),[8] as we will now see, there exists a tangible instance—perhaps the first instance—of organized civil disobedience on the subcontinent, and while not overtly committed to the principle of nonviolence in the same way that Gandhi and King were, Śrī Chaitanya's actions serve to quell a potentially violent episode, in which tens of thousands[9] could have perished. Indeed, the march on the Chand Kazi's home could have been one of the bloodiest battles in history, but instead it ended in both sides joyfully chanting Krishna's holy name, with no harm perpetrated on a single individual.

Before relating the Chand Kazi narrative, it would be useful to note some important distinctions between our relatively recent political heroes and Śrī Chaitanya: Gandhi and King were both modern figures, ensconced in the politics of their time. Śrī Caitanya, on the other hand, was neither from the present-day nor a politician, and neither Gandhi nor King ever mentioned him as a precedent for their politics. Gandhi and King worked for decades on their political projects, and this work constituted their main concern. Śrī

Chaitanya, conversely, rarely engaged directly with political leaders, even keeping himself at a distance from the Gajapati king Pratāparudra, merely because of the latter's political or worldly affiliation. There are no historical indications that Śrī Caitanya's movement was ever meant to bring about overt political change in premodern India (whether Bengal or Orissa), which is precisely what Gandhi and King wanted to do vis-à-vis British colonial rule in India/Pakistan/Bangladesh and white supremacy in America, respectively. Most significantly, perhaps, Gandhi and King were mortal, while Śrī Chaitanya is viewed as God, Krishna himself, and thus his involvement with civil disobedience, such that it was, is part of his *līlā*, or divine sport, say his followers, with spiritual implications that transcend ordinary politics. In other words, Śrī Caitanya's movement was ultimately meant to create a spiritual revolution, not a political one.

That said, Gauḍīya Vaishnava philosophy, when properly practiced, does not neglect life in the material world, for when people's hearts are truly changed by spiritual realization, they behave in an exemplary way both materially and spiritually, feeling compassion for all souls. As Joseph T. O'Connell, the late Professor Emeritus in the Study of Religion at the University of Toronto, Canada, writes,

> Certain authoritative Chaitanya Vaishnava writers appealed to the principle of *lokasaṅgraha* (holding the world together/maintaining the general welfare), a principle also enunciated in the *Bhagavad-gītā*, by way of explaining how to participate responsibly in the environing mundane world without fundamentally violating one's basic commitment to *krishna-bhakti*. Rather than occasion unnecessary difficulties and distractions,

> Vaishnavas should put up with less than ideal conditions in the mundane, or *laukika*, sphere. The Chaitanyaite interpretation of *lokasaṅgraha* justifies participating in public affairs, even under Muslim regimes (as well as under the British colonial and independent Indian regimes). Chaitanya Vaishnavas may also accede to many Brahmanic ritual-social customs even though these may be judged to be devoid of sacral legitimation in and of themselves. However, if governmental or Brahmanic or other interests were to interfere seriously with their exercise of *krishna-bhakti*, then devotees would be expected to object and seek redress, preferably through discreet, negotiated settlements. ... For example, a boisterous mass protest (of a Muslim qāzī's ineffectual attempt to stop public *kīrtana* singing) leading to polite negotiation is celebrated in biographies of Chaitanya. Typically, issues of strain between devotees and civil authorities have been managed without the boisterous protest. There is virtually no history of violent conflict with authorities and attendant martyrdom in the Chaitanya Vaishnava tradition.[10]

It is against this backdrop—with a focus on how Gauḍīya Vaishnavism plays out in the material world when a dominating political regime tries to obstruct the practice of Krishna-bhakti, in this case by banning Harināma *saṅkīrtana*, or the public congregational chanting of the holy name—that we might now explore the incident known as *Kazi dalan*, or "the humbling of the Kazi."

Śrī Chaitanya and the Chand Kazi: A Synopsis

The Saṅkīrtana movement commences with the Lord's initiation in Gayā. Ostensibly, Śrī Chaitanya, then known as Nimāi, had traveled to this district in Bihar from Navadvīpa to conduct his father's funeral rites and to offer oblations to his forefathers. But his real reason, say his biographers, was to reunite with his spiritual master Īśvara Purī and to take initiation from him. As the texts opine, just after the initiation, Śrī Chaitanya experienced a substratal shift in consciousness, exhibiting feelings of divine separation from Krishna. From that moment, his absorption in the holy name took prominence in his daily life.[11] On his return journey to Navadvīpa, he chanted like a man possessed. So alluring was his ecstatic singing that people along the way would join in. This is *saṅkīrtana*.

Prior to going to Gayā, he had opened a school, teaching such subjects as Sanskrit, grammar, rhetoric, and logic. But when he returned, his students were shocked by his "God-intoxicated" behavior, resulting in the annulment of his school. His lectures were no longer about lofty intellectual subjects but about chanting the holy name. According to Vrindāvandāsa's *Chaitanya-bhāgavata*, Madhya 1 (405), Śrī Chaitanya instructed his students as follows, "What you have heard and read for many days now make perfect by chanting the holy names of Lord Krishna."[12] The chanting became contagious, and his students began to follow his example, chanting aloud whenever possible.

"Hearing the *kīrtana*," Vrindāvandāsa tells us, "all who

lived in neighboring homes ran toward the sound." Seeing the Master's ecstatic trance upon chanting, the Vaishnavas felt great wonder. Madhya 1 (411-419) tells us that the devotees gathered, one by one, at the Master's house. "Haribol! [Chant Hari!]" Śrī Chaitanya roared, his voice reverberating in all directions. Then he fell to the ground, shaking. No one could hold him still. Seeing these wonders, the devotees happily sang the holy names with him. Nothing could contain their ecstasy. In this way, Śrī Chaitanya began the Saṅkīrtana movement. As witnesses to this—and as participants—the devotees in Navadvīpa found that any suffering they may have previously experienced had become a thing of the past.[13]

During this period, too, Mahāprabhu began regular chanting sessions in Śrīvāsa Paṇḍita's courtyard, establishing a nocturnal school of *kīrtana*—and it was from this venue that *saṅkīrtana* really began to spread throughout Navadvīpa. His handpicked companions joined him in that courtyard, where he exhibited profound symptoms of divine love; such symptoms were nourished, he taught, by chanting God's names in the company of devotees. From Śrīvāsa's courtyard, and from other homes that now followed suit, *kīrtana* could be heard everywhere, spilling into neighboring streets, and this is where our story begins.

The Chand Kazi served as Navadvīpa's city magistrate under Hussein Shah (reigned 1493–1519), the independent sultan of Bengal, and he worked hard to please those under him, whether they were associated with his own Muslim tradition or the local *brāhmaṇa* community.[14] What is generally left unstated is that the Kazi and Mahāprabhu were sustaining a transcendental rivalry that goes back to their previous incarnations: Vaishnava luminary Bhaktivinoda Ṭhākura (1838–1914) expresses this esoteric dimension to the story in his work *Śrī Navadvīpa Dhāma Māhātmya*, Parikramā-khaṇḍa, Chapter 6: "King Kaṁsa of Krishna-līlā became Chand Kazi in Gaura-līlā. For that reason Gaurāṅga [Chaitanya] addressed the Kazi as his maternal uncle ... Under orders from Hussein Shah, who was the king of the Bengal Empire and Jarāsandha in Krishna-līlā, the Kazi caused disturbance during *kīrtana* performance ..."[15]

But as it played out in the material world, Śrī Chaitanya preached his doctrine of divine love throughout the Kazi's area of authority and gradually became more and more visible because of his large chanting parties. While the Muslim population remained tolerant, at least to some degree, it was the caste-conscious Hindus—*smārta brāhmaṇas*—who complained and created difficulty for Mahāprabhu's mission, their conventional understanding of Hinduism virtually forcing them to deprecate the Lord's ever-growing religion of love.

Thus, the Kazi, reacting to the complaints of his constituency, journeyed to Śrīvāsa Paṇḍita's courtyard and witnessed the *kīrtana* for himself. At that time, he warned the devotees that the congregational chanting should stop at once, especially in public (Śrīvāsa's courtyard was also considered public, for it had a large open area visible to the outside). He further told them that if they ignored his reprimand, he would have their instruments confiscated and even forcefully repeal their caste status, effectively converting them into Muslims! It was during this interaction that the

Kazi infamously broke their *mṛdaṅga* to show the seriousness of his warning.[16] In fact, the Kazi had been harassing devotees for some time, threatening to make their public chanting illegal. Moreover, say the texts, he would often beat them if he found them singing in the streets.[17] Indeed, his "breaking of the *mṛdaṅga*" was not an isolated incident: he had done this before.[18]

Nevertheless, it was, in particular, the unfortunate upheaval at Śrīvāsa's home that was brought to Mahāprabhu's attention. In response, he spoke out against the Muslims of Bengal, issuing severe verbal threats—just to show *his* seriousness. Although he was clearly infuriated by the Kazi's attempt to disturb his mission, in the end his methods were peaceful. He adhered to the principle of nonviolent resistance, as Prabhupāda, the founder of the modern-day Hare Krishna movement, opines in his commentary, a subject to which we will later return.

In reaction to the Chand Kazi's infraction, Mahāprabhu sent out word to the townspeople that they should take to the streets that evening, singing the holy names with torches in hand, to light up the night sky. In actuality, the masses with lit flames brought great fear to the Kazi and his constables. Many thousands gathered on Śrī Chaitanya's behalf, chanting and determined to help. They divided into fourteen groups, each one growing as they marched to the Kazi's home.[19] Their mood of protest was clear.

Upon their arrival, Mahāprabhu and a few of his main followers confronted the Muslim leader, who was visibly frightened, and a long conversation ensued. In the end, the Master communicated the essence of his Vaishnava tradition, as the Kazi did his, drawing on both the Vedic scriptures and the Koran.[20] They had agreed to let scripture be their guide. Among the many topics discussed were vegetarianism and the treatment of defenseless animals, since, in general, the Vaishnavas abstained from animal flesh while the Muslims were meat eaters. The Lord explained to him that while ancient Vedic sacrifices indeed included the killing of animals, such sacrifices are forbidden in the current age of Kali. Rather, the practice of *saṅkīrtana*—the congregational chanting disrupted by the Kazi and his men—was recommended for the current epoch of world history. The Kazi, touched by his words and person, began to cry, admitting that he was wrong to stand in his way, and that he could see divinity in Mahāprabhu himself. More, he felt pangs of ecstatic love merely by being in his presence. The Kazi then joined the chanting parties waiting right outside, and everyone rejoiced.

Interestingly, the Kazi had already, before their meeting, made up his mind to support the Saṅkīrtana movement. Apparently, as he told Mahāprabhu during their discussion, he had had a dream right after his breaking of the drum: "As I slept that night," said the Kazi, "I saw a greatly ferocious creature, roaring very loudly—his body was like a human being's but his face was like that of a lion. In my dream, the lion jumped on my chest, laughing and showing his sharp teeth. Placing his nails on my chest, he said in a scary voice, 'I shall immediately break open your chest as you broke apart the drum!'" The lion was, according to tradition, the half-man/ half-lion *avatāra* known as Nṛsiṁhadeva. After telling Mahāprabhu this story, the Kazi showed him his chest, which bore the actual marks of the lion's nails. Because of this, he had already asked his men to cease and desist, giving full endorsement to the Saṅkīrtana movement. Meeting Mahāprabhu served to further nourish and enhance his newfound devotional sentiments. Thus, the only real violence perpetrated during the Chand Kazi episode was the violence in his dream.

Was it Really Civil Disobedience?

As stated, the Chand Kazi episode is sometimes considered an early instance of "civil disobedience," predating both Mahatma Gandhi and Martin Luther King, Jr. Prabhupāda notes: "He was the first man in the history of India who started this civil disobedience movement. It is not Gandhi who is the originator of civil disobedience; it was Chaitanya Mahāprabhu."[21]

That said, Vrindāvanadāsa Ṭhākura's *Chaitanya-bhāgavata* (Madhya 23), whose version of the story is slightly different than that of Krishnadāsa Kavirāja's *Caitanya-caritāmṛta*, gives us reason to pause. His rendition is often more harsh, with little indication of "passive resistance" or "civil disobedience." Gone is the mood of reconciliation and the prolonged interreligious discussion between Mahāprabhu and the Kazi, which we do not find until the fuller version as revealed in the *Caitanya-caritāmṛta*.[22] It is Kavirāja Goswāmī who enables readers to see the episode as an instance of nonviolent civil disobedience.

To be sure, the Vrindāvandāsa version is more severe. But if looked at in terms of ultimate results, again, no one was harmed, and this remains true despite harsh, instigating language and property damage. In the end, it seems merely a judicious use of scare tactics, especially since the texts tell us that the Kazi "repeatedly abused and beat the Vaishnavas." Thus, although the *Caitanya-bhāgavata* version is more dramatic, with aggressive rhetoric, it is ultimately a very small and measured response to ongoing religious persecution of an entire community.

"I think what Caitanya attempted to do," writes Santanu Dey, Associate Professor in the Department of History at the Ramakrishna Mission Vidyamandira, "was to build up resistance against a patently unfair restriction of religious freedom by the Kazi. The Kazi's blanket threat against public performance by the Vaishnavas and his physical destruction of a *mṛdaṅga* was sufficient proof of the fact that he was abusing his position of authority with an intention to uphold the ideal of Sunni orthodoxy. Caitanya's counter threat ... may be read as an equally strong oppositional stance meant to neutralize an unfair religious hegemony imposed by the Kazi."[23]

In the entire encounter, Śrī Chaitanya utters only several sentences that could easily lend themselves to misunderstanding, and the most explosive of them should be addressed here. In the heat of the march, in the mood of retaliation, He says, "Today I will destroy all the *yavanas* [i.e., foreigners or Muslims]."[24] Brutal language, to be sure.[25] How, then, can Prabhupāda call this civil disobedience—in what sense is it civil, that is to say, courteous, or peaceful?

Prabhupāda's commentary on this verse (1.17.130) serves to clarify.[26] Representing the entire lineage of Gauḍīya Vaishnava teachers, he indicates that Mahāprabhu's locution is not meant to be taken literally, for such violence is not the purpose of his divine descent. Indeed, in other incarnations, the Lord came to this world to overtly kill demons. But not as Śrī Chaitanya. In this incarnation, he merely kills their demonic mentality.[27] Thus, Prabhupāda writes:

> ... Śrī Caitanya Mahāprabhu started His movement of nonviolent civil disobedience to the order of Chand Kazi. It is not necessary to commit violence to stop the opposition from hindering a movement, *for one can kill their demoniac behavior with reason and argument*. Following in the footsteps of Lord Caitanya Mahāprabhu, whenever there are obstacles the Hare Kṛṣṇa movement should kill the opposition with reason and argument and thus stop their demoniac behavior. [italics added]

Prabhupāda indicates that, in the Chaitanya Vaishnava tradition, it is not literal but metaphorical violence that must sometimes be brought to bear. That is to say, if some naysayer exhibits antagonistic mentality, trying to hinder the Saṅkīrtana movement, an attempt should be made to destroy that deviation of consciousness. To be clear: No action is to be taken against the bodies of such people, but the devotee should endeavor to dismantle the perpetrators' misconceptions. This is the traditional understanding passed down in disciplic succession, and it is particularly articulated in relation to the story of the Chand Kazi.

Additionally, this reading of the text simply makes sense, given that neither Chaitanya nor his followers actually killed the Kazi or his Muslims compatriots—and, given their numbers, they certainly could have done so. Likely, they were merely giving their adversaries clear indication of their seriousness. Indeed, it is one thing to show the stick, another to actually use it, and still another to go so far as to kill someone with it.

Cogen Bohanec, Assistant Professor in Jain Studies at Arihanta Academy, offers this perspective: "It seems to me that Mahāprabhu provided an alternative to violence, and was effective with his nonviolent approach, irrespective of the violent impulses that naturally arise in such situations. It isn't violence that ultimately persuaded the Kazi; it is nonviolence. Mahāprabhu anticipated Gandhi's playbook by treating the Kazi as a friend, not an enemy, e.g., acknowledging their mutual relationship, and so on. Ultimately, he showed the Kazi, through peaceful means, that the street *kīrtana* should go on, unimpeded."[28]

How the narrative is positioned in the text is also significant, particularly in the *Caitanya-bhāgavata* (Madhya Chapter 23) version of the story, which goes on for more than 500 verses. Instead of highlighting the interaction with the Kazi, which is relatively brief, the section focuses more on the massive *nagara saṅkīrtana* led by Śrī Chaitanya in the midst of his vast ocean of followers. The text presents almost 200 verses of descriptive elaboration, underlining Mahāprabhu's beauty, his otherworldly, ecstatic dancing, and the extraordinarily vibrant and colorful street festival of congregational chanting, all in ornate poetic language. One can easily lose the thread of the Chand Kazi story, which seems almost incidental in the midst of this disarmingly captivating—and peaceful—*saṅkīrtana* exposition. It is important to underscore that the impulse of Mahāprabhu and his followers was to pick up *mṛdaṅga* drums, not weapons.

Indeed, Ravi Gupta, who holds the Charles Redd Chair of Religious Studies at Utah State University and serves as the director of the University's Religious Studies Program, tells us, "On the whole, [the Chaitanya/Kazi exchange] was peaceful disobedience. We should remember, however, that the concept of a political march or civil disobedience is applied to the Kazi episode anachronistically. After all, this was before the time of nation-states, free speech, colonialism, equal rights, etc. For example, we have no record of Mahāprabhu giving a speech to the assembled protestors and laying down the rules of the 'protest.' So it would be a bit unfair to compare the highly organized protests of the colonial and modern period with the more spontaneous gatherings of premodern India. Yes, the Kazi episode embodied qualities of nonviolence that were developed into a political philosophy by Gandhi, but I wouldn't go too far with drawing a straight line from one to the other."[29]

As Gupta correctly observes, it is impossible to draw a straight line between the Chand Kazi narrative and Gandhian politics, chiefly because of chronological inconsistency, or the sequence of events. On the other hand, as Gupta also points out, our modern sensibility can clearly recognize a certain resonance inherent in the two phenomena, seeing a mood of "peaceful disobedience" in Mahāprabhu's action.

With all of this as background, it should be noted that Prabhupāda, in seeing this episode as an instance of civil disobedience, does not stand alone. The notion has been affirmed and reaffirmed by those who have meticulously studied the subject, highly qualified devotees and scholars, from the time of Gandhi onwards—in fact, it has existed from the time that Gandhian phrases like "civil disobedience" first came into being.[30]

For example, Dr. Sambidananda Das, a disciple of Śrīla Bhaktisiddhānta Sarasvatī (1874–1937) who did his Ph.D. work at the University of London in 1933, wrote in his dissertation (later published as a book): "Thousands formed themselves into groups of *Sankirtana* parties at Sri Nimai's house to protest against the unreasonable orders of the Kazi, by the method of non-violent civil disobedience in the shape of open performance of *Sankirtana* in the streets of the town."[31] This statement appears only three years after Gandhi's famous salt march. Similar proclamations appear throughout the 1940s:

> The Kazi *dalan* episode has been quite significant for most hagiographers but more so with latter day scholars who read contemporary meanings into it. The literary historian Sukumar Sen and the scholar-critic Girijashankar Raychaudhuri, who delivered a series of lectures on the subject of Chaitanya at the Calcutta University in the 1940s, referred to it as the first successful civil disobedience movement against an oppressive and unjust state.[32]

Contemporary scholars make the connection clear as well. To cite but one prominent example:

> *Saṅkīrtana* so disrupted the normal life of Navadvīp that the town's Muslim administration attempted to bar these public performances, but the restrictions ultimately had an opposite effect. In response, Caitanya organized massive *nagar-kīrtanas* (*kīrtanas* involving the entire town), parading through the streets in a jubilant but organized defiance, which some have cited as the

> original model for Gandhi's non-violent civil disobedience campaigns. The *kazi* (Muslim chief administrator) was supposedly won over by the sincerity of the masses and charm of their leader, subsequently authorizing *nagar-kīrtanas* by official proclamation.[33]

One last quote. Among the more well known Vaishnava savants to make the connection between the Chand Kazi episode and civil disobedience would be Sisir Kumar Ghosh (1840–1911), though, given the time period in which he is writing—and we may here remember Ravi Gupta's reservations—he is naturally unable to use Gandhian language. Still, what he describes is a nonviolent and even loving exchange. Ghosh, incidentally, was well known as a friend and coworker of Bhaktivinoda Ṭhākura, and perhaps one of the most well informed scholars of Śrī Chaitanya in his generation. Thus, his periodical *Amrita Bazar Patrika* and his widely read *Amiya Nimāi Carita*, a six-volume Bengali work on Śrī Chaitanya, have great historical significance. After carefully studying all of the literature on Bengali Vaishnavism, he writes:

> All these un-Vaiṣṇava-like proceedings were stopped as soon as the Lord appeared on the scene. The thoughtless crowds who formed the advance-guard had done all the mischief that was possible for them to do under the influence of their excitement, and under the belief that such proceedings would be pleasing to their Master; but when the Lord came up and saw their doings, he reproved them for their conduct and everyone was hushed into silence. The word flew from mouth to mouth that the Lord commanded silence and forbearance, and all these thousands of people submitted in an instant, cheerfully, without a murmur, forgetting

> all the injuries that they had sustained at the hands of the Kazee. ... The Lord inquired where the Kazee was and it was soon ascertained that he had fled into the inner apartments to protect himself and his family. He then deputed some of the leading men well known to the Kazee, to convey to him a message to the following effect: that he, the Kazee, should come out at once, and that he had nothing to fear. ... In the case of the Kazee, brutal ferocity succumbed to spiritual beauty, the flower garland vanquished the sword![34]

Conclusion

In volatile political situations, it is difficult to mobilize huge masses against an unjust government while avoiding mob mentality. Civil disobedience, in such a scenario, would involve having the courage to do precisely what has been forbidden as an intentional act of defiance/resistance, demonstrating that the activity itself—in this case, *saṅkīrtana*—cannot and should not be repudiated. This necessitates a certain kind of faith in a power that is larger than the oppressing governmental power being protested—the kind of faith we see in Mahāprabhu's followers. That it was accomplished without anyone getting hurt is a testament to Mahāprabhu's Vaishnavism.

Śrī Chaitanya did not hand out swords and spears to the assembled devotees, but instead armed them only with the holy name. That is telling.

In all civil disobedience movements, some modicum of violence finds its way to the fore, even if it comes in the form of a spectrum, from totally demure to something more menacing. This was acknowledged even in Gandhi's notion of civil disobedience. (See Endnote 5.) Since the devotees of Navadvīpa had already been victim to the Kazi's overt violence, what was needed in retaliation was surely more than a dreamlike peaceful march and the handing out of flowers. When violence takes so many insidious forms, nonviolence cannot be limited to a strictly defined monochromatic caricature. It is often more nuanced, as we see in the Chand Kazi episode. That said, the nonviolent means of Śrī Chaitanya clearly win out in the end.

One can fully appreciate Mahāprabhu's approach to civil disobedience by contrasting it with thesis and antithesis, such as we see in Gandhi and Subhash Candra Bose, or Martin Luther King and Malcolm X. Extremism rarely accomplishes its end. And so it may be that protest ideology needs an update, and that civil rights activists may benefit from the example of Śrī Chaitanya and his followers, finding in them a spiritual synthesis that underlies all worldly endeavors.

This is all to say that, in the end, Mahāprabhu's march on the Chand Kazi's house is most assuredly an instance of civil disobedience. "Civil disobedience is a refusal to obey an order from a civil authority or public nonviolent violation of a legal prohibition. It can be an individual or corporate act. Those undertaking civil disobedience seek to understand and act on a higher law." So says the AFSC's Guide to Civil Disobedience. Indeed, Mahāprabhu and his party refused to submit to the Kazi's abuse, nor would they entertain his mandate to stop public street chanting. This was based on a higher law. Much higher. It was, according to Mahāprabhu's followers, the law of the spiritual world.

As an addendum, let it be said that all religious traditions have known representatives who stand out for their doctrine of love and nonviolence—Jesus was a Jew, King was a Christian, Khan was a Muslim, and Gandhi was a Hindu. Śrī Chaitanya, who also preached a doctrine of love and nonviolence, promoted Vaishnava dharma, which is said to be a spiritual science that embodies the best in all religions. As Bhaktivinoda writes:

> The religion preached by Mahaprabhu is universal and non-sectarian. The most learned and the most ignorant are both entitled to embrace it. The learned people can accept it by studying the literatures left by the great *acharyas*. The ignorant can have the same privilege by simply chanting the name of the Lord and mixing in the company of pure Vaishnavas. The church of *kirtan* invites all classes of people, without distinction as to caste or clan, to engage in the highest cultivation of the spirit.[35]

The Kazi, after meeting Mahāprabhu, embraced this invitation with heart and soul.

Endnotes

1. See Henry David Thoreau, *Civil Disobedience*, 1849 (https://xroads.virginia.edu/~Hyper2/thoreau/civil.html) Although the term "civil disobedience" originated in the 1840s with the works of Henry David Thoreau, it was popularized in 1930 with Mohandas Gandhi's bold march to the sea in protest of the British monopoly on salt.

2. ibid.

3. Our retelling of the narrative is based primarily on Kṛṣṇadāsa Kavirāja Gosvāmī's *Caitanya-caritāmṛta* (Cc), as commented upon by His Divine Grace A. C. Bhaktivedanta Swami Prabhupāda. I will also selectively refer to an alternate account in the *Caitanya-bhāgavata*,

written by Vrindāvanadāsa Ṭhākura. Since Vrindāvanadāsa's work is earlier than the Cc and written in the region of Bengal, where the incident occurred, some scholars give it greater credence. However, Kavirāja Gosvāmī's version, though compiled much later (1615), has the virtue of being informed by the earliest diaries of Mahāprabhu's direct associates, the teachings of the Six Gosvāmīs of Vrindavan, and the hindsight afforded by an already fully developed religious tradition. To adherents, therefore, it is generally considered the more reliable version.

4. A number of Śrī Chaitanya's prominent followers held important posts in the Muslim regime of the day, either in judicial or governmental positions, as prominent ministers, or in the revenue collection agency throughout Bengal. Some examples are Rūpa and Sanātana Gosvāmīs, Guṇarāja Khan, and Sūryadāsa Sarakhela.

5. Many think of Gandhi's nonviolence as extremist and without nuance. But while nonviolence was clearly his preference, and adamantly so, he was also aware that sometimes there was no alternative to physical retaliation. A few statements should suffice: "I would risk violence a thousand times rather than risk the emasculation of a whole race." (M. K. Gandhi, *Young India*, August 4, 1920) "I have been repeating over and over again that he who cannot protect himself or his nearest and dearest or their honour by non-violently facing death may and ought to do so by violently dealing with the oppressor." (M. K. Gandhi, *The Way to Communal Harmony*, ed., U. R. Rao (Ahmedabad: Navajivan Publishing House, 1963, reprint).) "Though violence is not lawful, when it is offered in self-defense or for the defense of the defenseless, it is an act of bravery far better than cowardly submission. The latter befits neither man nor woman. Under violence, there are many stages and varieties of bravery. Every man must judge this for himself. No other person can or has the right." (M. K. Gandhi, *Non-Violence in Peace & War*, Volume II (Ahmedabad: Navajivan Trust, 1949)

6. See Gillian Brockell, "'To India I come as a pilgrim': Martin Luther King Jr.'s remarkable trip to honor his hero," *The Washington Post*, January 20, 2020 (https://www.washingtonpost.com/history/2020/01/20/martin-luther-king-india-gandhi/). Also see "India Trip," published by The Martin Luther King, Jr. Research and Education Institute, Stanford University (https://kinginstitute.stanford.edu/encyclopedia/india-trip)

7. Prominent personalities specifically influenced by Gandhi in the fight for nonviolent resistance would also include Nelson Mandela, Thomas Merton, the Dalai Lama, and many others.

8. A *kazi* (Qāḍī in Arabic) literally refers to a civil judge, a magistrate; the Chand Kazi, in particular, was a high-ranking officer in the kingdom of Emperor Hussein Shah in Bengal. "Although Vaishnava texts are silent about the [denomination] of the Kazi in question, I think he was almost definitely a Sunni Islamic jurist. ... Historically, Shia nobles from Persia (Iran) were rather rare, if not non-existent, in Bengal before the Mughal period. Bengal was ruled essentially by the Turko-Afghan immigrants from Central Asia who substantially followed the Sunni faith ..." says Santanu Dey, Associate Professor, Department of History, Ramakrishna Mission Vidyamandira (personal correspondence, October 23, 2022). Amiya Sen, Professor of modern Indian history at the Department of History & Culture, Jamia Millia Islamia, New Delhi, concurs: "In all probability, he was a local convert to Sunni Islam." (personal correspondence, October 23, 2022) The Chand Kazi also had a Sufi component and was generally considered the spiritual master of the Nawab Hussein Shah.

9. Several verses in the *Chaitanya-bhāgavata* describe that "millions and millions" marched on the Kazi's home, which could easily be understood as an exaggeration expressed for effect. For example, see Madhya-khaṇḍa 23.365: "Millions and millions of people are coming this way with Nimāi Ācārya [Chaitanya]. They are fully prepared. Who knows what they will do today." (*koṭi koṭi loka saṅge nimāi-ācārya sājiyā āise āji kibā kare kārya*) The Sanskrit *koṭi* is translated variously, "millions," "ten million," "countless," and so on, to indicate the greatest number imaginable.

10. See Joseph T. O'Connell, "Does the Chaitanya Vaishnava Movement Reinforce Or Resist Hindu Communal Politics?" *Journal of Vaishnava Studies*, Volume 5, No. 1 (Winter 1996-97), 197-216.

11. Of course, for practitioners, Śrī Chaitanya's gradual unfolding of divine love and his "evolution of consciousness" are only apparent, seen instead as *līlā*, i.e., divine pastime, here particularly to show how a devotee normally progresses on the path of transcendence once having taken initiation from a bona fide spiritual master.

12. These origins of the Saṅkīrtana Movement can be found in

the pages of the *Chaitanya-bhāgavata*, Madhya-khaṇḍa, chapters one and two, both entitled, "Śrī Saṅkīrtanārambha-varṇana ("Description of the Saṅkīrtana Movement's Beginning"). In Navadvīpa, just after the Master returned from Gayā, many Vaishnavas gathered in devotees' homes to chant with him (particularly in the homes of Śuklāmbara, Śrīvāsa, and Śacīdevī, all of whom were his dear associates). This is where the great sound of Mahāprabhu's *kīrtana* resounded for the first time, as well as among his students, as mentioned. See Śrīla Vṛndāvana dāsa Ṭhākura's *Śrī Caitanya-bhāgavata*, trans., Bhumipati Dāsa, in seven volumes, with English translation of the *Gauḍīya-bhāṣya*, commentary and chapter summaries of Śrī Śrīmad Bhaktisiddhānta Sarasvatī Gosvāmī Mahārāja (New Delhi: Vrajraj Press, 2008). Also see *Vrindāvandāsa Ṭhākura's Śrī Caitanya-bhāgavata* (Complete in One Volume), trans., Kuśakratha Dāsa (Alachua, Florida: The Kṛṣṇa Institute, 1994).

13. ibid.

14. Muslim presence in Bengal dates back three centuries prior to Mahāprabhu, when Muhammad Bhakhtyār and his troops defeated the Sena dynasty. This led to various sultanate regimes, which became a sustained dimension of North India's political and religious landscape. By the mid-14th century, the Ilyas Shāhī dynasty began to reign in Bengal and continued until just before Mahāprabhu's era, when Abyssinians, initially migrating from Africa as slaves, took power. It is with the end of Abyssinian rule, in 1493, that Husain Shāh brought the area under his influence. "Some say that the Kazi's full name was Maulānā Sirājuddin; others say it was Habibar Rahmān," writes Śrīla Prabhupāda. "His descendants still live in the vicinity of Māyāpur, and pilgrims regularly come from various quarters to see his nearby tomb, formally known as 'Chand Kazi's Samādhi.'" See *Caitanya-caritāmṛta*, Ādi 17.124, purport.

15. See Bhaktivinoda Ṭhākura, *Navadvīpa Dhāma Māhātmya* (http://www.krishnapath.org/Library/Goswami-books/Bhaktivinoda-Thakura/Bhakti-vinoda_Thakura_Sri_Navadvipa-Dhama-Mahatmya.pdf). As for how this is expressed in Chaitanya-līlā, the Kazi points out that he and Śrī Chaitanya have a natural "village relationship" through Nīlāmbara Cakravartī, Mahāprabhu's material grandfather (*māmā, bhāginā*), and in this way attempts to neutralize the situation. Clearly, there is more to the story than expressed in their documented

exchange, and Kavirāja Gosvāmī, at 17.151, notes this by saying that there is a hidden meaning here (*bhitarera artha keha bujhite nā pāre*). The hidden meaning is revealed by Bhaktivinoda Ṭhākura.

16. To this day, Śrīvāsa's house is called "Khol Baṅga Daṅga," i.e., "the place where *mṛdaṅga* was broken."

17. "One may wonder if there was another factor as well," says Dr. Abhishek Ghosh (personal correspondence, October 21, 2022). "Some say that Muslims in Bengal, especially at that time, considered it *haram* ("forbidden") to assemble for musical performance of any kind, a phenomenon seen in recent history in Afghanistan under Taliban rule." The Islamic tradition offers many diverse positions on music, ranging from strict avoidance to largely accommodating. Most modern Muslims have no problem with it. The Sufis in India, for example, primarily the Chishti Order, have always utilized devotional singing and accompanying instrumentation to great effect, even if other Sufi orders tend to ban it as sacrilegious. Qawwali, a distinct form of Sufi singing as practiced in both India and Pakistan, is highly musical and considered spiritual by its practitioners. Regarding the Kazi, it would be fruitful to carefully research his particular religious orientation and whether his specific denomination forbade music in general. To be sure, disparagement of music in Islam is generally found in the more "legal" schools of thought (*shari'a*), and the Kazi, as a judge, would have likely adhered to this, disallowing music altogether, even for religious purposes. Thus, his banning of *saṅkīrtana* would not only be in compliance with the demands of the *smārta brāhmaṇas* and his co-Muslims, but also a statement of his preference for Islam and, possibly, the more general observance of eschewing music on religious grounds.

18. See *Chaitanya-bhāgavata,* Madhya 23, text 105: "The Kazi beat whomever he caught. He broke the *mṛdaṅgas* and wreaked havoc ..." (*yāhāre pāila kājī, mārila tāhāre, bhāṅgila mṛdaṅga, anācāra kaila dvāre*). This verse and others suggests more than a singular occurrence. Moreover, the context makes clear that this particular verse does not refer to the incident in Śrīvāsa's courtyard, but rather to a more general series of events. It refers to the Kazi seeing regular townspeople engaging in *kīrtana* and running after them to do them harm. From these verses we can understand that beating devotees and breaking *mṛdaṅgas* was the Kazi's tendency, not a one-off occurrence. See also *Caitanya-caritāmṛta* 1.17.192-193.

19. By material calculation, this demonstration was tantamount to King's Montgomery Bus Boycott (1955), Gandhi's Salt March (1930), and the Estonian Singing Revolution (1988) all put together, with literally millions taking part for a higher cause.

20. See Ravi M. Gupta, "Toward a Caitanya Vaiṣṇava Interfaith Theology: Lessons from Śrī Caitanya's Dialogue with the Qāzī of Navadvīpa" in Graham M. Schweig, ed., *The Worldwide Krishna Movement: Half a Century of Growth, Impact, and Challenge* (Oxford University Press, forthcoming).

21. See A. C. Bhaktivedānta Swami Prabhupāda, morning walk conversation, Montreal, August 26, 1968 (https://vanisource.org/wiki/Category:Conversations_-_by_Date). Other references to the Chand Kazi episode as a primary instance of civil disobedience can be found in Prabhupāda's purports to *Caitanya-caritāmṛta* 1.10.67, 1.17.130, 1.17.140, 1.17.141, and 1.17.144, among others. See also the preface to his *Śrīmad Bhāgavatam* series, as well as his commentary to 4.29.57.

22. For a good summary of the *Chaitanya-bhāgavata*'s more violent version, see the work of Kiyokazu Okita: "Following Viśvambhara's [Chaitanya's] order, his followers destroy the qāzī's house, his flower garden, and the surrounding plantain forest. Vrindāvandāsa writes that they shout Krishna's names while performing these acts of violence. Then Viśvambhara orders his followers to set fire to the qāzī's house. In the midst of this, he also spreads his gospel of kīrtan." See Kiyokazu Okita, "Singing in Protest: Early Modern Hindu-Muslim Encounters in Bengali Hagiographies of Chaitanya," *Bhakti and Power: Debating India's Religion of the Heart,* edited by John Stratton Hawley et al. (University of Washington Press, Seattle, 2019), 159–170. To be sure, no fire actually occurred and no one was hurt. Mahāprabhu's followers ascertain that their march was all that was needed, since the Kazi had been sufficiently "insulted" (2.23.414) and will now recant his prohibition. So in the end, even the more severe version of the *Chaitanya-bhāgavata* merely amounts to inducing fear in a few individuals and some repairable damages to one house, without affecting anyone's livelihood or the Muslim community.

23. Santanu Dey, personal correspondence, October 25, 2022.

24. This intense proclamation is found in both *Chaitanya-bhāgavata* and *Caitanya-caritāmṛta*, at 2.23.389 and 1.17.130, respectively. Also

in *Chaitanya-bhāgavata,* Mahāprabhu orders his followers (2.23.398-399, 405) to burn down the Kazi's house (which, again, never actually happens); the townspeople also shouted harsh words, threatening the magistrate's life (2.23.371, 372); in the end, they only ransacked his garden and parts of his home (2.23.393, 394). This is confirmed in *Caitanya-caritāmṛta* 1.17.142.

25. Mahāprabhu sometimes manifests Rudra-bhāva (the mood of Lord Śiva), displaying a sort of Rudra-avatāra—see *Caitanya-bhāgavata* (2.23.409) for an example of this during the Chand Kazi episode. When Mahāprabhu adopts this persona, he embodies all the anger required for universal devastation—for Śiva is seen as the god of destruction. Mahāprabhu's manifestation of Śiva is mentioned in the *Caitanya-caritāmṛta* (1.17.100), Lochan Dasa's *Caitanya-maṅgala* (7.16.50-63), Kavi Karṇapūra's *Caitanya-caritāmṛta-mahākavya* (7.86-89), and elsewhere. Such instances are technically called Raudra-kopa-bhāva, or anger directed toward an enemy of Krishna, as seen throughout Krishna-līlā in general. However, given Mahāprabhu's merciful disposition, which is a defining characteristic of his particular *avatāra*, his anger is not used for vanquishing enemies, but rather only for doing away with their faults.

26. In this instance, Prabhupāda seems to concur with famous *Caitanya-caritāmṛta* commentator Śrī Rādhāgovinda Nāth, who says, "The nature or disposition (*svabhāva*) of the *yavana* is to oppose *kīrtana*. I will remove or destroy that aspect of his nature." (*saṁhāriba dhvaṁsa kariba, yavanera svabhāva kīrtanavirodhita, dura kariba*) Thus, the "destruction" referred to here, once again, is not a mandate to destroy material bodies, but rather to transform mental conceptions. (This is verse 124 in the Rādhāgovinda Nāth edition.) See *Śrī Caitanya Caritāmṛta of Kṛṣṇadāsa Kavirāja*, ed., Rādhāgovinda Nātha, in Bengali, 4th edition, 6 vols. (Calcutta: Sādhanā Prakāśanī, 1962).

27. There is only one other instance where Mahāprabhu exhibited such harsh behavior, and this is in his exchange with the ruffians Jagāi and Mādhāi, as found in *Caitanya-caritāmṛta* 2.16. Here again, in Prabhupāda's purport to 2.16.65, he writes, "When they injured Nityānanda Prabhu, Lord Caitanya became angry and decided to kill them with His Sudarśana cakra, but Nityānanda Prabhu saved them from the Lord's wrath and delivered them. In the incarnation of Gaura-Nitāi, the Lord is not supposed to kill demons but is supposed

to deliver them by preaching Kṛṣṇa consciousness." Thus, in this text we again learn that Śrī Chaitanya has no intention of killing living bodies. Instead, he seeks to destroy the demonic mentality. Tellingly, at the conclusion of the Jagāi and Mādhāi account, too, there is no overt violence. Instead, as in the Chand Kazi narrative, the Lord bestows compassion rather than anger, mercy rather than wrath. He seeks not to destroy but to transform. Jagāi and Mādhāi become supporters of his cause and much admired among the devotees.

28. Cogen Bohanec, personal correspondence, October 21, 2022.

29. Ravi Gupta, personal correspondence, October 17, 2022.

30. While such language goes back to Thoreau and the mid-1800s, it wasn't in vogue among Indians until Gandhi's usage of it, around the time of his famous salt march (1930).

31. Dr. Sambidananda Das, *The History &Literature of the Gaudiya Vaishnavas and their Relation to other Medieval Vaishnava Schools* (Chennai: Sree Gaudiya Math, 2007, reprint), 256.

32. Amiya P. Sen, *Chaitanya, A Life and Legacy* (New Delhi: Oxford University Press, 2019), 68.

33. Charles R. Brooks, "The Blind Man Meets the Lame Man: ISKCON's Place in the Bengal Vaishnava Tradition of Caitanya Mahaprabhu," *Journal of Vaishnava Studies*, Vol. 6, No. 2 (March-April 1998), 9.

34. Shishir Kumar Ghose, *Lord Gaurāṅga or Salvation for All*, Volume I (Calcutta: Piyush Kanti Ghose Patrika Office, 1923, Third Edition), 349, 350, 357.

35. Śrīla Bhaktivinoda Ṭhākura, *Chaitanya Mahaprabhu: His Life and Precepts* (https://bhaktivinodainstitute.org/chaitanya-mahaprabhu-life-and-precepts-his-precepts/).

Nine

The Golden Sannyāsī: Śrī Caitanya in the *Mahābhārata*

ŚRĪ CAITANYA MAHĀPRABHU appeared some five hundred years ago in West Bengal, India, as the most recent and most merciful of all of Kṛṣṇa's manifestations. In fact, He is said to be Rādhā and Kṛṣṇa combined, the epitome of transcendence. Among the many scriptural predictions foretelling Śrī Caitanya's appearance – some of which are no longer extant – the one in the *Mahābhārata*, specifically in the *Viṣṇu-sahasra-nāma* ("Thousand Names of Viṣṇu"), remains for me the most interesting.

Kṛṣṇadāsa Kavirāja Gosvāmī quotes the following verse three times in his *Caitanya-caritāmṛta*:

> *suvarṇa-varṇo hemāṅgo*
> *varāṅgaś candanāṅgadī*
> *sannyāsa-kṛc chamaḥ śānto*
> *niṣṭhā-śānti-parāyaṇaḥ*

"The Lord [in the incarnation of Śrī Gaurasundara] has a golden complexion. Indeed, His entire body, which is very nicely constituted, is like molten gold. Sandalwood pulp is smeared all over His body. He will take the fourth order of spiritual life [*sannyāsa*] and will be very much self-controlled. He will be distinguished from Māyāvādī *sannyāsīs* in that He will be fixed in devotional service and will spread the *saṅkīrtana* movement."[1]

Śrīla Prabhupāda, following our *ācāryas* in disciplic succession, refers to this same verse throughout his writing. For example, commenting on a famous text in the *Śrīmad-Bhāgavatam* (11.5.32), he writes:

> The incarnation of Caitanya Mahāprabhu is also described in the *Śrī Viṣṇu-sahasra-nāma,* which appears in Chapter 189 of the *Dāna-dharma-parva* of *Mahābhārata.* Śrīla Jīva Gosvāmī has quoted this reference as follows: *suvarṇa-varṇo hemāṅgo varāṅgaś candanāṅgadī.* "In His early pastimes He appears as a householder with a golden complexion. His limbs are beautiful, and His body, smeared with the pulp of sandalwood, seems like molten gold." He has also quoted, *sannyāsa-kṛc chamaḥ śānto niṣṭhā-śānti-parāyaṇaḥ:* "In His later pastimes He accepts the *sannyāsa* order, and He is equipoised and peaceful. He is the highest abode of peace and devotion, for He silences the impersonalist nondevotees."

One may note that Śrīla Prabhupāda offers no specific verse number and cites these two qualities – *suvarṇa-varṇo hemāṅgo* (golden complexioned) and *sannyāsa-kṛc* (taking *sannyāsa*) – separately. There is a reason for this. As we will see, these descriptions of Mahāprabhu originally appear in two separate *Mahābhārata* verses, spliced together for our convenience.

The Two Verses

The two original verses (13.135.75 and 13.135.92) appear in the Critical Edition of the *Mahābhārata* as follows, here rendered with the English translation of K. M. Ganguli.[2]

trisāmā sāmagaḥ sāma
nirvāṇaṁ bheṣajaṁ bhiṣak
sannyāsa-kṛc chamaḥ śānto
niṣṭhā-śānti-parāyaṇaḥ

"He that is hymned with the three Vedas (foremost Samans; He that is the singer of the Samans; He that is the Extinction of all worldly attachments (in consequence of His being the embodiment of Renunciation); He that is the Medicine; He that is the Physician (who applies the medicine); He that has ordained the fourth or last mode of life called renunciation (*sannyāsa*)[3] for enabling His creatures to attain to emancipation; He that causes the passions of His worshippers to be quieted (with a view to give them tranquillity of soul); He that is contented (in consequence of His utter dissociation with all worldly objects); He that is the Refuge of devotion and tranquillity of Soul. (13.135.75)

suvarṇa-varṇo hemāṅgo
varāṅgaś candanāṅgadī
vīrahā viṣamaḥ śūnyo
ghṛtāśīracalaścalaḥ

"He that is of golden complexion; He whose limbs are like gold (in hue); He that is possessed of beautiful limbs; He whose person is decked with Angadas made with sandal-paste; He that is the slayer of heroes; He that has no equal; He that is like cipher (in consequence of no attributes being affirmable of Him); He that stands in need of no blessings (in consequence of His fulness); He that never swerves from His own nature and puissance and knowledge; He that is mobile in the form of wind." (13.135.92)

I purposely use Ganguli's translation to show that even when rendered by a Sanskrit scholar who has no ostensible connection to a devotee community, the reference to Śrī Caitanya is self-evident, with these verses referring to a form of God who engages with the *sannyāsa āśrama*. Mahāprabhu is famous as the incarnation who entered the renounced order of life and bears a golden complexion (as Gaurahari He is well known as the "Golden Avatāra").[4]

The identification of Mahāprabhu with the divine *sannyāsī* predicted in the *Mahābhārata* goes back to the formative days of Gauḍīya Vaiṣṇavism. In Kavi Karṇapūra's *Caitanya-candrodaya-nāṭaka* (5.93), written in the middle of the sixteenth century, we see that Advaita Ācārya Himself articulates this truth: "Says Advaita: '[Other explanations] are all deception. You have accepted *sannyāsa* to fulfill the *Viṣṇu-sahasra-nāma's* prediction: "*sannyāsa-kṛc chamaḥ śānto niṣṭhā-śānti-parāyaṇaḥ* ["The Supreme Lord will appear as a peaceful devotee, a *sannyāsī*."]'"[5]

Similarly, in regard to Mahāprabhu being the Lord who famously appears with a golden complexion, this too is well known throughout the *sampradāya*, with numerous scriptural verses highlighting the "nonblackish" or "golden color" of the Lord, particularly in His form as Śrī Caitanya. And there is more. Gauḍīya teachers have pointed out that the word *varṇa* in this verse (and others) can also allude to the chanting of the holy name. Indeed, *varṇa* can mean "order of life," as in *varnāśrama*; "color," as in the Lord's bodily hue; and "syllables," as in the chanting of Hare Kṛṣṇa.

Consequently, *suvarṇa-varṇo* in this verse, although clearly pointing to Mahāprabhu's golden complexion, includes another, esoteric meaning, i.e., the Lord who always chants the names of the Lord.[6]

As for combining the two verses into one, this was the brainchild of Śrīla Jīva Gosvāmī in his *Krama Sandarbha*.[7] Kavirāja Gosvāmī followed suit. After this, in his *Nāmārtha Sudhā Bhāṣya*, Baladeva Vidyābhūṣaṇa, the famous eighteenth-century scholar of the Gauḍīya tradition, looked at the verses more thoroughly, specifically emphasizing six particular names and how they relate to Śrī Caitanya. According to David Buchta, Senior Lecturer in Sanskrit Classics at Brown University:

> Quoting Baladeva on the *Viṣṇu-sahasra-nāma*: "Now, revealing that he is Kṛṣṇa Caitanya, he speaks six names. He renounces, i.e., lives the life of a wandering mendicant. Thus he is called Renouncer (Sannyāsakṛt). He reveals (*śāmayati* = *ālocayati*) secrets about Hari. Thus he is called Revealer (Śama). This word contains the *curādi* (tenth-class) verbal root *śamā,* used in the sense of seeing. He restrains himself (*śāmyati* = *uparamati*) from objects other than Kṛṣṇa. Thus he is called Restrained (Śānta). Devotional sacrifices predominated by glorification of Hari are consummated in him. Thus he is called Consummation (Niṣṭhā) This is according to the *smṛti* text [ŚBh 11.5.32], 'The wise certainly worship, by a sacrifice consisting primarily of congregational chanting, him whose name is Kṛṣṇa, though he is not dark in complexion, along with his attendant weapons in the form of his limbs and ornaments.' All things contrary to devotion, headed by pure non-dualism, are destroyed (*śāmyanti*) by him. Thus he is called Destruction (Śānti). He is the highest refuge of the varieties of *bhāva* ending in *mahā-bhāva.* Thus he is called Highest Refuge (Parāyaṇa)."] This set of names in the *Viṣṇusahasranāma*

> came to be an important proof text for Caitanya's divinity shortly after Rūpa's time. Jīva Gosvāmin cites these and four other names in his own extensive discussion of Caitanya's divinity while commenting on the *Bhāgavata's* description of the *kali-yuga-avatāra*. In the *Caitanyacaritāmṛta,* Kṛṣṇadāsa Kavirāja likewise cites these names three times: once in its opening argument for Caitanya's divinity and twice in the mouths of devotees who had come to realize his identity. . . . The additional names cited by Jīva and Kṛṣṇadāsa, placed first, are from *Mahābhārata* 13.135.92a-b: *suvarṇavarṇo hemāṅgo varāṅgaś candanāṅgadī*. In Jīva's commentary, the line *niṣṭhā śāntiḥ parāyaṇam* is not included. Kṛṣṇadāsa's citations are found at 1.3.49 (in narratorial voice), 2.6.104 (in the voice of Gopīnātha Ācārya, trying to convince his brother-in-law Vāsudeva Sārvabhauma Bhaṭṭācārya of Caitanya's divinity), and 2.10.170 (in the voice of Brahmānanda Bhāratī). In introducing these names at 1.3.48, Kṛṣṇadāsa says that they consist of two sets of four names, one concerning the earlier part of Caitanya's life; the other, the later part. (*dui līlā caitanyera ādi āra śeṣa. dui līlāya cāri cāri nāma viśeṣa.*)[8]

Baladeva's esteemed predecessor Śrīla Viśvanātha Cakravartī mentions the two verses as well, telling us again that the *Mahābhārata* indirectly refers to Śrī Caitanya by highlighting His gold complexion and the fact that He took *sannyāsa*. Viśvanātha tells us more: Though these esoteric names are indeed found in the *Mahābhārata*, other *śāstras,* he writes, avoid them altogether. This is because these names speak to a highly confidential subject, Viśvanātha adds, and he illustrates this with a reference from scripture. Prahlāda Mahārāja states in *Śrīmad-Bhāgavatam* (7.9.38): *channaḥ kalau yad abhavas tri-yugo 'tha sa tvam*, "Because the

Lord appears in a hidden way in Kali-yuga, He is addressed as Triyuga." In other words, Mahāprabhu covered His original color and mood with a golden form and the garb of a renunciant so that the people of His time would not recognize Him. This was His method of experiencing earthly pastimes as a devotee, not as the Lord, for He came to this world to feel the *bhāva* of Śrī Rādhā. Viśvanātha is exceedingly clear on this point.[9]

The Names According to Gauḍīya Siddhānta

Below we outline all nineteen names found in the two verses as interpreted by Bhaktivinoda Ṭhākura (1838–1914), the saintly Vaiṣṇava *ācārya* who brought Gauḍīya Vaiṣṇavism into the modern world. His insights into these names are based on Baladeva's gloss and are specifically in tune with Vaiṣṇava philosophy, often bringing out the inner meaning of the texts themselves, especially when they apply to Śrī Caitanya. Both Baladeva's and Bhaktivinoda's elucidations are contained in the same volume, published by Bhaktivinoda:[10]

> Verse 75:
>
> *trisāmā* – Lord Kṛṣṇa, in His appearance as Śrīla Vyāsadeva, divided the original *Veda* into three parts; *sāmaga* – Śrīla Vyāsadeva took pleasure in singing the Vedic hymns; *sāma* – He taught those hymns to His disciples; *nirvāṇam* – He freed them from ignorance and liberated them from material bondage; *bheṣajam* – He administered the medicine of pure devotional service to Kṛṣṇa, which freed the devotees from the disease of material existence; *bhiṣak* – He is the greatest physician;

sannyāsa-kṛt – in His appearance as Lord Caitanya, He accepts the renounced order of life, *sannyāsa*; *sama* – Lord Caitanya is equipoised; śānta – He is peaceful; *niṣṭhā-śānti-parāyaṇa* – He is the abode of the highest peace and devotion, for He silences the impersonalist non-devotee philosophers.

Verse 92:

suvarṇa-varṇa hemāṅga – Lord Kṛṣṇa appears in Kali-yuga as Śrī Caitanya Mahāprabhu, and in His early years plays the role of a *brāhmaṇa* householder with a golden complexion; *varāṅga* – His limbs are beautiful; *candanāṅgadī* – His body, smeared with sandalwood pulp, seems like molten gold; *vīrahā* – He kills lust, greed and all other enemies of His devotees; *viṣama* – no one is equal to or greater than Him, who protects the devotees and kills the demons; śūnya – He is free from all material defects, and He made the entire world unsafe for the demons and atheists; *dhṛtaśī* – He grants all auspiciousness to His devotees; *acala* – He was unmoving in His determination to protect the Pāṇḍavas from all danger; *cala* – He broke His own promise not to take up any weapon in the Kurukṣetra war to keep the promise of His devotee Bhiṣma.[11]

In conclusion: Śrīla Bhaktisiddhānta Sarasvatī Ṭhākura (1874–1937), Śrīla Prabhupāda's beloved spiritual master, published a popular edition of Prabodhānanda Sarasvatī's classic *Caitanya-candrāmṛta* that included a commentary by an Odiya poet named Ānandī. In a poignant section toward the end of Prabodhānanda's work (12.141), Ānandī points out how, based on these two *Mahābhārata* verses, Kavirāja Gosvāmī composed a beautiful poem about Mahāprabhu's form and purpose. He is referring to *Caitanya-caritāmṛta,* Ādi 3.40–47:[12]

The religious practice for the Age of Kali is to broadcast the glories of the holy name. Only for this purpose has the Lord, in a yellow color, descended as Lord Caitanya. The luster of His expansive body resembles molten gold. The deep sound of His voice conquers the thundering of newly assembled clouds. One who measures four cubits in height and in breadth by his own hand is celebrated as a great personality.[13] Such a person is called *nyagrodha-parimaṇḍala.* Śrī Caitanya Mahāprabhu, who personifies all good qualities, has the body of a *nyagrodha-parimaṇḍala.* His arms are long enough to reach His knees, His eyes are just like lotus flowers, His nose is like a sesame flower, and His face is as beautiful as the moon. He is peaceful, self-controlled and fully devoted to the transcendental service of Lord Śrī Kṛṣṇa. He is affectionate toward His devotees, He is gentle, and He is equally disposed toward all living beings. He is decorated with sandalwood bangles and armlets and anointed with the pulp of sandalwood. He especially wears these decorations to dance in *śrī-kṛṣṇa-saṅkīrtana.* Recording all these qualities of Lord Caitanya, the sage Vaiśampāyana included His name in the *Viṣṇu-sahasra-nāma.*

"By performing the sacrifice of congregational chanting of the holy name, learned scholars in the Age of Kali worship Lord Kṛṣṇa, who is now nonblackish because of the great upsurge of the feelings of Śrīmatī Rādhārāṇī. He is the only worshipable Deity for the *paramahaṁsas,* who have attained the highest stage of the fourth order [*sannyāsa*]. May that Supreme Personality of Godhead, Lord Caitanya, show us His great causeless mercy."[14] Here, Śrī Caitanya's primary biographer, quoting Śrīla Rūpa Gosvāmī, mentions the two qualities highlighted in the *Mahābhārata* verses, suggesting that He appears with the golden hue of Śrī Rādhā (*dyuti-bharād akṛṣṇāṅgam*) and that He is Lord of all *sannyāsīs* (*caturtha-āśrama-juṣām*). What more needs to be said?

Endnotes

1. See *Caitanya-caritāmṛta,* Ādi 3.49, *Madhya* 6.104, and *Madhya* 10.170. Also see *Caitanya-bhāgavata, Madhya* 28.168.

2. Kisari Mohan Ganguli (1848–1908) is well known for his complete English translation of the Sanskrit epic *Mahābhārata*. See Ganguli, Kisari Mohan, trans., *The Mahabharata of Kṛṣṇa-Dwaipayana Vyasa* (Delhi: Motilal Banarsidass, 1991, reprint). For the two verses, see Volume 11, 341–343. In terms of the *Viṣṇu-sahasra-nāma*, the numbering of the divine names in these verses appears as follows: 13.135.75 includes names 576 through 587, and 13.135.92 includes 737 through 746. These numbers may vary depending on the edition used.

3. The word *sannyāsa-kṛc* can be understood in at least two ways, as "one who *creates* the *sannyāsa aśrama*" or "one who *takes sannyāsa*." Most Sanskritists would understand it here as the former, which would apply to any incarnation of God, since the *varṇāśrama* system is created by the Supreme. Gauḍīya Vaiṣṇava commentators, however, see in this verse the latter interpretation, for Śrī Caitanya is famously that manifestation of God who "takes" *sannyāsa* in His later pastimes. In fact, *kṛt* (*kṛc*) is an action noun formed from *kṛ*, which is among the most versatile verbs in the Sanskrit language. It can mean "make" (i.e., make or cause *sannyāsa*) or "do" (i.e., do or take *sannyāsa*), and so on. So one has to discern in each instance whether one meaning is preferable to another, which is usually done according to the specific context in which the verb is used. But here context is unhelpful, since this is a list of Viṣṇu's thousand names, without a plot or philosophical argument. In this case, then, the meaning will be determined by the reader according to his or her own philosophical conclusions, and, for reasons too numerous to express here, we would do well to honor the reading of the *ācāryas*.

4. These two verses contain other hints of Śrī Caitanya's *avatāra* as well: For example, *Sāmagāna* is not merely a name given to the melodious hymns of a particular Vedic *saṁhitā* but represents the overall philosophy of sound vibration on the spiritual platform. The word *sāma*, in fact, comes from the root *sāman*, meaning "a song of praise." The *Nārada-pañcarātra* tells us, "The essence of all Vedic knowledge – comprehending the three kinds of Vedic activity [*karma-kāṇḍa, jñāna-kāṇḍa,* and *upāsanā-kāṇḍa*], the *chandas*, or Vedic hymns, and the processes for satisfying the demigods – is included in the eight syllables Hare Kṛṣṇa, Hare Kṛṣṇa. This is the reality of all Vedānta. The chanting of the holy name is the only means to cross the ocean of nescience." Further, "Śrīla Jīva Gosvāmī states that the substance of all the Vedic *mantras* is the chanting of the holy name of the Lord. Every *mantra* begins with the prefix *nama oṁ* and eventually addresses by name the Supreme Personality of Godhead. By the supreme will of the Lord there is a specific potency in each and every *mantra* chanted by great sages like Nārada Muni and other *ṛṣis*. Chanting the holy name of the Lord immediately renovates the transcendental relationship of the living being with the Supreme Lord." See *Caitanya-caritāmṛta*, Ādi-*līlā*, 7.76, Purport. Caitanya Mahāprabhu is the foremost champion of the holy name. One other example of a name that clearly points to Caitanya is the final name of verse 75 – Parāyaṇa – which means the "great goal," or as Bhānu Swami translates it, "the refuge of persons of the highest *bhāvas* [spiritual sentiments]." This, say our Vaiṣṇava *ācāryas*, can only indicate Caitanya Mahāprabhu, the manifestation of Kṛṣṇa who is the very vessel of the topmost love (*mahābhāva*).

5. See Kavi Karṇapūra, *Caitanya-candrodaya-nāṭaka*, trans., Bhanu Swami (Chennai, Tamil Nadu: Bhanu Swami Books, 2018), 185–186. See also *Caitanya-candrodaya*, trans., Kuśakratha Dāsa (10 Volumes, The Krishna Institute, 1989), 5.93.

6. From the root *varṇ*, which means "to praise, explain, extol." For this confidential reading, see Śrīla Bhaktivinoda Ṭhākura, "Prema-Bhakti and Śrī Gaurāṅgadeva" (https://bhaktivinodainstitute.org/prema-bhakti-and-sri-gaurangadeva/): "*suvarṇa-varṇo hemāṅgaḥ* – His limbs are golden and He is continuously chanting..." Śrīla Prabhupāda, too, writes, "Śrīla Jīva Gosvāmī, the most authoritative *ācārya* of our *sampradāya*, has explained like this. *Kṛṣṇa-varṇam* means 'always chanting Hare Kṛṣṇa.' *Kṛṣṇaṁ varṇayati*, describing Kṛṣṇa, 'Hare

Kṛṣṇa, Hare Kṛṣṇa.'" (Lecture, London, March 10, 1975) Similarly, in Viśvanātha Cakravartī's *ṭīkā* to *Śrīmad-Bhāgavatam* 11.5.32, he writes, "Another meaning of *kṛṣṇa-varṇa* is 'he speaks about the pastimes of Kṛṣṇa.'" So, in the context of these names, *suvarṇa-varṇo hemāṅgo*, we can also see reference to "the Golden Avatāra who chants the Hare Kṛṣṇa *mahā-mantra*," as Prabhupāda himself sometimes translates it.

7. See Śrīla Jīva Gosvāmī, *Krama Sandarbha*, Volume 6 (Cantos 11 & 12), translated by Bhānu Swami, commentary on *Śrīmad-Bhāgavatam* 11.5.32 (Chennai, Tamil Nadu: Bhanu Swami, 2018), 95 and 609–610.

8. See David Buchta, "Pedagogical Poetry: Didactics and Devotion in Rūpa Gosvāmin's *Stavamālā*" (Ph.D. Thesis, University of Pennsylvania, 2014), 91–92. See especially fns. 45 and 46.

9. See *Śrīmad-Bhāgavatam, Daśama-skandha (Pūrvārdha)* with Bengali translation of Śrīla Viśvanātha Cakravartī's *Sārārtha-darśinī* by Śrī Vijana-vihārī Gosvāmī, Chapter 8, Text 13 (Iśodyāna, Śrīdhāma Māyāpura: Śrī Caitanya Vāṇī Press, 2001), 181–182. Also see Viśvanātha Cakravartī, *Sārārtha-darśini,* Chapter 8, Text 13 (Vrindavan: Radha Book Trust, 2013), 256–257.

10. Here both Baladeva Vidyābhūṣaṇa and Bhaktivinoda Ṭhākura confirm the esoteric reading of *suvarṇa-varṇo* as referring to one who chants Kṛṣṇa's name. See endnote 6.

11. See *Śrī Śrī Viṣṇu-sahasra-nāma Stotram* (Medinipur, West Bengal: Śrī Caitanya Āśrama, 1974), with Śrī Śrīmad Bhaktivinoda Ṭhākura's Bengali translation of Śrī Śrīmad Baladeva Vidyābhūṣaṇa's *Nāmārtha-sudhā* commentary (edited by Bhakti Kumuda Santa Gosvāmī Mahārāja), 60–61, 77–79. We have just included Baladeva's gloss, although in the text itself, Bhaktivinoda further elaborates.

12. See Śrīla Prabodhānanda Sarasvatī, *Śrī Caitanya Candrāmṛtam*, with commentary of Śrīla Bhaktisiddhānta Sarasvatī Ṭhākura and Ānandī, trans., Sarvabhāvana Dāsa (Vrindavan: Rasbihari Lal & Sons, 2004), 517–518.

13. Medieval Bengali texts do not offer measurements in either inches and feet or meters and centimeters, and so Mahāprabhu's exact height remains unknown, though tradition teaches that he was quite tall. Commenting on this verse, however, Tony K. Stewart, one of the foremost academic authorities on Caitanya Vaiṣṇavism in the modern era, estimates the Lord's height: "[Caitanya] measured, by the measure

of his own arms, four arms or hands (*hatha*) tall; Rādhāgovinda Nātha says that one hand is from the tip of the middle finger of one hand to the tip of the middle finger of the other when the arms are outstretched, but that is clearly impossible. More likely the measure is from the tip of the middle finger to the elbow, an average of eighteen inches. Caitanya, then, was perhaps taller than 6' 2", extremely tall for a Bengali of the period. Such great height is one of the marks of a great man, a *mahāpuruṣa*, for so Kṛṣṇa himself is called in *BhP* 10.40.4 and in many other places." See Edward C. Dimock, Jr., trans., and Tony K. Stewart, ed., *Caitanya Caritāmṛta of Kṛṣṇadāsa Kavirāja: A Translation and Commentary,* Harvard Oriental Series, vol. 56 (Cambridge, MA: The Department of Sanskrit and Indian Studies, Harvard University, 1999), 180, fn. 33.

14. This verse is from the *Stava-mālā* of Śrīla Rūpa Gosvāmī, quoted in *Caitanya-caritāmṛta*, Ādi 3.58.

Ten

Coming Home: Śrī Chaitanya's Journey to Vrindavan

ŚRĪ CHAITANYA, WHO IS Krishna in the mood of his own topmost devotee, Rādhā, showed great determination in his earthly pastimes to travel to Vrindavan, to bask in the very land where Krishna once walked and played and loved. Why? Why the determined effort, which, as we will see, was considerable? Was it the aspiration born of his devotee side, wanting to be near his lotus-eyed Lord and to thus develop greater love for him? Or was it simply a matter of Krishna "coming home," since Vrindavan is Krishna's natural playground, and, again Śrī Chaitanya is Krishna himself? As we will see: In the story of Chaitanya, both dimensions are at play.

Vrindavan is known by several names—for example, Braj (Vraja) and Brajbhumi, among others—but whatever one calls it, to devotees, it is the spiritual world. More, it is the highest portion of the spiritual world, the narrative landscape of Krishna-līlā (the divine play of God).

It exists in two forms, that is, in Uttar Pradesh, India, where its central portion is known as Gokula, and in the spiritual world, where it is known as Goloka. In Gokula,

God is said to have manifested on Earth some 5,000 years ago; and in the transcendental Goloka, he abides eternally. Though he is always in Gokula, too, only the purest souls can see him there.

The Sanskrit root *vraja* refers to "an enclosure of herdsmen," or to "a place where cows wander," indicating the pastoral nature of Krishna's eternal cowherd environment. As for Vrindavan (Vṛndāvana), it means "the forest of Vṛndā" (another name for the sacred *tulasī* plant), so dear to Lord Krishna.

Located just over 100 miles south of Delhi, Braj is today identified as a specific area covering 35 square miles in Uttar Pradesh, at least in terms of geography. To Vaishnavas, however, "Braj," like Vrindavan, represents so much more. It is a place in the heart that manifests when love for Krishna arises, and it is the ultimate manifestation of the kingdom of God.

The Yamunā River flows on the eastern end of Braj, while on the west one sees the Aravalli mountain range, including Govardhana Hill, famously lifted by Krishna on his small finger. Largely consisting of thousands of small temples and agricultural fields of wheat, millet, beans, and sugarcane, visitors are reminded of Krishna when they see the few remaining pockets of woodland and pasture throughout the region, though today the area is quickly turning into a metropolis, a fact that local people and pilgrims greet with mixed emotions.

The ancient city of Mathurā (where Krishna was born) lies inside the heart of Braj, with Gokula, Vrindavan, Barsana, Rādhā-kuṇḍa, Govardhana, Nandagaon, and other holy places peppered throughout—all of these places mark various events in the story of Krishna's earthly sojourn.[1] We mainly know of these sacred regions today because they were unearthed by Śrī Chaitanya and his followers in the 16th century, as we will see.

Overall, Braj consists of 12 large forests (*vanas*) and 24 smaller ones (*upavanas*), with over 100 groves and numerous hills and lakes. The ancient texts describe it as an ecologically rich environment, but much of its flora and fauna are now a thing of the past.

Pollution has overtaken the once vibrant fields and lakes of Braj, and even the holy Yamunā, due to sewage, makes ritual bathing a loving chore. Nonetheless, those with higher vision, say the Gauḍīya teachers, still see it for what it is, and vast numbers of pilgrims travel there on a regular basis, hoping to gain spiritual advancement through proximity.

Indeed, the *Padma Purāṇa* (Pātāla-khaṇḍa) says, "Anyone who spends even one day in Mathurā/Vrindavan will attain Hari-bhakti. i.e., devotion to God." (*aho madhupuri dhanya, vaikunthac ca gariyasi, dinam ekam nivasena, harau bhaktih prajayate*)[2] And the *Brahmaṇḍa Purāṇa* concurs, saying, "One achieves the bliss experienced at the stage of *prema* [divine love] just by setting foot in Mathurā" (*parananda-mayi siddhir mathura-sparsha-matratah*)[3]

Along similar lines, Śrīla Rūpa Gosvāmī tells us that, "The essence of all advice is that one should utilize one's full time—twenty-four hours a day—in chanting and remembering the Lord's divine name, transcendental form, qualities and eternal pastimes, thereby gradually engaging one's tongue and mind. *In this way, one should reside in Braj* and serve Krishna under the guidance of devotees. One should follow in the footsteps of the Lord's beloved devotees, who are deeply attached to his devotional service." (*tan-nāma-rūpa-caritādi-sukīrtanānu-smṛtyoḥ krameṇa rasanā-manasī niyojya tiṣṭhan vraje tad-anurāgi janānugāmī kālaṁ nayed akhilam ity upadeśa-sāram*)[4] [emphasis added]

Śrī Rūpa calls this "the essence of all advice," so important is Braj in the practice of Bhakti-yoga, the yoga of devotion. In fact, he cites residence in its holy environs as one of the five most important principles of devotional service, along with having faith in serving the Deity, relishing the *Śrīmad Bhāgavatam*, keeping the company of devotees, and chanting the Holy Name (*Bhakti-rasāmṛta-sindhu* 1.2.90-92).

The Four Attempts

It is no wonder, therefore, that Śrī Chaitanya, whose purpose was to play the role of a perfect devotee, showing by his own example how one might live as the consummate Krishna-bhakta, took great pains to get to Braj. In fact, it was not until his fourth attempt that he actually set foot on its sacred ground. This is significant. By repeatedly trying to approach the land of Krishna, he shows the common devotee just how important such pilgrimage is—he was relentless, and finally he arrived.

Of course, he is Krishna himself, so his arrival in Braj has special meaning. He was returning home, as it were, since Krishna's natural habitat is Vrindavan. Truth be told, and as we learn from Vaishnava texts, Vrindavan is home to us all—the phrase "going back to Godhead" means nothing more or less than returning to Braj, at least in terms of "Braj Consciousness," a point to which we will later return.

As for Mahāprabhu's four attempts to reach Braj: Although often overlooked by historians, his first attempt occurred immediately after being initiated by Īśvara Purī. At that time, he would have been roughly sixteen or seventeen years old, in circa 1502.[5] According to the *Caitanya-bhāgavata*, the initiation marked a major turning point in his earthly pastimes. Intoxicated through recitation of the Krishna mantra, he immediately wanted to "go to Mathura," to see "the Lord of my life, Śrī Krishnacandra." In Śrīla Bhaktisiddhānta Sarasvatī's commentary, he tells us, "He loudly addressed Krishna in a piteous tone and displayed the pastime of searching for Krishna." But after traveling for some time, "the Lord heard a voice from the sky say, "O crest-jewel of the *brāhmaṇas*, don't go to Mathurā now. ... You will go when the appropriate time comes. Now you should return to your house in Navadvīp."[6]

The Lord's second attempt can be found in *Śrī Caitanya-caritāmṛta*, Madhya-līlā, Chapter Three. Here we learn that he decided to go to Vrindavan shortly after accepting *sannyāsa*, the renounced order, at age twenty-four (January-February, 1510). Nityānanda Prabhu, his chief associate, tricked him into thinking that the Gangā, which flows through Navadvīpa, West Bengal, was Vrindavan's river Yamunā, and thereby redirected him back to his devotees in Śāntipura.[7] Mahāprabhu was so intensely absorbed in thoughts of Vrindavan that he jumped into the Gangā. But Advaita Ācārya, another leading associate, working conjointly with Nityānanda Prabhu, was waiting close by with a boat to bring him back. Upon seeing Advaita, Mahāprabhu realized where he was, but at that point, it was inconsequential—he was happy to be with his loving devotees in Bengal. Advaita Ācārya took Mahāprabhu to his nearby home, where the Lord's mother, Śacīmātā, was awaiting his arrival. On her request, the Lord proceeded to Jagannātha Purī, where he would spend a large part of his remaining years.

However, in 1514, the need to go to Vrindavan arose in his heart once more, and for a third time he set out to meet his beloved Krishna. But instead, on the way, he met the two brothers Dabīra Khāsa and Sākara Mallika in Rāmakeli, West Bengal. At the time, they were highly posted government officials. But Mahāprabhu knew who they really were—they would soon become Rūpa and Sanātana Gosvāmīs, in many ways the most significant patriarchs of the Gauḍīya tradition. Prior to meeting him, they had written him lengthy letters, expressing dissatisfaction with their employment under Islamic rule and political life in general. They wanted to participate in his Saṅkīrtana movement but felt their entanglement in mundane affairs too overwhelming, stopping them from pursuing spiritual life with the commitment it warranted. It was important that he nurture them for the future of his movement, and this he did. Spending time with these two exceptional brothers, however, meant that he would once again not consummate his trip to Vrindavan.

That summer, he returned to Purī, as the *Caitanya-caritāmṛta* (Madhya 18) tells us. But his return was not merely a matter of being diverted by Rūpa and Sanātana. There were pragmatic concerns as well. In the *Caitanya-bhāgavata*, we learn more about those reasons: While visiting the two brothers and touring the rest of Bengal, crowds of people started flocking to his side—hundreds if not thousands that wanted his association.

Although he still proceeded in the direction of Mathurā, the king himself sent warning to be careful while traveling in great numbers, lest envious people try to do him harm. And so he acquiesced, returning to Purī.

But by the autumn of 1515 (some say it was the prior year), when he was twenty-nine, he set out for Vrindavan once more, overcome with bliss. This time, on his fourth try, he set foot in the holy land of Braj.[8]

Śrī Chaitanya in Braj

The journey to Vrindavan was itself significant, even before his arrival. Remembering the sage advice to avoid the multitudes, he took the forest route via Jhārikhaṇḍa, in the Chota Nagpur plateau,[9] assisted only by a single follower named Balabhadra Bhaṭṭācārya.

Traveling by foot across the dense forest, the Lord incessantly chanted the name of Krishna. The resident creatures, seeing his transcendental form and hearing him chant, were touched deep in their souls, temporarily setting aside their animal nature. Indeed, they responded to his presence by joyfully dancing together—tigers with deer, wild boar with pheasants—creating an idyllic image of the perfect world. In fact, hearing Śrī Chaitanya chant the holy names, tradition teaches, all the animals miraculously responded in their respective tongues.

According to the *Caitanya-caritāmṛta* (Madhya 17.29), "The Lord said, 'Chant the holy name of Krishna!' And the tiger immediately got up and began to dance and to chant 'Krishna! Krishna!'" Similar incidents occurred with other creatures. Thus, the otherwise perilous forest transformed into a facsimile of the fabled "peaceable kingdom" mentioned in the Bible, a phrase that has come to mean "a state of harmony among all creatures," as prophesied in *Isaiah* (11:1-9). Indeed, although on the outskirts of Braj, he felt as though he was already there. As the *Bhāgavatam* (10.13.60) says, "Though naturally inimical, both human beings and fierce animals live [in Vrindavan] together in transcendental friendship" (*yatra naisarga-durvairāḥ, sahāsan nṛ-mṛgādayaḥ, mitrāṇīva*).

And then he arrived.

According to Vaishnava scholar, O. B. L. Kapoor:

> At Vṛndāvana the intensity of his love for Kṛṣṇa increased a thousand-fold.[10] He wandered through the forests ... seeing all the places connected with Kṛṣṇa-līlā, and himself [founded] the sites of Rādhā-kuṇḍa and Śyāma-kuṇḍa. ... Kṛṣṇadāsa has given a vivid description of Śrī Caitanya's state of mind during his journey to Vṛndāvana and his wanderings in the holy forests, where he found every creeper and blade of grass vibrating with the spiritual associations of Kṛṣṇa-līlā. He chanted the Name of Kṛṣṇa, danced and wept and occasionally fell senseless on the ground, exhibiting in unprecedented form all the *aṣṭasāttvika-bhāvas,* or the bodily manifestations of divine love. His personality was so charged with the current of divine love that his very sight generated the feeling of devotion and compelled people to chant the name of Kṛṣṇa.[11]

In Śrīla Bhaktivinoda Ṭhākura's *Amṛta-pravāha-bhāṣya,* summarizing data culled from the *Caitanya-caritāmṛta*, we learn that the Lord spent time in Krishna's birthplace, Mathurā; the village of Āriṭ-grāma; discovered Rādhā-kuṇḍa and Śyāma-kuṇḍa, as Dr. Kapoor notes above; visited Govardhana Hill; encountered the famous Gopāla Deity; made His way to Keśī-ghāṭa, Rāsa-sthalī, Cīra-ghāṭa, Āmli-talā, Nandīśvara, Pāvana-sarovara, Śeṣaśāyī, Khelā-tīrtha, Bhāṇḍīravana, Bhadravana, Lohavana, Mahāvana, Gokula, and so many more, all places that today, for Vaishnavas, have deep meaning.

How long did Mahāprabhu stay in Braj? It is traditionally understood that he was there for no more than two months, from November of 1514 to early January 1515.[12] But theories abound.[13] What we do know is that, due to his presence, the crowds again began to swell, mainly with well-wishers and pious people—in the thousands—clamoring to get his *darśana*, and because his well-wishers feared for his safety, they opted to bring him back to Purī.

And so he left Vrindavan: It was winter, and he journeyed via Allahabad, which was then called Prayag. There he spent ten days with Rūpa Gosvāmī, instructing him in the details of man's relationship with God, information that Rūpa would later organize into the many books he would produce for the Gauḍīya tradition. He then sent Rūpa to Vrindavan (to unearth long lost holy places and to build temples) and left for Vārāṇasī, now Benares, on the road back to Purī. At Benares, he instructed Sanātana Gosvāmī in Vaishnava minutiae for some two months. After explaining these things at length, Mahāprabhu asked Sanātana to go to Vrindavan as well (to work with Śrī Rūpa).[14] While in Benares, too, Mahāprabhu converted one of India's most famous monists, Prakāśānanda Sarasvatī, at least according to Kavirāja Gosvāmī's version, who brought thousands of followers to Mahāprabhu's feet through his own surrender.

In that same year, by age 30, Mahāprabhu settled in Purī, never to leave again. Everything he needed to do outside of that sacred area was already accomplished. So in the association of his most intimate followers, such as Rāmānanda Rāya and Svarūpa Dāmodara Goswāmī, he allowed himself to be fully captivated by Rādhā-bhāva, the ecstasy of Rādhārāṇī's love for Krishna. For 18 years, while in this state of enhanced spiritual ecstasy, he engaged in loving pastimes with the devotees in Odisha, pastimes that are especially detailed by Kavirāja Goswāmī in his *Caitanya-caritāmṛta*.

Being in Vrindavan: A Deeper Meaning

What can be said about Mahāprabhu's journey to Braj? While it clearly held deep meaning for him, as we can understand through his persistent endeavor to get there, he did not stay, which is also an important part of his philosophy, as we shall now see. While the scriptures are forthright in saying that residence in Braj is an urgent devotional principle, as discussed above—indeed, "the essence of all advice"—we would like to conclude this article with several ruminations on what that actually means.

Without doubt, the ability to physically live in Braj is a blessing. But not everyone will be able to accomplish that, nor is it always desirable. Accordingly, Bhaktivinoda Ṭhākura defines "living in Braj" as follows:

> To live in a solitary place with transcendental emotion is called Braja-vāsa [living in Braj]. One should chant the holy names of the Lord with a prescribed number of rounds and engage in the service of the Lord twenty-four hours a day. One should engage in favorable service to the Supreme Lord in such a way that it does not create any impediment in the maintenance of his livelihood. (*Jaiva Dharma*, Chapter 40)[15]

Interestingly, the Ṭhākura does not specify Braj as such. Any spiritual environment that fosters intense *sādhana*—*that* is Braj. Śrīla Prabhupāda says much the same: "One who lives in such consciousness is actually living in Vṛndāvana. He may live anywhere; material location doesn't matter. When by the grace of Kṛṣṇa one thus advances, he becomes completely uncontaminated by the material body and mind and at that time factually lives in Vṛndāvana." (*Caitanya-caritāmṛta,* Madhya 8.139, purport) Or further, "The mind's activities are thinking, feeling and willing, by which the mind accepts materially favorable things and rejects the unfavorable. This is the consciousness of people in general. But when one's mind does not accept and reject but simply becomes fixed on the lotus feet of Kṛṣṇa, then one's mixnd becomes as good as Vṛndāvana.

"Wherever Kṛṣṇa is, there also are Śrīmatī Rādhārāṇī, the *gopīs,* the cowherd boys, and all the other inhabitants of Vṛndāvana. Thus, as soon as one fixes Kṛṣṇa in his mind, his mind becomes identical with Vṛndāvana. In other words, when one's mind is completely free from all material desires and is engaged only in the service of the Supreme Personality of Godhead, then one always lives in Vṛndāvana, and nowhere else." (*Caitanya-caritāmṛta,* Madhya 13.137, purport)

Indeed, there are many who live in Vrindavan, but are not qualified to do so. As Śrīla Prabhupāda writes in his purport to *Caitanya-caritāmṛta*, Madhya-lila, 16.281:

> The *prākṛta-sahajiyās* [imitationists] proclaim themselves *vraja-vāsī* or *dhāma-vāsī*, but they are mainly engaged in sense gratification. Thus they become more and more implicated in the materialistic way of life. Those who are pure devotees in Kṛṣṇa consciousness condemn their activities. The eternal *vraja-vāsīs* like Svarūpa Dāmodara did not even come to Vṛndāvana-dhāma. Śrī Puṇḍ-arīka Vidyānidhi, Śrī Haridāsa Ṭhākura, Śrīvāsa Paṇḍita, Śivānanda Sena, Śrī Rāmānanda Rāya, Śrī Śikhi Māhiti, Śrī Mādhavīdevī and Śrī Gadādhara Paṇḍita Gosvāmī never visited Vṛndāvana-dhāma. Śrīla Bhaktisiddhānta Sarasvatī Ṭhākura points out that we have no authorized documents stating that these exalted personalities visited Vṛndāvana.

In this way, Prabhupāda's makes the additional point that exemplary devotees who were clearly accomplished in their practice attained their position without overtly entering the land of Braj. He even refers to them as "*vraja-vāsīs*," or "inhabitants of Braj," despite their never having traveled there. It might be argued that, given their exalted spiritual status, they didn't *need* to go to Vrindavan. But such souls live to set an example for others, and if going to Vrindavan, physically, was an absolute necessity to advance on the spiritual path, they would have shown us by their example that this was the proper course of action. Prabhupāda's point is clear: While going to geographical Braj is beneficial, it is far from mandatory.[16]

In fact, Gauḍīya teaching insists that merely *visiting* Braj, as Mahāprabhu did, is probably best, as opposed to actually "living" there, which, if one is not ready, can in fact be detrimental. When Mahāprabhu's dear devotee, Jagadānanda Paṇḍita, requested permission to go to Vrindavan, the Lord said, "You should remain in Vrindavan for only a short time" (*śīghra āsiha, tāhāṅ nā rahiha cira-kāla*). Prabhupāda writes in his purport, "In his *Amṛta-pravāha-bhāṣya*, Śrīla Bhaktivinoda Ṭhākura advises that one avoid remaining in Vrindavan for a very long time. As the saying goes, 'Familiarity breeds contempt.' If one stays in Vrindavan for many days, he may fail to maintain proper respect for its inhabitants. Therefore those who have not attained the stage of spontaneous love for Kṛṣṇa should not live in Vrindavan very long. It is better for them to make short visits." (*Caitanya-caritāmṛta*, Antya 13.39)

While Mahāprabhu, as God, could have stayed in Vrindavan for as long as he likes—and indeed, in a spiritual sense, he is in Vrindavan eternally—he set the example of a true devotee, humbly relishing the Braj environment for two or three months, and then bringing "Braj" back with him, wherever he went. Śrī Chaitanya emphasized "Braj consciousness," that is, wherever one is, one should turn that place into Braj, for by absorption in Krishna, especially by chanting his holy names, such a spiritual transformation occurs as a matter of course.

The tension between the mandate to live in Braj, which is echoed throughout Gauḍīya texts, and the more accommodating notion of visiting Braj with marked enthusiasm, or even imbibing Braj as a state of consciousness, which is also endorsed throughout the tradition, is nowhere as sharply represented as in *Bhakti-rasāmṛta-sindhu* 1.2.295-296. Śrīla

Rūpa Gosvāmī says, in the very first line, "One should always live in Braj" (*kuryād vāsaṁ vraje sadā*), but Śrīla Jīva Gosvāmī, in his commentary on this very same verse, adds necessary nuance: "If one is able, then one should physically reside in geographical Braj, which is the residence of Śrī Nanda Mahārāja" (*sāmarthye sati vraje śrīman-nanda-vrajāvāsa-sthāne śrī-vṛndāvanādau śarīreṇa vāsaṁ kuryāt*).

The key word here is *sāmarthya*, i.e., "able," "fit," "adequately prepared." It is a question of *adhikāra* ("qualification"), and many are simply not ready to fulfill Śrī Rūpa's mandate, for various reasons. With this as a backdrop, Śrī Jīva continues, "If one cannot live in Vrindavan physically, then he should go there mentally." (*tad-abhāve manasāpīty arthaḥ*) Viśvanātha Cakravartī's commentary concurs. Both notions are fundamental to the Gauḍīya tradition. In other words, there are undeniable virtues awaiting those who live in Krishna's holy land, but bringing this same sacred space into your heart of hearts, through meditation, wherever you happen to live, is equally meritorious, and for those of us who are not pure, much less of a risk.

Conclusion

In contemplating Mahāprabhu's sojourn in Braj, one would do well to remember his promise 4,500 years earlier, when he manifested on Earth as Lord Krishna: "I will return" (*āyāsye iti*). We are introduced to this notion in the *Śrīmad Bhāgavatam* (10.39.35): "As he departed, that best of the Yadus saw how the gopīs were lamenting, and thus he consoled them by sending a messenger with this loving promise: 'I will return.'" (*tās tathā tapyatīr vīkṣya sva-prasthāne yadūttamaḥ/sāntvayām āsa sa-premair āyāsya iti dautyakaiḥ//*) We encounter similar words six chapters later (10.45.23), "Now you should all return to Vraja, dear father. We shall come to see you, our dear relatives who suffer in separation from us ..." (*yāta yūyaṁ vrajaṁ tāta vayaṁ ca sneha-duḥkh-itān/jñātīn vo draṣṭum eṣyāmo vidhāya suhṛdāṁ sukham//*) And in the following chapter, the great devotee Uddhava delivers the same message (10.46.35): "Having killed Kaṁsa, the enemy of all the Yadus, in the wrestling arena, Kṛṣṇa will now surely fulfill his promise to you by coming back." (*hatvā kaṁsaṁ raṅga-madhye pratīpaṁ sarva-sātvatām/yad āha vaḥ samāgatya kṛṣṇaḥ satyaṁ karoti tat//*)

We may take recourse in the well known Vaishnava teaching, "Krishna never steps foot out of Vrindavan,"[17] indicating that when he and Balarāma left for Mathurā, he was still in Vrindavan for those who love him. The tradition is clear: It was Vasudeva Krishna, an expansion, and not Braj Krishna (the original form of Godhead), who ventures outside. Śrīla Viśvanātha Chakravartī states in his commentaries to the 10th canto that Braj Krishna remained in Vrindavan and enjoyed continuous pastimes with all his devotees there, if clearly on a different level, i.e., it was *aprakaṭa*, invisible to those without the proper *adhikāra* (qualifications). Simultaneously, Vasudeva Krishna left for Mathurā, enabling "separation pastimes" (*viraha-līlā*) for the inhabitants of Vrindavan, situating them in the highest echelon of love of God.

Did Krishna ever return to Braj?[18] Ask the flora and fauna in those forests, the fortunate entities who were there when Śrī Chaitanya entered the sacred terrain some 500 years ago: "Thus all the moving and nonmoving living entities of Vṛndāvana became very jubilant to see the Lord. It was as if friends were made happy by seeing another friend." (*Caitanya-caritāmṛta* Madhya 17.202) It was that warm feeling of seeing an old, long lost friend. All the Braj residents knew who he was—it was Krishna coming home, fulfilling his promise.

Ultimately, in the end, Mahāprabhu's journey to Vrindavan teaches us two things. Since he is both the perfect devotee and Krishna in the mood of Rādhā as well, we see (1) the importance of a devotee making the effort to go to Braj. On that score, Mahāprabhu would not accept defeat, and though it took four tries, he would not abandon his endeavor until he finally arrived. This shows the determination with which a devotee should hanker after being in Braj. But also, (2) as Krishna, it was a journey home. The Lord in his original form is a *vraja-vāsī*, i.e., a resident of Braj, and Mahāprabhu's determined effort to get there was nothing less than the intense desire to go home. May we all have such a blessing.

Endnotes

1. Gokula and Vrindavan, while literally referring to two specific forests in the Braj area, are also used generically for Krishna's divine playground as a whole.

2. See *Bhakti-rasāmṛta-sindhu* 1.2.237.

3. *ibid.*, 1.2.212.

4. See *Upadeśāmṛta* 8.

5. See Śrīla Bhaktivinoda Ṭhākura, Śrī Chaitanya: His Life

and Precepts (https:// bhaktivinodainstitute.org/chaitanya-mahaprabhu-life-precepts-the-life-of-sri-chaitanya-mahaprabhu/).

6. See *Caitanya-bhāgavata,* Ādi-khaṇḍa 17.124-30.

7. One may wonder how anyone can trick the Supreme Personality of Godhead. The scriptures tell us that for the sake of loving exchange, the Lord allows Himself to be covered by His Yogamāyā potency, playing like an ordinary being for the sake of *rasa*, or the relish that comes from interpersonal relationship.

8. Coincidentally, Śrīla Prabhupāda, too, was twenty-nine when he first visited Vrindavan in 1925.

9. Jhārikhaṇḍa refers to the forests south of Bihar and east of Orissa, which at the time was largely a tribal area.

10. As God, how is it that Śrī Chaitanya's love had opportunity to increase? Is his love not already perfect? It is. In Vaishnavism, there is the conception of "perfect, more perfect and most perfect." In other words, God's nature need not conform to logic, and, accordingly, his love is ever-increasing, even if already perfect. Additionally, Śrī Chaitanya is playing the role of a devotee, whose love increases when in proximity to the Lord, and proximity is nowhere as pronounced as in Vrindavan. As for a scriptural basis for Śrī Chaitanya's ever-growing love, see *Caitanya-caritāmṛta* (Madhya 17.227): "The Lord's ecstatic love increased a thousand times when He visited Mathurā, but it increased a hundred thousand times when He wandered in the forests of Vṛndāvana."

11. See O. B. L. Kapoor, *The Philosophy and Religion of* Śrī *Caitanya* (New Delhi: Munshiram Manoharlal, 1977), 30-31.

12. As stated in the Gaudiya Math periodical, *The Harmonist*, edited by Śrīla Bhaktisiddhānta Sarasvatī Ṭhākura: "The narrative of the circumambulation performed by Sri Chaitanya Mahaprabhu is found in the Charitamrita. After His return to Puri from the South in 1514 A.D. the Supreme Lord wished to visit Sree Brindaban. He started from Puri in the Autumn of the same year in the beginning of Aswin (Sept-Oct) with a single attendant Balabhadra Bhattacharyya to accompany Him during the journey on foot through the forest of Jharikhanda (Orissa Garhjats and Choto Nagpur). Sree Chaitanya reached Mathura towards the end of the month of Kartik (early November) via Benares and Prayag (Allahabad). He set out on the circumambulation of Sree

Brajamandal early in Agrahayana (middle of November). He completed the tour of the Sphere of Braja before Magh (January) was far advanced when He began the return journey to Puri via Prayag (Allahabad)." See *The Harmonist*, Vol. 29, No. 5 (November 1931), 129-130. According to Sambidananda Das, the Vrindavan visit was postponed for one year, commencing in the fall of 1515 and lasting until January 1516. See Dr. Sambidananda Das, Bhaktisastri, *Sri Chaitanya Mahaprabhu* (Madras: Sree Gaudiya Math, 1958), 149– 157.

13. There are various theories about how long Mahāprabhu stayed in Braj, all based on documentary evidence. Some propose that he stayed for three months, from Mid-October 1515 to Mid-January 1516. See Khonika Gope-Kumar, "Constructing an Approximate Time-line of Mahaprabhu's Life Events in Gregorian Calendar" (https://iskcondesiretree.com/profiles/blogs/constructing-an-approximate-time-line-of-mahaprabhu-s-life-events). Mahanidhi Swami offers a variant saying that Mahāprabhu's visit lasted some four-and-a-half months. See "Mahaprabhu: Four Months in Vraja" (https://www.mahanidhiswami.com/mahaprabhu-four-months-in-vraja (https:// www.mahanidhiswami.com/mahaprabhu-four-months-in-vraja/). Finally, according to Vaishnava scholar and priest Shrivatsa Goswami, Mahāprabhu is said to have stayed in Braj for a full nine months (but I would speculate that this would likely include his extended travel time there and back). See Acharya Shrivatsa Goswami, "Chaitanya Mahaprabhu" in Alon Goshen-Gottstein, ed., *Interreligious Heroes: Role Models and Spiritual Exemplars for Interfaith* (Eugene, OR: Wipf & Stock, 2021), 22.

14. The project of reclaiming and refurbishing Braj did not begin with Rūpa and Sanātana Gosvāmīs, though they developed it beyond anyone's wildest dreams. Mahāprabhu had sent Lokanāth and Bhūgarbha Gosvāmīs to unearth the lost holy places of this region as far back as 1509, prior to his taking *sannyāsa*, and it was indeed these two *sādhus* who initiated the proceedings. Also prominent in the re-creation of Braj were Vallabhācārya and his followers, and special mention should be made of Nārāyaṇa Bhaṭṭa, a contemporary of the Gosvāmīs, whose *Vraja-Bhakti-Vilasa* is to this day one of the most important guidebooks for pilgrimage in Krishna's holy land. For more on Nārāyaṇa Bhaṭṭa, see Leena Taneja, "The Forgotten Story of

Narayan Bhatt" in *Journal of Vaishnava Studies*, Volume 15, Number 2 (Spring 2007), 35–50.

15. See Śrī *Bhaktivinoda Vāṇī Vaibhava*, ed., Śrīpāda Sundarānanda Vidyāvinoda, trans., Bhumipati dāsa (Kolkata: Touchstone Media, 2016), 570.

16. It should perhaps be underlined that physically being in Vrindavan is an extraordinary experience. Although ultimately Vrindavan is a state of consciousness, the geographical region is not unimportant. It embodies a sublime atmosphere that even conditioned souls can experience and appreciate. It is inspirational, powerful, emotional, and mere proximity leads to spiritual advancement. Living in the temple town known as Vrindavan is, in a sense, like living in the spiritual world, where all components work together as reminders of Krishna: the bells, the cows, the peacocks, the holy name, the Deities, the endless stream of devotees—all permeate the environment. Naturally, a pure soul can experience the holy atmosphere of Vrindavan anywhere, even if he or she particularly relishes Vrindavan proper, but the conditioned soul, especially, is more likely to experience it when visiting or living in that specific terrain.

17. See *Viṣṇu-yāmala-tantra*, quoted in Rūpa Gosvāmī's *Laghu-bhāgavatāmṛta* 1.5.461, *vṛndāvanaṁ parityajya pādam ekaṁ na gacchati.*

18. The *Śrīmad Bhāgavatam* leaves the question open, supporting the notion that although Lord Krishna is always in Braj spiritually, and within the hearts of all souls (particularly that of his devotees), he did not return in terms of his *prakṛta-līlā*. The Six Gosvāmīs, on the other hand, including Sanātana, Rūpa, and Jīva, have revealed an esoteric dimension to this narrative, in which Krishna in fact returned to Braj to satisfy the intense longing of his special *vraja-vāsī* associates. Among other texts in support of this conclusion, the reader may look to *Bṛhad-bhāgavatāmṛta* 2.6.354-355 and 2.6.348; *Laghu-bhāgavatāmṛta* 1.5.480; and especially Chapters 22-37 of Jīva Gosvāmī's *Gopāla-campū*. For context and elaboration, see Jan K. Brzezinski, "Does Kṛṣṇa Marry the Gopīs in the End? The Svakīya-vāda of Jīva Gosvāmin," in *Journal of Vaishnava Studies*, Vol. 5, No. 4 (Fall, 1997), 49–110.

Eleven

The Mystery of the Pañca Tattva in Light of the Christian Trinity

pañca-tattva—eka-vastu, nāhi kichu bheda
rasa āsvādite tabu vividha vibheda

"There are no spiritual differences between these five (*pañca*) truths (*tattvas*), for on the transcendental platform all spiritual phenomena are absolute. Yet there are also varieties in the spiritual world, and in order to taste these spiritual varieties one should distinguish between them."[1]

TO BEGIN, THE FIVE TRUTHS of the Pañca Tattva should be identified: Śrī Chaitanya Mahāprabhu, Śrī Nityānanda Prabhu, Śrī Advaita Ācārya, Śrī Gadādhara Prabhu, and Śrī Śrīvāsa Ṭhākura. These five divine entities, appearing in Bengal, India, some five centuries ago, represent or constitute various aspects of the Absolute Truth. In that sense, they are all on the same platform and are spiritually equal. Still, one naturally distinguishes between them, for they are, in the end, distinct individuals, manifesting God's glories in diverse ways. According to the principle of Acintya-bhedābheda ("inconceivable and simultaneous oneness and difference"), spiritual personalities and phenomena may be one and different at the same time, as we will explain elsewhere.

Although divine, these five beings manifest as devotees: *Bhakta-rūpa* (Śrī Caitanya), *bhakta-svarūpa* (Śrī Nityānanda) and *bhakta-avatāra* (Śrī Advaita) are manifestations of the Supreme Personality of Godhead himself, his immediate manifestation, and his plenary expansion, respectively, and they all belong to the Vishnu category. In other words, they are God himself—still, they appear as devotees. Similarly, Gadādhara and Śrīvāsa, though manifestations of the Lord in the form of his own energy, manifest as devotees to assist in Chaitanya Mahāprabhu's project of tasting what it means to be a devotee who is fully in love with God.[2]

To reveal their identities a bit more, Chaitanya Mahāprabhu is a combined manifestation of Rādhā and Krishna; Nityānanda Prabhu is Balarāma (Krishna's elder brother); Advaita is Sadāśiva (or Mahāvishnu); Gadādhara is Rādhārāṇī (Krishna's eternal consort and internal energy), and Śrīvāsa Ṭhākura is an incarnation of Nārada (who represents the ideal devotee). The Gauḍīya saint and scholar Bhaktisiddhānta Sarasvatī Thākura has summarized these truths in the following way: Caitanya Mahāprabhu, Nityānanda Prabhu, and Advaita Ācārya are in the category of *śaktimān-tattva*. In other words, they are the energetic source of everything that exists. Gadādhara and Śrīvāsa, as representatives of the internal energy and marginal energy of the Lord, respectively, are forms of *śakti-tattva*. Together, all five comprise the Pañca Tattva.

Clearly, there is a certain intricacy here that can lead to confusion, for embedded in these truths are theological details that require much research and realization to fully understand. How is it that one God manifests as five?

Historically, the Christian tradition has had to grapple with similar complexity: The Holy Trinity.[3] Here, the Supreme manifests as three. "For the Christian," Professor Klaus Klostermaier tells us, "the Trinity represents the deepest mystery of faith. If one took literally the symbolism of the Son being eternally generated by the Father, for example, one could come up with all kinds of mundane crudities and perversions. Similarly, the Rādhā-Kṛṣṇa relationship cannot be fathomed by paralleling it with romantic love poetry or late medieval Marian devotion, as some writers have tried to do. The mystery of these things goes very deep, and there is no earthly symbolism that can accurately convey its truth."[4]

The notion of the Father, the Son, and the Holy Ghost (or Holy Spirit) has challenged Christian philosophers for centuries. In a way not unlike the Pañca Tattva, these three divine Christian truths are seen as both one and different, serving varied functions of divine revelation while still partaking of the same essence, as we will describe below. The Trinity thus forces Christian philosophers to confront the complexity of God as he manifests in a variety of forms, even while he necessarily remains one.

For most Vaishnava thinkers, the Christian Trinity is often compared to *ātmā*, or *jīva*, Paramātmā, and Bhagavān, that is to say, the soul (the Son), the indwelling Lord in the heart (the Holy Spirit), and the Supreme Personality of Godhead (the Father). As Prabhupāda writes, "Regarding the Christian's Trinity, I believe it is called God, the Holy Ghost, and the son. Person in Krishna Consciousness accepts this by the name Vishnu, Paramātmā, and Jīva. God is a Person, the holy spirit or the Supersoul is a person, and the living entity is also a person. Also, Mary is the representation of the energy of God. Either as internal energy Rādhārāṇī or as external energy Durgā, the energy of Godhead can be considered the mother of the living entities. But there is no clash between the Bible and the Vedas . . ."[5] Prabhupāda's reference to Mary/Rādhārāṇī is pertinent here, too, for in the early Christian tradition the Holy Spirit is identified as the feminine divine, as we shall see below.[6]

Another way of expressing Prabhupāda's view of Vishnu, Paramātmā, and Jīva, with a slight variation, would be as follows: Bhagavān, *bhakti*, and *bhakta*. In the Gaudiya tradition, all three are considered transcendental phenomena. Bhagavan, of course, refers to Krishna, the Supreme Lord; *bhakti*, or devotional service, is a feminine word and is often envisioned in female form, thus finding resonance with the Holy Spirit (even if this female dimension has been lost in modern conceptions of the Holy Spirit doctrine); and the *bhakta* is the devotee, epitomized as "the perfect son," or the ideal servant of God—in the understanding of most Christian denominations, solely evoking Jesus and no one else. We will see how these categories overlap with the Pañca Tattva and how these truths point to transcendental phenomena that is beyond ordinary understanding.

God is One

By definition, God is One, the unequaled source of everything. This is as true for Vaishnavas as it is for

Christians. According to the Vedic scriptures, *nityo nityānām cetanaś cetanānām,* "There is one supreme eternal being who is maintaining all others, who are subordinate." (*Kaṭha Upaniṣad* 2.2.13) In fact, names of God that refer to his oneness are ubiquitous in traditional Vaishnava texts: Ekanātha, Ekeśa, Ekendra, and many others. These names stem from the Sanskrit *eka,* "one," the Hebrew derivative of which is *echod* (as in *Deuteronomy* 6.4: "Hear O Israel, the Lord our God, the Lord is one") and in Arabic, it is *ilah* (as in the Islamic Creed of Faith: "There is one God and that is Allah…"). The great monotheistic traditions boldly proclaim God's exclusive position as the original cause of all causes. All major world religions say it in their own way: "the Lord our God is One."

Interestingly, despite insisting on God's oneness, the Bible refers to him with pluralized names, such as Elohim. For example, consider *Genesis* 1.26: "Let us make humanity in our image, after our likeness." The Jewish prophets repeatedly use such terms throughout the Bible.[7] Biblical commentators assert that such verses attempt to evoke an aristocratic "we" (instead of "I"), often used by sovereigns and high officials and also by English editors and writers of various disciplines. It does not, they say, refer to a literal plurality.

Some commentators go so far as to say that these verses are actually referring to God's angels and not to God himself, although there is no evidence to support this in the texts themselves. In the Christian tradition, the doctrine of the Trinity has exacerbated this ambiguity: "Is God one or three?" It is often answered that he is both, inconceivably, for the Lord need not be confined by our laws of logic, which he created.

That said, Jewish and Islamic philosophers tend to see Christianity as polytheistic, specifically because of its Trinitarian doctrine. But Christianity, of course, does not see itself that way. In fact, the tradition has a long history of monotheistic teaching, with countless theologians internally confirming the religion's adherence to the doctrine of one Supreme God.

If the Judaeo-Christian tradition, which is monotheistic, acknowledges pluralistic names for the Supreme and even the conception of a triune God, then the Vaishnava teaching of the Pañca Tattva should be equally plausible. Indeed, although Vaishnavism acknowledges a plethora of Divine manifestations, it considers itself monotheistic, and, like Christianity, has centuries of confirmation from scholars and philosophers inside the tradition.

The Trinity[8]

Regarding the Trinity, early Christian theologians had to address criticism from several points of view, including that of Jewish monotheists, Greek philosophers, who favored polytheism, and neo-Platonists, among others. Briefly, monotheists refused to acknowledge that one God could manifest as three, while those who were inclined to polytheism refused to accept that three divine persons could in some way be one.

Today, however, most of the Christian world accepts the idea of the Father, the Son, and the Holy Spirit. This is so even though the word "Trinity"—and even the specifics regarding the doctrine itself—is never mentioned in the Bible. Still, *the idea of the Trinity,* it has been argued, is implicit in New Testament texts, and so even the *Nicene Creed,* which was composed at the Council of Nicaea (325 CE.), is today considered a statement in orthodoxy, fully affirming the Christian belief in the triune God.

This is not to say that the majority of Christians believe in three gods, which would be polytheism, but rather that they believe in three complete persons composing one God. Believers in the Pañca Tattva, too, accept one God who manifests in five features (as compared to the Christian three). This ability to expand into various personalities is evidence of God's incomprehensible nature, and is detailed in all scriptures from the Bible to the Vedic literature.

In order to express the mystical union of three persons composing one God, Christian theologians and philosophers have traditionally used such terms as the Greek *perichoresis*, or the Latin *circumincessio*, both of which indicate that each divine person of the Godhead contains the other; they interpenetrate in a way that is unique to them; in a word, they are not three, but one—statically and/or ecstatically combined in essence while remaining separate as individuals. Such a truth is said to be inconceivable.

The tradition is clear about how the three personalities of the triune God unite and how they diverge. The monistic combination of the three divine personalities refers only to their substance; their personhood distinguishes them. According to Christian tradition, then, the proper conception of God views the Father, Son, and Holy Spirit as partaking of the same spiritual substance—this refers to their unity—but they are considered separate in terms of their personalities, and because of this they reflect different aspects of divinity and serve different functions in their devotees' lives.

To further elucidate the theology of unity in trinity and trinity in unity, St. Augustine (354-430 CE) offered several analogies. To cite but one, he compared the triune God to mind (heart), knowledge and love. Clearly, each of these terms contains the others: one cannot love without the mind (and heart); to exhibit knowledge, one must have a mind; and to love, both mind and knowledge are indispensable, and so on. Such analogies offer a dim reflection of a greater and yet more subtle truth, showing a oneness and difference between the various elements of the trinity.

A practical example of the above can be seen in *John* (10:30), when Jesus says, "The Father and I are one." A glance at the original Greek reveals that Jesus is not referring to numerical oneness, for which the Greek word is *heis.* Instead, Jesus uses the word *hen,* which means "we are together." Jesus uses the same word eight verses later, when he says, "The Father is in me, and I am in my Father." Biblical scholarship has shown that in these verses (and in others like them) union presupposes differentiation. If my father and I are "in each other," then we are two separate individuals. The very fact that we can talk about "being one," indicates that we are in some way "two." Ultimately, the truth alluded to here is the inconceivable, simultaneous oneness and difference between various manifestations of

God and between God and ordinary living beings, mentioned earlier as Acintya-bhedābheda.

Gauḍīya Vaishnavism asserts that both God and the living entity are substantially the same in terms of quality; it is in quantity that they differ. The traditional analogy given is that of gold and a gold mine. Or a drop of water and the ocean. When chemically analyzed, they are the same. But the gold mine holds more than the small piece of gold; the ocean is greater than the drop of water. Similarly, God has unlimited greatness, beauty, knowledge, strength, wealth, fame, and so on; the living entities share these same qualities but in minute quantity. Gauḍīya Vaishnavas see a similar interrelationship between various manifestations of God: such manifestations are the same yet different, much in the same way that the Trinity is one God in substance but several in terms of personality. This truth is nowhere as prevalent as in the Pañca Tattva.

In the Christian tradition, there is a hierarchical aspect to the Trinity. Jesus referred to his own subservience to the Father, just as often as he affirmed his oneness with him. In regard to the Holy Spirit, there are various points of view. Traditionalists often perceive the Holy Spirit as the Indwelling God. Here the Holy Spirit was at times seen as greater than Jesus, who worked through "the power of the Spirit." (See *Luke* 4.14) Early Syrian and Jewish texts, as well as later mystical literature, saw the Holy Spirit as feminine, "the Holy Mother," who worked in the world through her Son.[9] This harkens back, of course, to Prabhupāda's allusion to divine feminine energy when discussing the Christian Trinity, as stated above. In this early literature, Jesus, who was said to have been "conceived" by the Holy Spirit, was seen as being "nurtured" by her, and as being prepared by her for his mission. In this conception the Holy Spirit would sometimes take prominence in a hierarchical sense, as Jesus's true mother, whereas at other times it was Jesus who would take a more prominent position.

Conclusion: The Doctrine of Love

Having established that one God can manifest in a variety of forms, and that these forms are simultaneously one and different, one question remains: Why would One Supreme Being manifest as three (or five)?

Great Western thinkers—from Plato through Augustine and Bonaventure to the medieval Franciscan school—have considered this question. Basically, their collective mystical intuition can be expressed as follows: God is much more than merely a Perfect Spirit—he is Highest Good or Supreme Love, seeking to share that perfection, goodness, and love with all creation.

The inherent property of Perfection, Goodness, and Love—especially when embodied in a conscious being—is to spread and communicate itself, to go out from itself and share itself with others. In Vaishnavism, this is called the Saṅkīrtana principle—to passionately give God's essence to others. Even God, say the Gauḍīyas, partakes in this glorious activity.

As the infinite loving principle expands, it reveals itself as Son or Word, which is of the same nature as its spiritual source and yet which is accessible and approachable in the world. This is the guru, seen in the Christian tradition as fully embodied in Jesus only, but in the Vaishnava tradition as any perfect *bhakta*, who has distinguished himself or herself on the path, in the eyes of God. In other words, it is through this medium that the love of the Father can reach others, can extend itself through human interaction. It can also be understood that this love is communicated from Father to Son to World through the Holy Spirit or, as expressed in Vaishnava terms, through *śakti,* the Energy, the Mother—Śrī Rādhikā.

Gauḍīya Vaishnava thinkers concur that the One becomes Many to exchange and disseminate Divine Love. Kavirāja Gosvāmī has written in the *Caitanya-caritāmṛta* (Ādi 7.21) that the characteristics of Krishna are understood to be like a storehouse of transcendental love. Although this loving repository certainly accompanied Krishna when he was present in the world (five thousand years ago), it was sealed, protected from those who might abuse it or take it for granted. But when the Pañca Tattva arrived (five hundred years ago), they broke the seal and plundered the storehouse to drink transcendental love of Krishna, which was among their reasons for appearing in the world of three dimensions.

The more they tasted it, the more their thirst for it grew. This is the peculiar nature of love. It is dynamic—a constant surge upward. The more it is relished, the more it is desired. It follows, then, that if God has more love than any other being—indeed, he is considered to be the very embodiment of love itself—then his yearning for love must be greater than anyone else's as well (as is his potency to fulfill that yearning).

But love is not enjoyed alone, in a vacuum; it is shared between people. Therefore, the One becomes Many. First, he expands into his eternal consort, Śrī Rādhā, and into his plenary expansions and incarnations, and then into the multifarious living entities (although the ordinary living beings are removed expansions and therefore constitute an entirely separate category of divine energy, known as *jīva-tattva).* The two primary living beings, Rādhā and Krishna, reunite in the form of Chaitanya Mahāprabhu, and so the expression of love that the Lord manifests in this feature is beyond the ken of ordinary and extraordinary perception.

Just as in the Christian conception God's love is passed to the world through the Son and the Holy Spirit, Kavirāja Gosvāmī tells us (Ādi 7.22) that the Pañca Tattva danced together, again and again, and thus made it easier to drink the sweet love of the spiritual realm. They danced, laughed, cried and chanted like madmen, and in this way they distributed love of Godhead. This is an important point. The union-communion-*perichorsis* opens outward like a lotus, inviting human beings and the rest of the universe to insert themselves in the divine *līlā,* or the play of God: "May they become one in us *(hen)* . . . that they may be one as we are one." (John 17.21-2)

Endnotes

1. See *Caitanya-caritāmṛta*, Ādi 7, Text 5. Key words in this verse: *pañca-tattva*—the five subjects; *eka-vastu*—they are one in five. Thus, the five transcendental personalities of the Pañca Tattva—Chaitanya, Nityānanda, Advaita, Gadādhara, and Śrīvāsa—though distinct individuals, are spiritually one and the same.

2. While the notion of God being nondifferent from his energy, Rādhā/Gadādhara, is easily understandable, one might balk at the

idea of Śrīvāsa, a devotee, generally identified as a *jīva*, or an ordinary soul, being included in this divine stratification. Let it be known: The tradition views Śrīvāsa as a *nitya pāriṣada*, or an eternal associate of the Lord, and as such he partakes of divine status in a way that most ordinary entities do not. In Gauḍīya Vedānta, the Lord's *śakti* (of which Śrīvāsa is decidedly a component) is inseparable from Krishna, and even referred to as a special category of being: *vibhinnāṁśa*, or the Lord's separated parts.

3. I originally explored the comparison between the Trinity and the Pañca Tattva in my Introduction to *Śrī Pañca Tattva: The Five Features of God* (New York: Folk Books, 1994).

4. See Klaus Klostermaier, "Vaiṣṇavism and Christianity" in Steven J. Rosen, ed., *Vaiṣṇavism: Contemporary Scholars Discuss the Gauḍīya Tradition* (Delhi: Motilal Banarsidass, 1994), 225.

5. Letter from Śrīla Prabhupāda to Śivānanda, New York, April 19, 1968). Some have alternately compared the Trinity to Brahman, Paramātmā, and Bhagavān, though this analogy is fraught with imprecision. Briefly, Brahman is God as an abstract force; Paramātmā is God as he indwells all people and phenomena; and Bhagavān is the Personality of Godhead. In this reading, Brahman may be compared to an amorphous Holy Spirit and the son might be compared to Paramātmā, for the Lord in the heart is the Chaitya-guru, and his outward manifestation is the guru or the teacher—the perfect son, i.e., Jesus. (By other estimations, the Paramātmā is said to be the Holy Spirit.) Finally, God, the Father, is clearly analogous to Bhagavān. However, when thoroughly analyzing Brahman, Paramātmā, and Bhagavān in terms of this Trinity schema, we may note that Brahman is traditionally understood as having no activity or relation to variegatedness of any kind, which sets it apart from the Holy Spirit. Similarly, Paramātmā is described as being neutral to all living beings and has no birth in the material world: It would thus be impossible to crucify him because he never "becomes flesh." Thus, overall, it can be vexing to indulge in interreligious comparisons, here leading to a compromise in *siddhānta* for both Gauḍīyas and Christians. Nonetheless, with that caveat, it is clearly tempting to find points of similarity and can be useful in one's spiritual understanding. As an addendum, in a general sense, without reference to the Christian Trinity, most Hindus think of their own trinity in terms of the Creator (Brahma), the Preserver

(Vishnu), and the Destroyer (Śiva), sometimes expressed in the modern era with the acronym G.O.D. ("Generator, Operator, and Destroyer").

6. See Van Oort J., 2016, "The Holy Spirit as feminine: early Christian testimonies and their interpretation," *HTS Teologiese Studies/Theological Studies* 72(1), a3225. http://dx.doi.org/10.4102/hts.v72i1.3225. Also see Susan Ashbrook Harvey, "Feminine Imagery for the Divine: The Holy Spirit, the Odes of Solomon, and Early Syriac Tradition," *St. Vladimir's Theological Quarterly* 37, nos. 2-3 (1993): 111-120.

7. See *Genesis* 3.22, 11.7; also *Isaiah* 6.2-3.

8. For more on the Christian Trinity, see Matthew W. Bates, *The Birth of the Trinity* (New York: Oxford University Press, 2015); Paul Fiddes, *Participating in God: a pastoral doctrine of the Trinity* (London: Darton, Longman, & Todd, 2000); Marian Hillar, *From Logos to Trinity: The Evolution of Religious Beliefs from Pythagoras to Tertullian* (New York: Cambridge University Press, 2012); William J. La Due, *The Trinity guide to the Trinity* (New York: Continuum International Publishing Group, 2003); and Eugene Webb, *In Search of The Triune God: The Christian Paths of East and West* (Columbia, MO: University of Missouri Press, 2014).

9. See Van Oort J., 2016, "The Holy Spirit as feminine: early Christian testimonies and their interpretation," op. cit. Also see Susan Ashbrook Harvey, "Feminine Imagery for the Divine: The Holy Spirit, the Odes of Solomon, and Early Syriac Tradition," *op. cit.* In Kabbalistic literature and in the writings of the Christian mystics, reference is often made to the *Shekinah,* a word pointing to a feminine Deity—often identified with the Holy Spirit. While the Hebrew word is indeed grammatically feminine, the notion of a consequent female Deity has had its detractors. Nonetheless, the earliest mystical literature of the Jews and Christians contains much information about God in female form. Parenthetically, the "feminine" Holy Spirit is often seen to be a variation on Mary, who is known as Theotokos, the Mother of God Incarnate. For details on the *Shekinah,* see the *Jewish Encyclopedia* (https://www.jewishencyclopedia.com/articles/7833-holy-spirit).

Eleven

The World's First Deity Forms of Śrī Chaitanya: A Precedent for ISKCON Temples

WALK INTO ANY ISKCON center, and the golden form of Śrī Chaitanya (1486–1534), Krishna Himself in the mood of His own devotee, will not be far away. Whether in His Deity manifestation, i.e., a visible icon, or *mūrti* (resembling a statue), or in the form of a painting, Śrī Chaitanya dominates the ISKCON landscape, and rightly so. Even the first "Deity" of ISKCON, in 1966, soon after Śrīla Prabhupāda had founded the movement at 26 Second Avenue in New York, was a painting of Śrī Chaitanya and His associates as rendered by Jadurani Devī Dāsī, one of Prabhupāda's first female disciples. Clearly, ISKCON is a manifestation of the Gauḍīya Vaishnava tradition, complete with its unique emphasis on Śrī Chaitanya.

What is often left unsaid is that Deity forms of Śrī Chaitanya are not some modern-day innovation peculiar to ISKCON. Worship of such Deities goes back to the earliest days of the Hare Krishna movement, some 500 years ago in Bengal, India. What's more, these Deities are imbued with Śrī Chaitanya's very essence so that these forms are nondifferent from Him, just as Deities of Rādhā and Krishna are nondifferent from Them. Thus, the worship of Chaitanya Deities was a part of the fledgling Gauḍīya Vaishnava movement of 16th-century India, and it continues on today, worldwide. Below, I give two examples of Chaitanya Deities from the early days of Gauḍīya Vaishnavism, though there are several.

Gaurīdāsa Paṇḍita's Deities

According to traditional Vaishnava texts, such as Śrīla Vṛndāvanadāsa Ṭhākura's *Chaitanya-Bhāgavata*, Śrīla Narahari Chakravatī Ṭhākura's *Bhakti-ratnākara*, and Murārilāla Adhikārī's *Vaishnava Digdarśanī*, the earliest Chaitanya Deity made His appearance in the presence of Gaurīdāsa Paṇḍita, one of Śrī Chaitanya's direct associates, who is clearly not an ordinary soul. It is stated in the *Gaura-gaṇoddeśa-dīpikā*, verse 128, that in his previous life, he was Subāla, one of the cowherd boyfriends of Krishna and Balarāma in Vṛndāvana.

Gaurīdāsa lived in a town known as Ambikā-kālanā, in the Purba Bardhaman district of West Bengal, off the western bank of the Bhagirathi River. Even today, one finds in Ambikā-kālanā a temple that was constructed generations ago by a wealthy landowner from Burdwan, whose name we no longer know.[1] This Gaura-Nitāi temple is forever associated with Gaurīdāsa and his family.

Once, just prior to taking *sannyāsa* (the renounced order of life), Śrī Caitanya visited Gaurīdāsa at Ambikā-kālanā, accompanied by Nityānanda Prabhu, the incarnation of Balarāma who was among Mahāprabhu's chief companions.

Understanding that the Lord was about to renounce the world and also embark on a pilgrimage to South India, which meant that such friendly visits would now be few and far between, Gaurīdāsa became overwhelmed with grief. Thus, without any other recourse, he begged his dear ones, Gaura-Nitāi, Chaitanya and Nityānanda, to stay with him for an extended period in his home.

It was not to be, or so it seemed. The Lord told Gaurīdāsa that, as much as They'd love to stay, it would not be possible to honor his request. But as a consolation, He allowed the carving of two life-like Deity forms made of pure *neem* wood — and He permitted these first ever Deities of Gaura-Nitāi to be worshiped by Gaurīdāsa and family for the remainder of their lives. The life-sized forms stood beside each other with Their long arms raised in the air, a semblance of Their ecstatic dancing postures in real life. Gaurīdāsa's bliss was beyond words.

"Gaurīdāsa," said Śrī Chaitanya, "My Deity form is non-different from Me." The Lord continued, "In this way, Nitāi and I will forever remain in your home to accept your service." Gaurīdāsa boldly if also somewhat humorously replied, "If these Deities are as good as You, why don't You just stay here with me and let Them go where They need to go?!"

Taking the request of His devotee to heart, Śrī Chaitanya and Nityānanda Prabhu immediately stepped onto Gaurīdāsa's altar, raising Their arms high in the air (simulating the newly carved forms) and transforming Themselves into wooden Deities. To further prove that They were identical, the carved Deities stepped off of the altar and walked out the temple door.

Gaurīdāsa was naturally awestruck by this transformation, and, not wanting to inconvenience the Lord, asked the Deities to return to the altar. When the Deities stepped back onto the altar, Śrī Caitanya and Nityānanda resumed Their original forms and began to leave, with the Deities in Their place. Seeing this, Gaurīdāsa again approached Them, asking Them to stay, and escorted Them back onto the altar. Meanwhile, the other forms of Gaura-Nitāi — the original forms — began to walk away yet again. This repeated several times.

Eventually, it was no longer clear to Gaurīdāsa who were the original forms of the Lord and who were the wooden Deities. Thus, the point was driven home — The Lord and His Deity form are nondifferent. In this way, the first Deities of Gaura-Nitāi made Their appearance in the world of three dimensions.[2] These Deities are still worshiped by Gaurīdāsa Paṇḍita's descendants in the temple of Ambikā-kālanā.[3]

Dhāmeśvara Gaurāṅga

When considering which of the Chaitanya Deities in India are among the first, carved and worshiped in the 16th century, mention must be made of Dhāmeśvara Gaurāṅga, sometimes known as Dhāmeśvara Mahāprabhu.[4] This blissful, grace-bestowing form of Śrī Chaitanya, again made from *neem*, is said to be the Deity that Śrīmatī Viṣṇupriyā — Mahaprabhu's wife and primary *śakti,* or energy, of the Lord — worshiped in her later years, assuaging the pain of separation after her husband took *sannyāsa*. Tradition avers that she worshiped this Deity for some 80 years, until her earthly demise at 96. Today, visiting devotees and pilgrims can have *darśana* of this very same Deity in the present town of Navadvīpa. The story runs as follows.

"O Jīva [Gosvāmī], listen to My confidential words," said Nityānanda Prabhu. "Śrīmatī Viṣṇupriyā's Deity of Śrī Gaurāṅga [Chaitanya] illuminates the world. In the future, *brāhmaṇas* in the lineage of Jagannātha Miśra [Mahāprabhu's father] will bring this jewel-like Deity to Saṭṭīkāra Dhāma [Navadvīpa]. Four hundred years after the appearance day of Śrī Gaura, the worship of the Deity will be set to the highest standard.[5] And so it was.

After the Lord's acceptance of *sannyasa*, Śrīmatī Viṣṇupriyā rarely left her home. The only exception was her daily bath in the Ganges, and Śrīmatī Śacīdevī [Mahāprabhu's mother] would aways accompany her. Together, they would constantly chant the holy name of Krishna. It is said that Viṣṇupriyā would place two earthen pots, one empty and one full of rice, on the ground beside her, one to her right and the other to her left. After each round of *japa* (108 beads), she took one grain of rice and placed it in the empty pot. Thus, she chanted for hours on end. At the end of the day, when her regulated chanting was complete, the accumulated grains in the once empty pot were cooked and offered to the Lord with love and devotion. This was her daily practice.

In their daily chores, Śacīdevī and Viṣṇupriyā were always assisted by their devoted house-servants, Īśāna Ṭhākura and Vaṁśīvadana Ṭhākura, who, on Mahāprabhu's order, looked after them for the remainder of their many years. It may be noted that Śrī Chaitanya's family servant throughout his early life was Īśāna Ṭhākura, a disciple of Advaita Ācārya.[6]

Īśāna was the dedicated servant of the Miśra household from early on, and was especially stationed as young Nimāi's attendant and caretaker.

After the Lord took *sannyāsa*, Īśāna continued to follow Mahāprabhu's order of protecting and caring for Śacī and Viṣṇupriyā. However, at that time or soon thereafter, Īśāna began to receive assistance from Vaṁśīvadana Ṭhākura. Together, they spent day and night serving the Lord's loved ones. Vaṁśīdāsa, as he was also called, was known amongst the higher devotees as an incarnation of Lord Krishna's flute.[7] His story is inextricably intertwined with that of Dhāmeśvara Gaurāṅga, as we will see.

When Śrīnivāsa Ācārya arrived in Nadiya, during the second generation of Mahāprabhu's followers, Vaṁśīdāsa introduced him to Śacīdevī, Viṣṇupriyā and Īśāna Ṭhākura, who were very old at the time. After the passing of Śacīdevī, Vaṁśīdāsa devoted full time to the service of Viṣṇupriyā and Īśāna Ṭhākura. These pastimes are elaborated upon in the *Bhakti-ratnākara*.

After most of the devotees in Bengal were no longer on the planet, and, especially, after the heartrending demise of Viṣṇupriyā, Vaṁśīdāsa took Dhāmeśvara Gaurāṅga and Viṣṇupriyā's family westward to Navadvip, where the Deity is currently worshiped. They had been on eastern side of the Gaṅgā, in Māyāpur, but after their house was washed away by the river's ever-changing tide, Vaṁśīdāsa moved family and Deity to Kulīnagrāma (also known as Kuliyā-Pāhāḍapura, and previously as Koladvīpa) on the western side of the river. This is now known as the modern town of Navadvīpa. As they settled, Vaṁśīdāsa particularly took up the service of Viṣṇupriyā's younger brother, Yādava Miśra (also known as Yādavāchārya). Since Śrī Chaitanya was the son-in-law of the family in charge of the temple — i.e., Viṣṇupriyā's relatives — to this day their descendants worship the Deity with great devotion as their transcendental son-in-law.

Conclusion

With such a glorious beginning, it is easy to see why Mahāprabhu worship has spread around the world. Of course, this ubiquitous presence is largely due to the efforts of His Divine Grace A. C. Bhaktivedanta Swami Prabhupāda, the founder/*ācārya* of the International Society for Krishna Consciousness, and his industrious disciples. Indeed, from that first painting at 26 Second Avenue, New York, Śrī Chaitanya Mahāprabhu blossomed throughout Prabhupāda's movement. While many ISKCON temples naturally have, as their central Deities, forms of Rādhā and Krishna — and even in these temples one finds Gaura-Nitāi, or Śrī Chaitanya, somewhere on the premises as well, perhaps on a subsidiary altar or in the form of a painting — there are also many in which Śrī Chaitanya is the primary Deity.

A quick survey brings to light several temples that have Śrī Chaitanya front and center, such as those in Atlanta and Long Island (America), Hamburg (Germany), Belfast (UK), Ljubljana (Slovenia), Budapest (Hungary), Warsaw (Poland), Zagreb (Croatia), Almviks Gard and Stockholm (Sweden), Rome (Italy), Split (Croatia), Albettone (Italy), Belgrade

(Serbia), Skopje (Macedonia), Christchurch (New Zealand), Johannesburg (South Africa), Buenos Aires (Argentina), Istanbul (Turkey), Hong Kong, Beijing (China), Mayapur (West Bengal, India) and others.

Śrī Chaitanya's pervasiveness should not be surprising. He was, some might say, a Christlike personality who spread love and wisdom wherever He went, an alluring manifestation of Godhead whose very presence could instill love for the Divine. Consequently, He is easily appreciated by thoughtful and sensitive people from all walks of life, regardless of religious orientation. Apropos of this, we conclude with the interesting insight of Christian theologian John Moffitt, who, while not exactly articulating the Gauḍīya Vaishnava conception of Śrī Chaitanya, does manage to vividly depict a particular aspect of His personality that is universally appealing:

> If I were asked to choose one man in Indian religious history who best represents the pure spirit of devotional self-giving, I would choose the Vaishnavite saint Chaitanya, whose full name in religion was Krishna-Chaitanya, or "Krishna consciousness." Of all the saints in recorded history, East or West, he seems to me the supreme example of a soul carried away on a tide of ecstatic love of God. This extraordinary man, who belongs to the rich period beginning with the end of the fourteenth century, represents the culmination of the devotional schools that grew up around Krishna. ... Chaitanya delighted intensely in nature. It is said that, like St. Francis of Assisi, he had a miraculous power over wild beasts. His life in the holy town of Puri is the story of a man in a state of almost continuous spiritual intoxication. Illuminating discourses, deep contemplation,

moods of loving communion with God, were daily occurrences.[8]

Gauḍīya Vaishnavas, who follow in Śrī Chaitanya's line, hope to achieve a fraction of His loving mood, which He manifested as an example for all.

Endnotes

1. There is a famous tamarind tree in front of this temple. It was here that Gaurīdāsa Paṇḍita is said to have met and conversed with Śrī Caitanya Mahāprabhu. Today, not far from that very tree, pilgrims are offered *darśana* of a bark/leaf manuscript of the *Bhagavad-gītā*, said to have been handwritten by Śrī Caitanya. Also at this temple one is shown the oar that Mahāprabhu used to cross the river.

2. Although these Deities are often considered the first of Gaura-Nitāi, there are certainly other contenders. For example, Gauḍīya commentator Rādhā Mādhava Dāsa writes about a famous Chaitanya Deity in East Bengal: "This deity was originally worshiped in Sylhet in the Srihatta district by Srimati Shobha Devi, Sri Chaitanya Mahaprabhu's beloved paternal grandmother. It was manifested from Mahaprabhu himself when he was only sixteen years old in the year 1502 AD, thus making it the first Mahaprabhu deity that we know of. It is also one of only a few deities of Mahaprabhu as a *sannyasi* — his hands sporting the *mudras* of holding a *daṇḍa* and *kamaṇḍalu.* It is also the only deity of Mahaprabhu that we have heard of who has dilated *cakā-dolā* eyes that are somewhat like those of his beloved Lord Jagannath. ... [This deity is] still worshiped today at the Naba Dhaka-dakshin temple in Srikona, near Silchar in Assam." See "Puri—The inner Chamber of Sri Chaitanya's Home, Part 1," *Sri Krishna Kathamrita Bindu*, Issue 484 (October 13, 2020), 2.

3. The Gaura-Nitāi Deities established in Gaurīdāsa Paṇḍita's temple at Ambikā-kālanā are mentioned by Murāri Gupta in *Śrī Caitanya-Carita*, one of Mahāprabhu's earliest biographies (4.14.12-15).

4. Wooden shoes allegedly worn by Śrī Chaitanya and given as a

gift to Viṣṇupriyā are kept in this temple; they are shown to pilgrims as a blessing for their journey to this holy place.

5. See Śrīla Bhaktivinoda Thakura, *Śrī Navadvīpa-dhāma-māhātmya*, 5.94-96.

6. See Haridāsa Dāsa, *Gauḍīya Vaiṣṇava Abhidhāna* (Navadvīpa: Hari-bola Kuṭīra, 1957). Volume 3, page 1,153, has three entries for Īśāna: (1) Īśāna (Mahāprabhu's childhood servant); (2) Īśāna Ācārya (identified with Mauna Mañjarī); and (3) Īśāna Nāgara (author of *Advaita Prakāśa*).

7. See Kavi Karṇapūra's *Gaura-gaṇoddeśa-dīpikā*, 179.

8. John Moffitt, *Journey to Gorakhpur: An Encounter with Christ Beyond Christianity* (New York: Holt, Rinehart, and Winston, 1972), 129, 135–136.

Twelve

Sanātana Gosvāmī in Benares: Focusing in on Deity Worship and the *Ātmārāma* Verse

Part I: The Importance of Deity Worship

After visiting Vrindavan, the holy land of Krishna, Śrī Chaitanya Mahāprabhu (1486–1534), who was God Himself in the form of His own devotee, began His return journey to Jagannath Puri. As He proceeded via Benares (also known as Kashi and Varanasi), which is on the way, He met His beloved follower, Śrī Sanātana Gosvāmī, who had by now abandoned his duties for the Islamic occupational government in Bengal and was on his way to Vrindavan, according to plan. His intention was to live there as a monk, establishing temples and writing texts in the service of Śrī Chaitanya's mission.

We learn from the *Caitanya-caritāmṛta* (Adi 7.160, purport) that the actual purpose of Śrī Chaitanya's stay in Benares on His return journey was specifically to meet Sanātana Gosvāmī and to teach him the nuances of Gauḍīya siddhānta. This is indeed what took place, with

Śrī Chaitanya spending a full two months instructing His enthusiastic disciple.

Through the empowerment thus received from Śrī Chaitanya, Sanātana Gosvāmī—in conjunction with his brother Śrī Rūpa and others—would soon fulfill the Lord's inner desire by discovering the lost holy places of Vrindavan, establishing the service of Krishna deities, and compiling several important *bhakti* texts. Specifically, Sanātana wrote the *Bṛhad-bhāgavatāmṛta*, which is the first book of the Gauḍīya Vaishnava *sampradāya*; the *Krishna-līlā-stava*, which describes Krishna's pastimes up to His stay in Mathurā; the *Bṛhad-vaiṣṇava-toṣaṇī*, a commentary on *Śrīmad-Bhāgavatam*'s Tenth Canto; and the *Hari-bhakti-vilāsa*, a mammoth text on Vaishnava culture and behavior, which we will discuss below.

While in Benares, Śrī Chaitanya enlightened Sanātana in the various truths of *bhakti*, including *sambandha* (the relationship between the living entity, matter, and God), *abhidheya* (the means by which one attains the Supreme), and *prayojana* (the ultimate end, which culminates in love of God). Śrī Chaitanya also specifically taught him about the various forms of God, including His exitence in the spiritual world; how He manifests as various *avatāras*, incarnations Who descend into our world of three dimensions; and the forms of Krishna Deities, or the three-dimensional icons that Vaishnavas worship in temples or in their homes. In regard to worshipping these Deities, Śrī Chaitanya taught Sanātana the intricacies of Vaishnava behavior and ritual, which was later passed on to the Gosvāmīs' peers and students. One of the most important instructions that Śrī

Sanātana received in Benares was to establish the methods and procedures of Deity worship. Indeed, the practice of such worship would become a primary component in the Six Gosvāmīs' reclamation of Vrindavan and in the lives of devotees to this day.

Vaishnava history tells us that the Gosvāmīs found ancient Deities—Govindadeva, Dāmodara, Madan-mohan, and others—long lost in the sands of Vraja, and worshiped Them in a simple way, as the spirit moved them. While it is true that these great souls, and others like them, were ensconced in spontaneous devotion, and lovingly served their Deities according to their own inner guidance and feelings of affection, they simultaneously established standards as well as rules and regulations for the common person, so that anyone practicing Vaishnavism might get the most out of Deity worship.

This becomes clear upon carefully studying the *Caitanya-caritāmṛta*, especially the section that tells us just what Mahāprabhu and Sanātana Gosvāmī discussed while in in Benares. For example, at Madhya 24, Texts 112 and 113, we read, "Even a liberated soul merged in the impersonal Brahman effulgence is attracted to the pastimes of Kṛṣṇa. He thus installs a Deity and renders the Lord service. Although Śukadeva Gosvāmī and the four Kumāras were always absorbed in the thought of impersonal Brahman and were thus Brahmavādīs, they were nonetheless attracted by the transcendental pastimes and qualities of Kṛṣṇa. Therefore they later became devotees ..." Here we may note that Mahāprabhu mentions Krishna's form and how it attracts even greatly advanced, liberated souls. The full significance of this statement will become clear below, in Part II of this article. But for now, we can at least see that Mahāprabhu highlights the importance of installing a Krishna Deity along with its commensurate worship.

Having been instructed to compile texts on this and related Vaishnava subjects, Sanātana then asks how to pursue writing about the practice of *bhakti*, specifically for a text that later became the *Hari-bhakti-vilāsa*. Mahāprabhu says in Madhya 24, Text 329, "Because you asked Me for a synopsis, please hear these few indications. In the beginning describe how one must take shelter of a bona fide spiritual master." Text 330: "Your book should describe the characteristics of the bona fide guru and the bona fide disciple. Then, before accepting a spiritual master, one can be assured of the spiritual master's position. Similarly, the spiritual master can also be assured of the disciple's position. The Supreme Personality of Godhead, Kṛṣṇa, should be described as the worshipable object, and you should describe the *bīja-mantra* for the worship of Kṛṣṇa, as well as that for Rāma and for other expansions of the Supreme Personality of Godhead." Text 331: "You should discuss the qualifications necessary for receiving a mantra, the perfection of the mantra, the purification of the mantra, initiation, morning duties, remembrance of the Supreme Lord, cleanliness and washing the mouth and other parts of the body." This is preliminary data, the embracing of which qualifies the aspiring disciple for worshiping the Deity of Krishna.

Mahāprabhu then specifically describes Deity worship, making sure that Sanātana includes it in his work, and, as history will show, this specific aspect of Krishna-bhakti becomes a major focus of the *Hari-bhakti-vilāsa.* As Mahāprabhu tells him: Text 334: "Also describe Deity worship, wherein one should offer food to Kṛṣṇa at least five times daily and in due time place Him on a bed. You should also describe the process for offering *ārati* and the worship of the Lord according to the list of five, sixteen or fifty ingredients." Text 335: "The characteristics of the Deities should be discussed, as well as the characteristics of the *śālagrāma-śilā.* You should also discuss visiting the Deities in the temple and touring holy places like Vṛndāvana, Mathurā and Dvārakā." Text 336: "You should glorify the holy name and explain that one must carefully give up offenses when chanting the holy name. You should also describe the symptoms of a Vaiṣṇava and explain that one must give up or nullify all kinds of *sevā-aparādha,* offenses in Deity worship." Text 337: "The items of worship, such as water, conchshell, flowers, incense and lamp, should be described. You should also mention chanting softly, offering prayers, circumambulating [the temple] and offering obeisances. All these should be carefully described." Text 338: "Other items you should describe are the method of performing *puraścaraṇa* [fundamental rituals)], taking *kṛṣṇa-prasādam* [food offered to Krishna], giving up unoffered food and not blaspheming the Lord's devotees." Text 343: "Whatever you say about Vaiṣṇava behavior, the establishment of Vaiṣṇava temples and Deities, and everything else should be supported by evidence from the Purāṇas."

Indeed, the completed version of the *Hari-bhakti-vilāsa*, compiled by painstakingly following the instructions of

Mahāprabhu in Benares as well as detailed notes generated by Gopāla Bhaṭṭa Gosvāmī, who had served as a priest in the Śrīraṅgam temple of South India (where rules and regulations of Deity worship are meticulously observed), includes elaborate sections on Deity worship: In the eighth *vilāsa* (section), for example, there is a description of how Deities should appear visually and on how to set up incense, *ghee* lamps, and other paraphernalia for Their worship. This *vilāsa* also includes guidelines for offering prayers and obeisances and counteracting offenses. In the eleventh *vilāsa*, there are elaborate details of how to conduct Deity worship and how to chant the holy name of the Lord for the Deity's pleasure, and how to avoid offenses committed while chanting for the Deity. The sixteenth *vilāsa* discusses duties to be observed in the month of Kārtika (October-November) and other auspicious time periods for Deity worship. In this section there are also descriptions of Govardhana-pūjā and Ratha-yātrā and how to serve the Deity in the midst of such festivals. The seventeenth *vilāsa* discusses preparations for Deity worship, and how to use various mantras for pleasing the Deity. The nineteenth *vilāsa* discusses the establishment of the Deity and the rituals observed in bathing Him before installation. Finally, the twentieth *vilāsa* discusses the construction of temples, referring to those that had already been built by great devotees of the past. Considering all of the above, one can see how the *Hari-bhakti-vilāsa* has a marked emphasis on Deity worship.

Part II: The *Ātmārāma* Verse

At the meeting in Benares, Sanātana Gosvāmī was also keen to hear Mahāprabhu's explanation of the *ātmārāma* verse (see below), for the Lord had earlier explained this verse to the Vedāntic scholar Sārvabhauma Bhaṭṭācārya, converting him to Vaishnavism through His brilliant exposition of it. And after meeting Sanātana, while still in Benares, the Lord would bring the famous impersonalist philosopher, Prakāśānanda Sarasvatī—along with thousands of his followers—to the shores of Vaishnava practice. He did this by thoroughly explaining the intricate text known as the *Vedānta-sūtra* from a Vaishnava point of view, by glorifying the special efficacy of the *mahā-mantra*, Hare Krishna Hare Krishna, Krishna Krishna Hare Hare/Hare Rāma Hare Rāma, Rāma Rāma Hare Hare, and by chanting it in their presence—and, yes, by explaining the *ātmārāma* verse.

As we will see, the *ātmārāma* verse is not unrelated to Mahāprabhu's emphasis on Deity worship. This is so because the verse itself makes the point that the Lord's form—whether in the spiritual world, or as an *avatāra* in this world, or in the form of the Deity in the temple—is so attractive that even those who have attained the topmost realization in terms of the impersonal Brahman are still drawn to it. That is to say, Those elevated souls, who do not have any material desires or attractions, are still desirous of and attracted to the Lord's form. This is because His form is not material and is higher than anything one can possibly imagine. As Śukadeva Gosvāmī himself says in *Śrīmad-Bhāgavatam* (2.1.9): "O saintly King, I was certainly situated perfectly in transcendence, yet I was still attracted by the delineation of the pastimes of the Lord, who is described by enlightened verses."

Without further ado, then, the *ātmārāma* verse, originally found in the *Śrīmad-Bhāgavatam* (1.7.10), runs as follows: "Sūta Gosvāmī said: 'All different varieties of *ātmārāmas* [those who take pleasure in the *ātmā*, or spirit self], especially those established on the path of self-realization, though freed from all kinds of material bondage, desire to render unalloyed devotional service unto the Personality of Godhead. This means that the Lord possesses transcendental qualities and therefore can attract everyone, including liberated souls.'" (*sūta uvāca, ātmārāmāś ca munayo, nirgranthā apy urukrame, kurvanty ahaitukīṁ bhaktim, ittham-bhūta-guṇo hariḥ*)

Some background on this verse may be in order: "The *ātmārāma* verse" writes Śrīla Prabhupāda, "was discussed at Naimiṣāraṇya at a meeting of many great sages, headed by Śaunaka Ṛṣi. They questioned Śrīla Sūta Gosvāmī, who presided at the meeting, about why Śrīla Śukadeva Gosvāmī, a *paramahaṁsa* already in the transcendental position, was attracted to a discussion of the qualities of Kṛṣṇa. In other words, they wanted to know why Śrī Śukadeva Gosvāmī engaged in the study of *Śrīmad-Bhāgavatam*." (Madhya 6.190, purport)

The verse just prior to the *ātmārāma* verse is informative as well: "Śrī Śaunaka asked Sūta Gosvāmī: 'Śrī Śukadeva Gosvāmī was already on the path of self-realization, and thus he was pleased with his own self. So why did he take the trouble to undergo the study of such a vast literature?'" Prabhupāda writes in his purport: "*Ātmā* means self, and *ārāma* means to take pleasure. Everyone is searching after the highest pleasure, but the standard of pleasure of one may be different from the standard of another. Therefore, the standard of pleasure enjoyed by the *karmīs* is different from that of the *ātmārāmas*. The *ātmārāmas* are completely indifferent to material enjoyment in every respect. Śrīla Śukadeva Gosvāmī had already attained that stage, and still he was attracted to undergo the trouble of studying the great *Bhāgavatam* literature. This means that *Śrīmad-Bhāgavatam* is a postgraduate study even for the *ātmārāmas*, who have surpassed all the studies of Vedic knowledge."

Śrīla Prabhupāda's spiritual master, Śrīla Bhaktisiddhānta Sarasvatī Ṭhākura, elaborates on the verse's overall meaning: "The actual purport of the *ātmārāma* verse is that Kṛṣṇa, the object of worship, is the original truth of all. Those persons who are completely liberated from all forms of material bondage are qualified to achieve devotional service to Kṛṣṇa. The qualities of Kṛṣṇa are very powerful. Those people who desire material enjoyment not related to Kṛṣṇa are conditioned souls averse to the worship of Kṛṣṇa." (*Caitanya-Bhāgavata*, Antya 3.89, commentary) And the Vaishnava stalwart Śrīla Viśvanātha Cakravartī Ṭhākura goes further: "Can *bhakti* deliver the already liberated? Can the *Bhāgavatam*, a scripture on *bhakti*, deliver those who have surpassed scriptures? Can a work discussing a server and the served (the Lord) deliver those who have given up all identities of ego? Can the rules of *bhakti* described in the *Bhāgavatam* deliver those who have given up all rules and prohibitions? To destroy all such protests, the verse says *itt-tam-bhūta-guṇa*: the Lord has such attractive qualities that even *ātmārāmas* become attracted."

Sanātana Gosvāmī, who heard the explanation of this verse directly from Mahāprabhu's lips, explains it succinctly in his *Bṛhad-bhāgavatāmṛta* (Verse 2.2.206): "When those who take pleasure in the self obtain the association of pure devotees by the mercy of Bhagavān [God], they are able to completely give up attachment for Brahman and enter the path of *bhakti*." (*ātmārāmaś ca bhagavat-kṛpayā bhakta-saṅga-taḥ, santyajya brahma-niṣṭhātvaṃ bhakti-mārgaṃ viśanty ataḥ*) Śrīla Jīva Gosvāmī writes in his *Krama Sandarbha* commentary to *Śrīmad Bhāgavatam* 1.7.10: "Kṛṣṇa is beyond the *anirvacanīya* [furthest grasp] of those who are Brahman-realized and therefore *bhakti* has the quality of being the most attractive element of all (*atyanirvacanīya-paramākarṣa-ka-bhakti-guṇatvād ity arthaḥ*) The word *atyanirvacanīya* means "unutterable" or "indescribable" or "beyond anything we are able to grasp."

There is a certain logic expressed in these explanations: Staying close to the words of the verse itself, certain rare souls are *ātmārāma*, i.e., they take pleasure in contemplating the self (the individual soul) or on a higher level even the Supreme Self (the Supersoul), the Lord in the heart. By that exclusive contemplation, often earned after years of serious austerities and meditation practice, they enjoy such pleasure (*rāma*) that they are no longer bound to this world by the knots of material desire (*granthā*). They've cut all such knots and are therefore *nirgranthā*. Simply put, they are constantly enjoying the pleasure of *brahmānanda* and are thus liberated. Still, when they hear of Lord Krishna's name, form, qualities, and pastimes (or, like the Kumāras, when they smell the fragrance of the *tulasī mañjarīs* on His lotus feet) they are so attracted that they desire to perform pure, loving devotional service to the Lord eternally. Ergo, pure devotional service to Lord Krishna is the highest spiritual phenomena, the highest yoga, and yields the most intense, endless, ever-increasing bliss for the living entity, surpassing any other form of spiritual pleasure.

I draw this conclusion from Śrīla Jīva Gosvāmī's *Tattva-Sandarbha* (Anuccheda 49):

> Further clarifying these in-trance realizations of Śrī Veda-vyāsa, the verse "*ātmārāmāś ca* ..." is spoken as the answer to a question by Śrī Śaunaka. This verse upholds Vyāsadeva's realization by citing the experience of all kinds of self-satisfied persons [*ātmārāmas*] and by giving a logical reason: Those who are "free from restrictions" [*nirgrantha*] are either beyond Vedic injunctions and prohibitions or free from the knots of false ego. The word "causeless" [*ahaitukī*] means "without looking for profit." To remove any doubt about the claims made about the *ātmārāmas*, the words "such are His qualities" [*ittham-bhūta-guṇaḥ*] are spoken. His qualities are such that they naturally attract even the self-satisfied." (Gopiparanadhana Prabhu's translation)

Or as Śrī Jīva sums up in his *Bhagavat Sandarbha*, also in Anuccheda 49 (see Bhanu Swami's translation): the Lord's qualities must be unique and extraordinary—otherwise why would they attract even the *ātmārāmās*?

The logic of the *ātmārāma* verse, then, can thus be presented in the form of a syllogism:

a. Śukadeva is not attracted to anything material.
b. Śukadeva is attracted to Krishna and the *Bhāgavatam*.

c. Therefore, Krishna and the *Bhāgavatam* are not material.

Syllogistic thinking can also be applied to another aspect of the verse:

a. Śukadeva is already on a very high spiritual platform.
b. Still, Krishna and the *Bhāgavatam* have the power to attract him.
c. Therefore, Krishna and the *Bhāgavatam* represent a level of spiritual perfection that surpasses his previous realization.

Conclusion

Devotees of the Krishna Consciousness Movement will likely be familiar with the fact that Śrī Chaitanya miraculously recited 61 readings of the *ātmārāma* verse—extemporaneously—as related in the *Caitanya-caritāmṛta*. I will not elaborate on them here, for the Lord's compositions are based on subtle rules of Sanskrit grammar and are difficult to understand for those who are not trained Sanskritists. Still, Śrīla Prabhupāda has given the world three chapters of eloquent English explanation—Chapters 15, 16, and 26 of his *Teaching of Lord Chaitanya*, and also his direct translations in the *Caitanya-caritāmṛta* (Madhya 24)—and the reader is encouraged to thoroughly study these chapters to fully understand this most important verse.

Śrīla Prabhupāda sums up the entire subject nicely in his purport to the *Caitanya-caritāmṛta* (Madhya-līlā 6.198):

That Kṛṣṇa is all-attractive is verified by the activities of the four ṛṣis and Śukadeva Gosvāmī. All of them were liberated persons, yet they were attracted by the qualities and pastimes of the Lord. It is therefore said, *muktā api līlayā vigrahaṁ kṛtvā bhagavantaṁ bhajante*: "Even liberated persons are attracted by the pastimes of Lord Kṛṣṇa and thus engage in devotional service." (Cc. Madhya 24.112) From the very beginning of their lives, Śukadeva Gosvāmī and the four Kumāras, known as *catuḥ-sana*, were liberated and self-realized on the Brahman platform. Nonetheless, they were attracted by the qualities of Kṛṣṇa, and they engaged in His service. The four Kumāras were attracted by the aroma of the flowers offered at the lotus feet of Kṛṣṇa, and in this way they became devotees. Śukadeva Gosvāmī heard *Śrīmad Bhāgavatam* by the mercy of his father, Vyāsadeva, and he was consequently attracted to Kṛṣṇa and became a great devotee. The conclusion is that the transcendental bliss experienced in the service of the Lord must be superior to *brahmānanda*, the bliss derived from realizing the impersonal Brahman.

Therefore, as Sūta Gosvāmī says near the conclusion of the entire *Śrīmad-Bhāgavatam* (12.12.69): "Let me offer my respectful obeisances unto my spiritual master, the son of Vyāsadeva, Śukadeva Gosvāmī. It is he who defeats all inauspicious things within this universe. Although in the beginning he was absorbed in the happiness of Brahman realization and was living in a secluded place, giving up all other types of consciousness, he became attracted by the most melodious pastimes of Lord Śrī Kṛṣṇa. He therefore mercifully spoke the supreme Purāṇa, known as *Śrīmad-Bhāgavatam*, which is the bright light of the Absolute Truth and which describes the activities of Lord Kṛṣṇa."'

In this way, the *ātmārāma* verse was explained to Sārvabhauma Bhaṭṭācārya (*Caitanya-caritāmṛta*, Madhya 6.187-198); Prakāśānanda Sarasvatī (Madhya 25.156-166); and most elaborately to Sanātana Gosvāmī (Madhya 24.4-314), affirming Krishna Consciousness as the highest level of spiritual life. Indeed, in worshiping the Deity in the temple, one is fulfilling the innermost meaning of this verse, for one is well on the way to surpassing all levels of self-realization and becoming absorbed in the Personal Absolute, Lord Krishna.

Fourteen

Śrī Chaitanya and His Pillar of Ecstasy:
The Garuḍa-stambha in the pastimes of the Lord

"Staying near the Garuḍa-stambha [pillar], the Lord would look upon Lord Jagannātha. What can be said about the strength of that love? On the ground beneath the column of the Garuḍa-stambha was a deep ditch, and that ditch was filled with the water of His tears."

—*Caitanya-caritāmṛta* 2.2.54

IT IS A SCENE NOW familiar to the followers of Śrī Chaitanya Mahāprabhu, the Lord Himself in the role of His topmost devotee, come to Earth some 538 years ago in Bengal, India. While in Jagannātha Purī, where Śrī Chaitanya lived in the latter portion of His life, He would often humbly stand at a distance from the Deities He loved so dearly—Jagannātha, Baladeva, and Subhadrā, i.e., Lord Krishna, His immediate expansion, and His energy (*śakti*), respectively—hoping to get a glimpse of Them. Each viewing would send Him into waves of ecstasy. At one point, this became a daily event, as He regularly adopted His now legendary position peeking out from behind the Garuḍa-stambha (pillar),[1] offering heartfelt prayers while singing and dancing before Lord Jagannātha. Each day, He humbly congregated with devotees by this same pillar, waiting to see the Upala-bhoga (midday refreshments) offered at noon, hoping to receive even a speck of the Lord's remnants.[2]

But Śrī Chaitanya had not always stood in the distance, far away from the altar that serves as home for His beloved Lord. Initially, He was not in the least bit reserved, running up to Lord Jagannātha with full enthusiasm, ready to embrace Him with the totality of His existence—and to fully manifest this urge with physicality, albeit transcendental physicality. Such a display, of course, would create a disturbance in the temple, and consequently had to be curtailed. The following article is about this change from boldness to reservedness, how it came to be, and why it is so important, even for fledgling practitioners.

Before exploring this subject, however, it would be useful to look at a corollary pastime in pre-history, as brought to us by Śrīla Sanātana Gosvāmī in his *Bṛhat-bhāgavatāmṛta.* One aspect of the life of Gopa-kumāra, as mentioned in that text, serves as a precursor to the Mahāprabhu pastime, showing us how ecstasy manifests in a devotee who is spiritually advanced, and how such a devotee behaves with restraint, despite having intense feelings of love.

Gopa-kumāra's initial viewing of Lord Jagannātha created ecstatic symptoms in him, much as they would famously manifest years later in the body of Chaitanya Mahāprabhu: "I was eager to go near Śrī Jagannātha," said Gopa-kumāra, "but was unable to walk forward. My mind had become helplessly deprived of will and, due to ecstatic love, all my limbs were trembling. My [bodily] hairs stood erect and I lost control of my body as tears blocked my vision. With great difficulty, I somehow caught hold of the Garuḍa pillar and stood there."[3]

Due to his ecstatic love, the Lord gave him special *darśana*, enabling him to truly see Jagannātha, not as He normally appears in Purī, but rather as Vrajendranandana Krishna, the original Personality of Godhead. Both forms of Krishna are, in fact, identical, even if Their external appearance is dissimilar: "From that very spot I saw the Lord. His bluish form, smeared with sandalwood pulp, was bedecked with divine clothes, ornaments, and garlands. Sitting playfully on a throne, He was accepting huge amounts of delectable foodstuffs. Thus, He was increasing the joy in the minds and eyes of those who were seeing Him."[4] This presages how Mahāprabhu would see Lord Jagannātha as well: "Śrī Caitanya Mahāprabhu stayed behind the huge column called the Garuḍa-stambha and looked upon Lord Jagannātha, but as He looked He saw that Lord Jagannātha had become Lord Kṛṣṇa, with His flute to His mouth." (*Caitanya-caritāmṛta* 3.16.85)

Again in Mahāprabhu-like fashion, Gopa-kumāra's body is overcome by ecstasy, and he falls to the ground, losing the use of his senses: "When I saw the wonderful opulence of Śrī Jagannātha-deva, the refuge of infinite glories, I fell unconscious to the ground." (2.1.170) But then, upon regaining consciousness, he did something that caused him some trouble: "Beholding the Lord, I became maddened and rushed to embrace Him. . . . As soon as I moved forward [in this way], the doorkeepers beat me with canes, barring me from entering inside. Realizing what I had done, I felt ashamed, but I considered being stopped in this manner to actually be the mercy of the Lord. When I went outside, I received *mahā-prasāda* [Jagannātha's food offerings] without even asking for it." (2.1.171-173)

Mahāprabhu was more fortunate. When He, in an even more intense mood of ecstatic love, ran toward the Deity, with the same intention as Gopa-kumāra, He also at first fainted, but He was then brought to Sārvabhauma Bhaṭṭācārya's home and soon regained consciousness. Sārvabhauma was a great scholar, and when he came to know of Śrī Chaitanya's divinity, many others became aware of it too. Furthermore, Sārvabhauma gave Him good counsel, as we shall see below, and although the Lord could have merely run up and embraced the Deity again and again, He chose instead to stay back at the Garuḍa-stambha, for the sake of social sanity. The story behind how this came to be is described in slightly diverse ways in the *Caitanya-bhāgavata* (3.2.424-488) and in the *Caitanya-caritāmṛta* (2.6.3-63).

Following the latter version, we see that just like Gopa-kumāra, "Lord Śrī Caitanya Mahāprabhu went swiftly to embrace Lord Jagannātha, but when He entered the temple, He was so overwhelmed with love of Godhead that He fainted to the floor." When Śrī Caitanya fell unconscious, Sārvabhauma Bhaṭṭācārya happened to see Him and brought Him to his home. But just prior to this, when the temple guards saw Him charging toward the Deities, they threatened to beat Him, just as their predecessors had beaten Gopa-kumāra. By divine grace, Sārvabhauma immediately forbade them, for upon seeing the personal beauty of Lord Chaitanya, as well as the transcendental transformations wrought on His body due to love of Godhead, he could understand that this was no ordinary personality. In the end, when Śrī Chaitanya was apprised of the events surrounding His loss of consciousness, He did not want to instigate any further uproar, nor did He want to upset the local temple-goers. To be safe, in fact, Sārvabhauma requested Him to never again go by Himself to see the Deity, but rather to be accompanied by Sārvabhauma or his men.

Considering all that had happened, Mahāprabhu said, "I shall never enter the temple again, but shall always view the Lord from the side of the Garuḍa-stambha." (Madhya 6.63) The *Chaitanya-bhāgavata* says it more bluntly: "I declare that from today on I will take *darśana* of Lord Jagannātha from outside. (Antya 2.487) I will not enter the temple. I will see the Lord only while standing next to Garuḍa." (Antya 2.488)[5]

Indeed, the Garuḍa-stambha lay outside the precincts of the temple's inner chamber. It is in a section of the temple known as the Nāṭa-maṇḍapa (where singing and dancing are enacted for the Lord's pleasure), standing more than 100 feet (30 meters) away from the altar area, or perhaps as much as 200 feet. So Mahāprabhu would gaze at His beloved Jagannātha from quite a distance. The Garuḍa-stambha, made of neem wood, is around ten- to eleven-feet high, rising up from a two-foot-high pedestal.[6] This is how I visualize it based on descriptions by those who have actually been there.

As a Westerner, I have never seen the pillar, nor have I even been allowed inside the Jagannātha temple. This is because of their age-old policy of keeping foreigners out.[7] Despite my reservations about this policy, I know that the

Garuḍa-stambha is quite important in Mahāprabhu's pastimes. Consequently, I have asked various friends—devotees and scholars who were actually fortunate enough to visit it—to express exactly what it's like to see the Deities from that vantage point. Here are some of their comments:

> Ravi Gupta (Radhika-ramana Dasa): "I have had darshan of Lord Jagannatha from the Garuda-stambha, and yes, it is quite a distance. It's been a while, so I can't estimate the exact length, but I do remember that the experience was both distant and intimate at the same time. Because the throngs are far ahead of you, and the Lords are on a high altar, it feels like they are looking straight at you, over the heads of those who are nearer. Standing at a distance feels just right for one as unqualified as me, and yet the Lord draws you in close by his gaze. One important note: you cannot see all three murtis together from the Garuda-stambha, because the entry door of the main room is too narrow. You can see Subhadra Devi, but then you have to move slightly left or right to see Jagannatha or Baladeva, one at a time.[8]
>
> Frédérique Marglin: The Garuda Stambha is in the Nata Mandapa. The latter is today considered part of the main temple structure. To the east and in continuation with it is the Garbha Griha, where the images of Jagannatha, Subhadra and Balabhadra are enshrined, and to the west of the Nata Mandapa—but in continuation with it—is the Bhoga Mandapa, all as one long structure. Outside are many other shrines/temples to other deities, as well as the kitchens to cook what will become *maha-prasad*. The whole temple compound is really a small city and is enclosed by a high wall.[9]
>
> Saheli Datta: I'm not a good judge of distances. [Mahaprabhu's] hand and shoulder impressions are on the Garuda Stambha and His footprints are beside it,

but they're not distinct, just clearly worn out where someone of His size stood over and over again. If you're facing Jagannath, it's on the right side of the Stambha. It's perhaps the most powerful *darshan* I have ever had. Honestly, even *darshan* of Jagannnath Himself is not as awe inspiring. I sincerely pray that you will one day get to see it.[10]

Murali Prathik: The *stambha* is after the *jaga-mohana*—between the *nata-mandapa* and the *bhoga-man-dapa*. People do curl around it [to this day] and see Jagannatha, reminding one of how Mahaprabhu would have had *darshan*. ... You are correct in saying that we can't see all four deities well [from this vantage point]. Subhadra is clearly visible. We cannot see Sudarshana. But we can see Baladeva and Jagannatha depending on our viewing position.[11]

Ujaan Ghosh: It is in the Nata-mandira. There is also a finger imprint of Chaitanya on the stone wall behind it. The distance to the altar is somewhat formi-dable, but you can see the three images from there if the crowd is minimal. But yes its really far given the lintel of the door of the Garbha-griha, which makes seeing the deities somewhat restrictive.[12]

Abhishek Ghosh: Mahaprabhu would stand at the Garuda-stambha, which is in the third part of the com-plex, the nata-mandir (dancing hall)—it's like three temples but connected on the inside so that one can see straight through from the Garuda-stambha to the altar, with the deities under the highest of the temple domes. The furthest dome away from the deities is where the *bhoga* room is, which is usually closed. ... The left side of the door has Mahaprabhu's fingerprints where the stone melted on his touch and the footprint was there, too, but because people were stepping on it they removed it and made a separate temple outside to worship his footprints

> on the northern side of the temple. The Garuda-stambha is more than a hundred feet [from the altar] and you can only see the right half of Jagannath's face from where Mahaprabhu stood.[13]

It might be noticed that some of these informants mention that Mahāprabhu's point of reference was limited, in the sense that He could only see a sliver of the altar from where He generally stood—focusing on Jagannātha and not on the other Deities. There is an esoteric reason for this, known mainly to Vaishnavas from Purī. They say that this position in viewing the Deities was intentional and hints at Mahāprabhu's identity as Krishna in the mood of Rādhā. As Purī expert and ISKCON scholar Madhavānanda Dāsa notes:

> Regarding the second question as to why particularly did Chaitanya Mahāprabhu have *darśana* from the left side of Garuḍa and from the left side of the doorway: Our *ācāryas* have described Śrī Chaitanya Mahāprabhu as *rādhā-bhāva-dyuti-suvalitaṁ naumi kṛṣṇa-svarūpam*—Krishna in the mood of Rādhārāṇī. Śrīmatī Rādhārāṇī becomes shy when she gets around Balarāma and Subhadrā. She wants to focus on Krishna. According to the local tradition in Jagannātha Purī, it was for this reason that Mahāprabhu stood on the left side, because from that vantage point you can only see Jagannātha and not his brother and sister. Mahāprabhu took *darśana* from those places because he was in the mood of Rādhā, who only wanted to see her Prāṇa-vallabha Śyāmasundara Krishna.[14]

There is yet another reason to position oneself at the Garuḍa-stambha while viewing the Deities—one that might speak to us more generally, since most of us are not on the level of Mahāprabhu or Gopa-kumāra.

According to Śrīla Bhaktisiddhānta Sarasvatī Ṭhākura: "We will stand behind our guru, Garuḍa. Jagannātha will look at Garuḍa because Garuḍa is His devotee. Then He will also cast His merciful glance upon us."[15]

After taking personal *darśana* of Lord Jagannātha, Śrīla Bhaktisiddhānta Sarasvatī expanded on this comment. One of the great master's earliest disciples, Ananta Vasudeva Prabhu, recalled how in June 1918, shortly after taking *sannyāsa*, Śrīla Sarasvatī Ṭhākura, along with 23 disciples, went to preach in Odisha. At the end of June, they arrived in Purī and, naturally, went directly to the Jagannātha Temple. While there, Śrīla Sarasvatī Ṭhākura stood behind the Garuḍa-stambha and from that vantage point, received *darśana* of the Lord. After this, he addressed his disciples with the following words:

> We should have *darśana* of Śrī Jagannātha standing behind the Garuḍa-stambha. Śrī Jagannātha is not the object of vision (*dṛśya*), but the One who looks (*draṣṭā*). Only when the *jīva* [the soul] gives up the view of himself as a seer (*draṣṭā*) and is fully established in the understanding of his pure nature (*śuddha-svarūpa*), which is that he is the object of Jagannātha's vision (*dṛśya*) and the object of Jagannātha's pleasure, then he becomes disposed to serve Him (*sevonmukha*), and thanks to such eyes, anointed with love in the inclination to serve (*sevonmukha-prema*), the soul receives *darśana* of Jagannātha. As long as we think, "I will go and see Jagannātha," we will *not* see Jagannātha, but only a tree, a stone, an object described in Buddhist literature [and the like] ... the object of our pleasure. And on the other

hand, when we can realize with all our hearts that He will see us, that we are an ingredient in *His* pleasure, in which we have no excuse for personal pleasure, that He is absolutely unlimited in His actions, then Jagannātha will reveal Himself us. But the people of this world, consciously or unconsciously, are deluded: "I will go and see Jagannātha and my flesh-made eyes will look at Sat-cit-ānanda-vigraha (the form of eternity, knowledge, and bliss) and will enjoy It." Therefore, even after such a so-called "*darśana*" of Jagannātha, their mind continues to look at various ugly forms of this world."[16]

Conclusion

Thus, it should be understood that there are two reasons why one might humbly stand in the back of the Jagannātha temple, near the Garuḍa-stambha, or in the back of any temple, for that matter.

One on the level of pure love would not want to create confusion in the minds and hearts of neophytes. Additionally, out of humility, such a person would not want to fully broadcast their love, and instead they take a back-seat, as it were, humbly allowing others to race towards the Lord according to their capacity. This truth was shown in the lives of both Mahāprabhu and Gopa-kumāra, where we see their full display of love leading to both suspicion and even brutality (as when Gopa-kumāra was beaten), and the corrective measures they took to act appropriately, setting an example for others.

Indeed, devotees are instructed not to let others know their level of advancement, lest it compromise their sense of humility and lead to envy and distrust. Best to always feel oneself fallen and to behave as a devotee who needs to adopt the basics of *bhakti* practice. This is the example generally seen in the topmost devotees. They do not reveal their true level of advancement.

Along these lines, the *Hari-bhakti-vilāsa* instructs: "If the disciple has a wondrous divine vision, either in dreams or in a waking state, he should not reveal it to anyone other than the guru."[17] In other words, one should not show, in action, words, or deeds, their level of advancement, or their vision of the Lord, if indeed they have one.

Similarly, Śrīla Jīva Gosvāmī, in his concluding instructions of the *Bhakti-sandarbha* (339) states: "Whatever confidential experiences are attained in connection with the practice and the goal given by the grace of Śrī Guru or Śrī Bhagavān, are one's very own treasure. They should not be revealed to anyone." Śrīla Narottama Dāsa Ṭhākura concurs in the concluding words of his *Prema-bhakti-candrikā*: "I will not disclose my path of worshiping the Lord to anyone and everyone. I will be extremely careful about it. Please do not get angry with me or take offense. I offer my respectful humble obeisances unto the lotus feet of the devotees."

All of this is to say that even if one has immense love for the Deity, one should act like a fledgling devotee, standing by the feet of one's guru and ready to serve him in all humility. This is the message of Mahāprabhu standing at the base of the Garuḍa-stambha. Moreover, such behavior harmonizes the positions of the advanced devotee and the neophyte—both are called upon to take a humble position and to keep their accomplishments within.[18]

It would serve all devotees well, then, to have the mind-set that Śrīla Sarasvatī Ṭhākura articulates above, humbly positioning ourselves near Garuḍa, praying that the Lord, while focusing His attention on His great devotee, the eagle-like carrier of Vishnu, might also cast His glance on His *other* humble servant, if much less qualified, who serves at his guru's feet.

Endnotes

1. Garuḍa-stambhas can be seen at many temples of Lord Vishnu/ Krishna, though few are as famous as the one in the Śrī Maṇḍira, or the Jagannātha temple of Purī. The story behind why these temples build such *stambhas* (pillars) at their entrance is ancient. We are told that Lord Vishnu had asked Garuḍa, a birdlike divinity mentioned throughout India's wisdom texts, to be His eternal mount (*vāhana*), and to serve Him as a vehicle, carrying Him throughout the cosmos. Naturally, the dedicated bird-devotee assented, and to this day we can see their inseparable relationship even in temple iconography: He is present in most Vishnu temples on a "Garuḍa-stambha" (a tall pillar), always waiting to serve his Lord according to his unique capabilities.

2. See His Divine Grace A. C. Bhaktivedanta Swami Prabhupāda, *Caitanya-caritāmṛta* 2.1.64: "Every day Śrī Caitanya Mahāprabhu used to see the *upala-bhoga* ceremony at the temple of Jagannātha . . ." Purport: "*Upala-bhoga* is a particular type of offering performed just behind the Garuḍa-stambha on a stone slab. That stone slab is called the *upala*. All food is offered within the temple room just below the altar of Jagannātha. This *bhoga*, however, was offered on the stone slab within the vision of the public; therefore it is called *upala-bhoga*."

3. Śrīla Sanātana Gosvāmī's *Śrī Bṛhad Bhāgavatāmṛtam*, Canto Two, Verse 2.1.168. See Śrī Śrīmad Bhaktivedānta Nārāyana Gosvāmī Mahārāja, trans., *Śrī Bṛhad Bhāgavatāmṛtam* (New Delhi: Pure Bhakti Books, 2005).

4. ibid., 2.1.169.

5. The current Jagannātha temple was refurbished into a virtually

new shrine in the 12th century by King Anangbarma Chodganga Dev of the Ganga dynasty, with additions to the main structure and various add-ons constructed well into the next few centuries. Thus, it is said that before Mahāprabhu's time, the Garuḍa-stambha was on the "outside" of the main temple, and even today it is not considered a part of the Garbha Griha (Sanctum Sanctorum). The temple is built in the Deula style, which has four components, namely, *vimana* (the structure containing the Deities, which is the temple proper), *jaga-mohana* (assembly hall), *nāṭa-maṇḍapa* (festival or dancing hall, where the Garuḍa-stambha stands), and *bhoga-maṇḍapa* (hall of offerings), each decreasing in height as it moves farther away from the main altar area, where one finds the seven major Deities of the temple: Jagannātha, Baladeva, Subhadrā, Sudarśana, Lakṣmī, Sarasvatī, and Nīla-Mādhava. There are numerous other shrines within the temple complex as well.

6. "Between the Bhoga *mandapa* and the Mukha Sala or Jagamohana, at 175 feet distance from the Ratna *simhasana* [where the altar is], the Garuda *stambha* rises, where generally people stand to take Darshan of Jagannatha. In this place Sri Chaitanya used to remain to contemplate Lord Jagannatha and his handprints can be seen on the pillar. . . . The Garuda *stambha* is made of *neem* wood, with Garuda on top of the pillar, with folded hands and looking at the feet of Lord Jagannatha. It is said that the pillar encases the Syamantaka jewel that blesses with wealth and health all those who touch it. Near the Garuda *stambha* a small water drain runs out of the main temple, carrying the bath water of the Deities." See Parama Karuna Devi and Rahul Acharyap, *Puri The Home of Lord Jagannatha* (Odisha: Jagannatha Vallabha Research Center, 2008), 241.

7. Many temples in India have strict policies regarding non-Hindus and foreigners, not allowing them entrance under any circumstances. Most notorious among these temples is the one in Purī. This is especially confounding because Jagannātha is known as "Lord of the Universe." Why would a universal Lord not accommodate all living beings? Why would a divinity with such an all-encompassing reach not allow certain entities within His domain? The official regulation began in 1803 while Odisha was under Maratha rule and continued until Indian independence in 1947. Just prior to Indian independence, Mahatma Gandhi and others began protesting on behalf of the lower castes so that these

castes may be allowed inside the Jagannātha Mandir and other temples of India. Accordingly, in 1948 lower castes were finally admitted into the temple, but the practice of barring various other sections of society continued. This included injunctions against the entry of foreigners. But the obvious question continued to loom large: Who is a true foreigner? Who is a true Hindu? Devotees — whether born in India or abroad — should not, according to Vaishnava philosophy, be considered foreigners, for they are Jagannātha's own. Thus, on principle, A. C. Bhaktivedānta Swami Prabhupāda, the founder of ISKCON, refused to go into Lord Jagannātha's temple when he visited Purī in January, 1977. Why? Because his disciples were not allowed to enter. They, too, he said, were devotees, and thus foreigners only in an external sense. But at the time his protest fell largely on deaf ears. Nonetheless, on July 5, 2018, the Supreme Court of India made a formal request to the management of the Jagannātha temple, asking them to allow, "every visitor irrespective of his faith, to offer respects and to make offerings to the deity." While this is a promising development, time will tell if the longstanding tradition changes. For more, See Madhavānanda Dāsa, "Jagannath Puri Dham: Two Opposites in One Container," *Journal of Vaishnava Studies,* Volume 27, No. 1 (Fall 2018), 123-156.

8. Personal correspondence, May 2, 2024.

9. Personal correspondence, May 3, 2024.

10. Personal correspondence, May 3, 2024.

11. Personal correspondence, May 1, 2024.

12. Personal correspondence, May 1, 2024.

13. Personal correspondence, May 5, 2024. O. B. L. Kapoor also notes, "Now, there were the 'Historic Foot-prints' of Śrī Caitanya on a slab of marble near the Garuḍa-stambha inside the Temple of Jagannātha—foot-prints marked on stone, converted into the consistency of clay by the magical tears that streamed down the cheeks and chest of Śrī Gaurāṅga, entranced at the sight of Lord Jagannātha. ... These sacred relics used to be trampled down by inadvertent strangers that came in crowds on the special occasions to have a look at Śrī Jagannātha. These foot-prints were removed, under orders of the Raja in the presence of his officers, to a spot in the adjoining yard within the temple. Barha Babaji Mahasaya had them tabernacled and duly

installed on a lotus of white marble." See O. B. L. Kapoor, *The Saints of Bengal* (South America: Sarasvatī Jayaśrī Classics, 1995), 116-117.

14. Personal correspondence May 5, 2024. This esoteric dimension has been extended to Lord Jagannātha's Ratha-yātrā festival as well, in explaining, for example, why there are three chariots as opposed to just one: "There is a phenomenon called *rasa-viparyāya* (a contradiction in moods). Because Rādhikā and the Vraja-gopīs would never meet with Krishna in the presence of Balarāma or Subhadrā, the latter two divinities travel separately. Balarāma leads the way and is followed next by Subhadrā. Krishna cannot act as a transcendental lover when surrounded by his brother and sister." See Śrīla Bhakti Vijñāna Bhāratī Mahārāja, "Ratha-yātrā Q and A" (https://www.visuddhacaitanyavani.com/single-post/2018/07/12/Ratha-yatra-QnA)

15. See Bhakti Vikāsa Swami, *Śrī Bhaktisiddhānta Vaibhāva*, Vol. 1 (Surat: Bhakti Vikas Trust, 2009), 181. See also Mahanidhi Swami, *Jagannath Puri Guide Book* (2009), 34-35, and Brijbasi Dasa, "About Garuda Stambha and Darshan of the Lord" (https://brijabasidas.wordpress.com/?s=Garuda+stambha) in *Gauḍīya-toṣaṇī* (2015).

16. Quoted from *Sarasvati-jayashri*, pp. 23-24, in Brijbasi Dasa, "About Garuda Stambha and Darshan of the Lord" (https://brijabasidas.wordpress.com/?s=Garuda+stambha) in *Gauḍīya-toṣaṇī* (2015).

17. See *Hari-bhakti-vilāsa* 2.143 (*svapne vākṣi-samakṣaṁ vā āścaryam atiharṣadam/ akasmād yadi jāyeta na khyātavyaṁ guror vinā//*)

18. That said, there are very specific instances when a devotee should highlight their own level of advancement, as in, for example, when he or she serves as guru. In such cases, it is important to be assertive, but this is solely to help less advanced devotees. Also, for those Vaishnavas who are somewhat accomplished on the path, the quality of enthusiasm (*utsāha*) may be allowed to flow without reservation. There is an example of such appropriate fervor that occurred right on the Garuḍa-stambha: "While Lord Chaitanya was at the temple to see the deity of Jagannātha, thousands of people were in front of Him also seeing the deity. Suddenly, a woman who was unable to see Jagannātha through the crowd, climbed the column of Garuḍa that was just in front of Chaitanya Mahāprabhu, placing her foot on His shoulder to get up. Govinda, Chaitanya Mahāprabhu's personal secretary, hastily got her down. Chaitanya Mahāprabhu, however, chastised Govinda for

this. When the woman came to her senses, she begged for forgiveness at the lotus feet of Lord Chaitanya. Chaitanya Mahāprabhu said, 'Lord Jagannātha has not bestowed so much eagerness upon Me. She has fully absorbed her body, mind and life in Lord Jagannātha. Therefore, she was unaware that she was putting her foot on My shoulder. Alas! How fortunate this woman is! I pray at her feet that she favor Me with her great eagerness to see Lord Jagannātha." See *Caitanya-caritāmṛta* 3.14.24-30.

Śrīla Raghunātha Dāsa Gosvāmī prays:

"Will Śacī's son [Mahāprabhu], always staying at His favorite place behind the Garuḍa-stambha and with the tears from His eyes bathing His splendid, tall form as He gazes with intense love at Lord Jagannātha, the master of Nīlācala [Jagannātha Purī], again walk on the pathway of my eyes?"

—Raghunātha Dāsa Gosvāmī, *Stavāvalī*, "Śacīsunvaṣṭakam" (Verse 6), trans., Śrīvasa Dāsa.

Fifteen

Books are the Basis: Śrī Caitanya's Discovery of *Śrī Brahma-saṁhitā* and *Śrī Kṛṣṇa-karṇāmṛta*

FOLLOWING THE KAVERI RIVER on foot, Śrī Caitanya Mahāprabhu (1486–1534), Krishna Himself in the form of His own devotee, traveled more than 500 miles across southern India, making His way through the tropical grasslands of Tamil Nadu to the southernmost border of the Bay of Bengal. His stay at various holy temples was punctuated by interaction with devotees, sharing the Holy Name of Krishna and spreading His mercy to all who would hear Him. In all, He spent some two years—from 1510 to 1512—unfurling His method of devotion to nearly every town and village in the Deccan before returning to His beloved Jagannath Puri.[1]

While touring the South, Mahāprabhu would have seen the region's idyllic coastline and lush mountain areas, along with its dense plantations and rich wildlife, as found even today in Cochin, Kovalam, Alleppey, and other surrounding villages. He would have also seen Munnar's rolling hills and deep valleys in the heart of Kerala, as He bathed at the auspicious confluence of the Muthirapuzha, Nallathanni and Kundali rivers. His main ports of call, of course, were the fabulous temples dotting the South, not only to see the age-old Deities who sanctified these holy pilgrimage sites, but also to encounter the throngs of visitors and pilgrims who frequented them. He had something special to share with the people, no doubt—i.e., the topmost loving ecstasies associated with the pure chanting of Krishna's holy name—and He also took something from them as well: While visiting the temples, He found two special books, to be detailed below, that would prove indispensable for His ever-growing mission.

Reaching Cape Comorin, the southernmost tip of southeastern India, Mahāprabhu began His return journey on the western side of the subcontinent, though He retraced some of the same districts He had encountered on the way down. He gradually reached Thiruvattoor Village (also known as Thiruvattaru) in Tamil Nadu, near Kerala. Upon arrival, He bathed in a local stream and then visited the well known Ādi-keśava Temple, a scenic fortresslike shrine surrounded on three sides by rivers, the Kothai, the Pahrali, and the Thamirabarani. The *Caitanya-caritāmṛta* (2.9.234-236) tells us: "Śrī Caitanya Mahāprabhu and His assistant Kṛṣṇadāsa arrived at the bank of the Payasvinī River. They took their bath and then went to see the temple of Ādi-keśava. When the Lord saw the Ādi-keśava temple, He was immediately overwhelmed with ecstasy. Offering various obeisances and prayers, He chanted and danced. All the people there were greatly astonished to see the ecstatic pastimes of Śrī Caitanya Mahāprabhu. They all received the Lord very well." He sang with great emotion for Ādi-keśava Perumāl, the Vishnu/ Krishna Deity housed in that temple.

The majestic Ādi-keśava *mūrti* is more than twenty-feet in length, depicted as lying down as per His Vishnu manifestation in the causal waters of eternity—He is said to be composed of 16,008 black *śāligrāma-śilās*, the sacred stones that are retrieved from the Gandaki River in Nepal for worship, and His entire form is spectacular. Unlike most Deities of Vishnu, which have four arms, this particular form has two arms, and He is depicted as "sleeping" with His head to the east and feet to the west—though Vishnu is usually depicted as lying in the opposite direction.[2] The Lord in the Ādi-keśava temple is lying on the couch-like coils of the celestial serpent Ananta, thus showing Vishnu enjoying His opulence, so revered in this part of India. The Deity is worshiped as both Vishnu and Krishna, according to the worshiper's desire and perspective.[3]

The Glorious *Brahma-saṁhitā*

It was at this Ādi-keśava temple that Mahāprabhu found the first of the two books explored in this article: the *Brahma-saṁhitā.* He read the text with great devotion and was so moved by its contents that he had ten men copy it down to bring it with Him, hoping to share it with His intimate associates. Copying texts was no easy task in the sixteenth century, for books in South India were still palm-leaf manuscripts and had to be copied by hand.[4] An arduous process, to be sure. Obviously, Mahāprabhu deemed this text well worth the effort. "There is no scripture equal to the *Brahma-saṁhitā*," says the *Caitanya-caritāmṛta* (Madhya 9.239-240), "as far as the final spiritual conclusion is concerned. Indeed, that scripture is the supreme revelation of the glories of Lord Govinda [Krishna], for it reveals the topmost knowledge about Him. Since all conclusions are briefly presented in the *Brahma-saṁhitā*, it is essential among all the Vaiṣṇava literatures."

The *Brahma-saṁhitā* is a Sanskrit text that captures the mood and prayers of Brahmā, the first created being in all of existence.[5] His focus of glorification: Śrī Krishna. Therefore, from the time of Mahāprabhu onward, the text has been relished as chief among religious scriptures within the Gauḍīya Vaishnava tradition. Unfortunately, the work had been lost over time, with only the 62 verses of its Fifth Chapter making its way into Mahāprabhu's hands. But these verses contain the summit of spiritual knowledge. Indeed, the text contains a highly esoteric description of Krishna in His supreme abode, Goloka, with details generally known only in the Gauḍīya tradition. No wonder Mahāprabhu was so taken with it: It reaffirmed Gauḍīya teachings in an unparalleled way and would support the conclusions of the *ācāryas*. Śrīla Prabhupāda underlines the unique nature of the text in his purport to *Caitanya-caritāmṛta* (2.9.239-240):

> The *Brahma-saṁhitā* is a very important scripture. Śrī Caitanya Mahāprabhu acquired the Fifth Chapter from the Adi-keśava temple. In that Fifth Chapter, the philosophical conclusion of *acintya-bhedābheda-tattva* (simultaneous oneness and difference) is presented. The chapter also presents methods of devotional service, the eighteen-syllable Vedic hymn, discourses on the soul, the Supersoul and fruitive activity, an explanation of Kāma-gāyatrī, kāma-bīja and the original Mahā-Viṣṇu, and a detailed description of the spiritual world,

> specifically Goloka Vṛndāvana. The *Brahma-saṁhitā* also explains the demigod Gaṇeśa, Garbhodakaśāyī Viṣṇu, the origin of the Gāyatrī mantra, the form of Govinda and His transcendental position and abode, the living entities, the highest goal, the goddess Durgā, the meaning of austerity, the five gross elements, love of Godhead, impersonal Brahman, the initiation of Lord Brahmā, and the vision of transcendental love enabling one to see the Lord. The steps of devotional service are also explained. The mind, *yoga-nidrā*, the goddess of fortune, devotional service in spontaneous ecstasy, incarnations beginning with Lord Rāmacandra, Deities, the conditioned soul and its duties, the truth about Lord Viṣṇu, prayers, Vedic hymns, Lord Śiva, the Vedic literature, personalism and impersonalism, good behavior, and many other subjects are also discussed. There is also a description of the sun and the universal form of the Lord. All these subjects are conclusively explained in a nutshell in the *Brahma-saṁhitā.*

Interestingly, Brahmā's description of Lord Krishna is quite specific, with a persona, identity, and particularity not found in most other religious scriptures when describing God, particularly in the West. Far from sketching out the Absolute as an impersonal vacuum; an overflowing burst of cosmic nothingness; a blinding white abstraction; or the oldest of souls, with a long white beard—as many do, even in India—we find in the *Brahma-saṁhitā* an all-attractive Personality of Godhead, complete with loving associates and a world where "every word is a song, and every step is a dance." (5.56) A few examples from Brahmā's text should make its position clear:

īśvaraḥ paramaḥ kṛṣṇaḥ
sac-cid-ānanda-vigrahaḥ
anādir ādir govindaḥ
sarva-kāraṇa-kāraṇam

Kṛṣṇa who is known as Govinda is the Supreme Godhead. He has an eternal blissful spiritual body. He is the origin of all. He has no other origin and He is the prime cause of all causes. (5.1)

cintāmaṇi-prakara-sadmasu kalpa-vṛkṣa-
lakṣāvṛteṣu surabhir abhipālayantam
lakṣmī-sahasra-śata-sambhrama-sevyamānaṁ
govindam ādi-puruṣaṁ tam ahaṁ bhajāmi

I worship Govinda, the primeval Lord, the first progenitor who is tending the cows, yielding all desire, in abodes built with spiritual gems, surrounded by millions of purpose trees, always served with great reverence and affection by hundreds of thousands of lakṣmīs or gopīs. (5.29)

veṇuṁ kvaṇantam aravinda-dalāyatākṣam-
barhāvataṁsam asitāmbuda-sundarāṅgam
kandarpa-koṭi-kamanīya-viśeṣa-śobhaṁ
govindam ādi-puruṣaṁ tam ahaṁ bhajāmi

I worship Govinda, the primeval Lord, who is adept in playing on His flute, with blooming eyes like lotus petals with head decked with peacock's feather, with the figure of beauty tinged with the hue of blue clouds, and His unique loveliness charming millions of Cupids. (5.30)

ālola-candraka-lasad-vanamālya-vaṁśī-
ratnāṅgadaṁ praṇaya-keli-kalā-vilāsam
śyāmaṁ tri-bhaṅga-lalitaṁ niyata-prakāśaṁ
govindam ādi-puruṣaṁ tam ahaṁ bhajāmi

I worship Govinda, the primeval Lord, round whose neck is swinging a garland of flowers beautified with the moon-locket, whose two hands are adorned with the flute and jeweled ornaments, who always revels in pastimes of love, whose graceful threefold-bending form of Śyāmasundara is eternally manifest. (5.31)

aṅgāni yasya sakalendriya-vṛtti-manti
paśyanti pānti kalayanti ciraṁ jaganti
ānanda-cinmaya-sad-ujjvala-vigrahasya
govindam ādi-puruṣaṁ tam ahaṁ bhajāmi

I worship Govinda, the primeval Lord, whose transcendental form is full of bliss, truth, substantiality and is thus full of the most dazzling splendor. Each of the limbs of that transcendental figure possesses in Himself, the full-fledged functions of all the organs, and eternally sees, maintains and manifests the infinite universes, both spiritual and mundane. (5.32)

advaitam acyutam anādim ananta-rūpam
ādyaṁ purāṇa-puruṣaṁ nava-yauvanaṁ ca
vedeṣu durlabham adurlabham ātma-bhaktau
govindam ādi-puruṣaṁ tam ahaṁ bhajāmi

I worship Govinda, the primeval Lord, who is inaccessible to the Vedas, but obtainable by pure unalloyed devotion of the soul, who is without a second, who is not subject to decay, is without a beginning, whose form is endless, who is the beginning, and the eternal *puruṣa*; yet He is a person possessing the beauty of blooming youth. (5.33)[6]

The Glorious *Śrī Kṛṣṇa-karṇāmṛta*

If the truth about Krishna's form and the spiritual world are revealed in the *Brahma-saṁhitā*, more specific and dramatic detail for meditating on that form is the subject of the second book: the *Kṛṣṇa-karṇāmṛta*. That is to say, the *Kṛṣṇa-karṇāmṛta* offers a series of snapshots of Krishna and His associates in the spiritual world, so that one might learn to enter into that world as the highest form of worship. Śrīla Bhaktivinoda Ṭhākura, the exemplar of *bhakti* practice and scholarship from the early 20th century, expresses this as follows: "The teachings of Śrī Mahāprabhu are clearly written in two texts. Teachings on *tattva* are in *Śrī Brahma-saṁhitā*, and teachings on *bhajana* are in *Śrī Kṛṣṇa-karnāmṛta*. Therefore, one who is a follower of Śrī Caitanya's teachings should recite *Kṛṣṇa-karnāmṛta* with special care every day."[7]

The *Kṛṣṇa-karṇāmṛta* was procured by Mahāprabhu on His return journey from South India. Apparently, He had heard the mellifluous text being artfully sung by a "gathering of *brāhmaṇa* Vaishnava *pandits* on the bank of the river Krishna,"[8] somewhere in Satara, Maharashtra.[9] The Lord's biographers do not say explicitly where He heard the *Kṛṣṇa-karṇāmṛta*, at least not as specifically as they do His discovery of the *Brahma-saṁhitā,* but we know the general area: "Śrī Caitanya Mahāprabhu next went to the bank of the Kṛṣṇa-veṇvā River, where He visited many holy places and the temples of various gods [such as those of Śiva or the Goddess]. The *brāhmaṇa* community there was composed of pure devotees, who regularly studied a book entitled

Kṛṣṇa-karṇāmṛta, which was composed by Bilvamaṅgala Ṭhākura." (Cc 2.9.304-6)

He had the book copied in much the same way that He had copied the *Brahma-saṁhitā*, and He would soon show both books to Rāmānanda Rāya, the devotional connoisseur and viceroy of the region, and others: "[W]ith great eagerness He had it copied and took it with Him. There is no comparison to the *Kṛṣṇa-karṇāmṛta* within the three worlds. By studying this book, one is elevated to the knowledge of pure devotional service to Kṛṣṇa. One who constantly reads the *Kṛṣṇa-karṇāmṛta* can fully understand the beauty and melodious taste of the pastimes of Lord Kṛṣṇa. The *Brahma-saṁhitā* and *Kṛṣṇa-karṇāmṛta* were two books that Śrī Caitanya Mahāprabhu considered to be most valuable jewels. Therefore He took them with Him on His return trip." (Cc 2.9.306-309)

The *Kṛṣṇa-karṇāmṛta* ("Nectar to Krishna's Ears") is likely a 12th- to 14th-century text, and while Bilvamaṅgala Ṭhākura (also known as Līlāśuka) is clearly the author of this work, the famous commentaries written by Caitanya Dāsa Gosvāmī (the brother of Kavi Karṇapūra), Gopāla Bhaṭṭa Gosvāmī, and Kṛṣṇadāsa Kavirāja Gosvāmī, are considered equally important.[10] Indeed, this most esoteric text on the love of Rādhā and Krishna needs commentary for us to understand what is really being said.[11] The author adopts the intense mood of hankering throughout the text. Verse after verse he begs for mercy, hoping to taste the love (*prema*) that is characteristic of Rādhā and the *gopīs*, to ascend to their heights of true love for Krishna. Unlike some other spiritualists, who are always ready to make public their so-called level of accomplishment, Gauḍīya *ācāryas* show a mood of humility, claiming that they are not yet there, praying for attainment that seems just beyond their reach. In this way, they gradually attain Rādhikā's mercy. Bilvamaṅgala Ṭhākura sets the perfect example of how to pine in the mood of the *gopīs*.

Interestingly, according to Bhaktivinoda Ṭhākura, we can learn the full gamut of spiritual life from Bilvamaṅgala Ṭhākura—from hovering on the platform of materialism, to the beginnings of the spiritual quest and its all-too-common impersonalism, to transcendental love of God.[12] Bilvamaṅgala, writes Bhaktivinoda, was born in a *brāhmaṇa* family in a village near the Kṛṣṇa-veṇvā River. In his earlier years he had become a sense enjoyer, and, after that, a follower of monistic philosophy, thinking himself the same as God. And finally, in his later years, he was able to go beyond the path of fruitive work and impersonal knowledge to become a pure devotee of Krishna. Bhaktivinoda tells us:

> If we deliberate on this story, we can understand that this is the course of the *jīvas* [souls] in this world. The *jīvas* of this world are under three categories—*prākṛta* (materialistic), *adhyātmika* (seeking impersonal liberation) or *aprākṛta* (seeking transcendence) according to their qualification. People say that there are six *darśanas* (philosophies); however, we divide all those *darśanas* into three types, namely, *prākṛta-darśana, adhyātmika-darśana*, and *aprākṛta-darśana*. Nyāya, Vaiśeṣika and Pūrva-Mīmāṁsā are *prākrta-darśanas*. Sāṅkhyā, Pātañjala and the *māyāvāda* commentaries on Vedānta are the three *adhyātmika-darśanas*. Vedānta itself is *aprākṛta-darśana*. This is how we may describe all the activities found within these threefold *darśanas*. Initially, Bilvamaṅgala

> Gosvāmī followed *prākṛta–darśana.* Taking refuge in *pāpa* [sin], he was extremely attached to the prostitute, Cintāmaṇi. Once, he crossed the Kṛṣnavenā off-season, and with great difficulty and went to see Cintāmaṇi. Observing Cintāmaṇi's renunciation and hearing advice from her, his initial interest in *adhyātmika–darśana* was born. He has expressed his two conditions in the *śloka*, *advaita-vīthī-pathikair upāsyāḥ* ("I was worshiped by those on the path of non-dualism"). Eventually, by the association and teachings of the Vaiṣṇavas, he became a devotee, and his attraction for *aprākṛta–darśana* was born. When that attachment became mature, *kṛṣṇa-rasa* manifested within him. *Aprākṛta-darśana* has three stages—*sādhakāvasthā* (the stage of *sādhana*), *bhāvāvasthā* (the stage of *bhāva*), and *premāvasthā* (the stage of *prema*). In *sādhakāvasthā*, one simply engages in *sādhana* of the nine limbs of *bhakti,* such as *śravaṇa, kīrtana,* etc. There is a difference between *vaidhi* and *rāgānuga* in *sādhakāvasthā.* By gradually following this, greed was aroused within Bilvamaṅgala Mahāśaya for *rāgānuga-bhakti.* In no other text has he described his *sādhana.* This book describes *premāvasthā.* The internal and external stages are indicated in all the *ślokas.*[13]

According to a list of temples and monasteries preserved in a Shankarite ashram in Dvaraka, Bilvamaṅgala Ṭhākura founded the Dvarakadhish temple of Gujarat, an outlet of Advaita Vedānta, the philosophy of oneness with God. History relates that after serving the Deity there for some time, he grew weary of the *brāhmaṇas* with whom he worked, for they philosophized that they were nondifferent from God—worshipping the Deity to realize that they were in fact one with Him! Gradually, Bilvamaṅgala turned the worship of the Dvarakadhish temple over to a disciple of

Vallabācārya named Haridās Brahmachari, and left in search of God.

As Bilvamaṅgala moved more and more beyond material life, and even pseudo spiritual life, he realized that his attraction for the opposite sex was at the heart of his inability to advance properly. "These eyes are my enemies!" he said. "May they now only look upon Krishna." And with that, he plucked out his own eyes, so he would not be tempted by worldly beauty. While the tradition does not encourage devotees to adopt such drastic measures, the story is meant to show the intensity of Bilvamaṅgala's determination on the spiritual path.

It was after this that he made his way towards Vrindavan, and as he neared its holy precincts, a young boy, seeing the difficulty that the now blind Bilvamaṅgala was enduring in his travels, took his hand and began leading him the rest of the way. The blind bard soon realized that the boy was Krishna himself. At one point as they journeyed ever closer to the land of Braj, Krishna pulled away from his hand. "I have to go now. My mother is calling Me. If I don't go now and take My lunch, she'll be very angry."

"No, you can't go," Bilvamaṅgala said. "I won't let You." But Krishna got away. He managed to pull His hand out of Bilvamaṅgala's, who then called after Krishna, "You can pull Your hand from mine, but You cannot take Yourself from my heart. I have imprisoned You there."

Arriving in Krishna's holy land, Bilvamaṅgala made a place for himself in Brahma-kuṇḍa, a sacred bathing place in Vrindavan, to perform austerities for the balance of his life.

One day, however, Krishna again came to Bilvamaṅgala. "My dear sir," He addressed the blind renunciant, "Why are you living so humbly, practicing such severe austerities? Why don't you take some milk?"

"Who are You, my dear boy?" Bilvamaṅgala inquired. "I am a cowherd boy," Krishna replied. "If you like, I can supply you with milk every day." Bilvamaṅgala agreed, and from then on Krishna daily brought him a small supply of milk. And in this way, Bilvamaṅgala lived out the balance of his life.

In his spiritual maturity, then, Bilvamaṅgala wrote the epic poem *Kṛṣṇa-karṇāmṛta*, which completely captures the essence of Krishna's identity and what it means to develop love for Him. Because of the insights of his work, his initiating guru, Somagiri, called him Līlāśuka, a name referring to his ability to sing like a parrot, recounting the inner meaning of Krishna's life and deeds again and again. It was this book that Mahāprabhu found in South India.

Returning to Puri from His journey south, Mahāprabhu wanted to set out for Vrindavan immediately, for as the consummate devotee of Lord Krishna, the ultimate place of pilgrimage is indeed Krishna's holy land, as seen in the life of Bilvamaṅgala Ṭhākura. However, due to the request of the local devotees, such as Rāmānanda Rāya, He stayed at Jagannath Puri for two more years, engaging in confidential pastimes with His intimates. But soon the desire to go to Vrindavan became unbearable, and so He immediately made plans to go. This journey to Vrindavan, of course, is the subject of an earlier chapter.

Endnotes

1. "He spent two years on His tour in South India." (*dui vatsara lāgila*) See *Caitanya-caritāmṛta* 2.16.84.

2. In the main temple of Śrī Raṅgam, for example, a similar two-armed form of Lord Vishnu is seen reclining on the divine serpent Ananta Śeṣa, though lying in the opposite direction, with His head to the west.

3. In the Śrīvaishnava tradition of South India, the distinction between Vishnu and Krishna is not as pronounced as it is in the Gauḍīya tradition. That said, Gauḍīyas, too, recognize that Vishnu and Krishna are the same Godhead in terms of *tattva* (philosophical truth), but different in terms of *rasa* (intimacy, relationship), for Vishnu is Krishna with majesty and opulence, whereas Krishna is epitome of beauty and intimacy. Additionally, Krishna is the source of Vishnu, i.e., the original *manifestor* of all divine manifestations. Proof-texts would run as follows. For the nondifference of Vishnu and Krishna: "Lord Kṛṣṇa and Lord Nārāyaṇa [Vishnu] are one and the same, but the pastimes of Kṛṣṇa are more relishable due to their sportive nature." (*Caitanya-caritāmṛta* 2.9.115) And the standard proof-text for Krishna as the source of all manifestations: "All of the above-mentioned incarnations are either plenary portions or portions of the plenary portions of the Lord, but Lord Śrī Kṛṣṇa is the original Personality of Godhead." *Śrīmad Bhāgavatam* 1.3.28.

4. Śrīla Bhaktisiddhānta Sarasvatī writes that Mahāprabhu made a copy of a *puñthi*, which refers to a palm-leaf manuscript. In Vrindavan and other northern areas at that time, hand-made paper derived from tree bark was the preferred medium for copying manuscripts, although the method was still in its infancy. In the South, however, it was palm leaves. They were cut into small rectangular sections, and then a metal stylus (made of iron, silver, or brass) was used to scratch the letters in horizontal lines on one or both sides. After that, powdered charcoal was used, either dry or wet, to fill the grooves with black letters. Finally, excess black was wiped off, revealing the words of the manuscript. Treating them with special Ayurvedic oils extended the life of such texts, which sometimes get brittle and turn to dust after many years. Śrīla Prabhupāda writes that (CC Madhya 1.120), "In the

olden days there were no presses, and all the important scriptures were handwritten and kept in large temples. Caitanya Mahāprabhu found the *Brahma-saṁhitā* and *Kṛṣṇa-karṇāmṛta* in handwritten texts, and knowing them to be very authoritative, He took them with Him to present to His devotees. . . . Now both the *Brahma-saṁhitā* and *Kṛṣṇa-karṇāmṛta* are available in print with commentaries by Śrīla Bhaktisiddhānta Sarasvatī Ṭhākura."

5. One might legitimately ask how it is possible that we currently have access to a series of prayers composed at the dawn of time. The great Vaishnava thinker and reformer Śrīla Bhaktivinoda Ṭhākura (1838–1914) anticipates this doubt in his brief Introduction to his Bengali commentary. He further suggests that some might prefer to believe that the book was actually composed by Mahāprabhu, rather than merely found by Him. To these thoughts, Bhaktivinoda responds as follows: "I simply wish to suggest that if this literature is accepted in the category of extremely ancient scriptures, it is exceptional evidence to support the doctrine of *Kṛṣṇa-bhakti*. Alternatively, one may argue that Śrī Caitanya Mahāprabhu must have written it Himself, since no mention of this scripture can be found anywhere in this region of Northern India. If such an opinion were to be established conclusively, what could possibly be a greater source of joy? The reason is that, in the Vaiṣṇava world, every last doubt about philosophical conclusions would at once be dispelled upon the discovery of a thesis of established philosophical truths written personally by Śrīman Mahāprabhu. Whatever one's opinion may be, this *Brahma-saṁhitā* is worshipable for Vaisnavas, and is also worthy of their thorough study." Of course, Bhaktivinoda does not accept the idea that Śrī Chaitanya wrote the text himself, but he is willing to entertain the notion as a theory, at least provisionally, to show that a true Vaishnava would relish anything comes from Mahāprabhu, whatever the circumstances. His See Śrī Śrīmad Bhaktivedānta Nārāyaṇa Mahārāja, *Śrī Brahma-saṁhitā: Fifth Chapter* (Vrindavan: Gauḍīya Vedānta Publications 2003), ii-iii.

6. For the full edition of verses and commentary of the *Brahma-saṁhitā*, see His Divine Grace Bhaktisiddhānta Sarasvatī Goswāmī Ṭhākura, *Śrī Brahma-saṁhitā* (Los Angeles: Bhaktivedanta Book Trust, 2023, reprint). This volume is a new and expanded edition of an English language version of the text published by the Gaudiya Math in

India in 1932, which was reprinted in 1958, 1973, and 1992. These earlier Indian editions featured the English translation and commentary of Śrīla Bhaktisiddhānta Sarasvatī (1874–1937), and the Sanskrit commentary of Śrīla Jīva Gosvāmī, the great Gauḍīya philosopher and one of the esteemed Six Gosvāmīs of Vrindavan. In the Bhaktivedanta Book Trust edition, the original *devanagari* text is shown for each verse of the *Brahma-saṁhitā*, as in the Indian editions, but here it is followed by Roman transliteration and a word-for-word translation into English, as per Śrīla Prabhupāda's request. Then, again replicating the Indian edition, the BBT includes Śrīla Bhaktisiddhānta Sarasvatī's full English translation and commentary—a commentary that closely follows the Bengali version of his father, Śrīla Bhaktivinoda Ṭhākura, the great Vaishnava saint and reformer.

It should be noted that the commentary ascribed to Śrīla Bhaktisiddhānta Sarasvatī Ṭhākura was actually rendered by two of his senior disciples, Bhakti Sudhākara (Professor Niśikānta Sānyāl) and B. P. Tīrtha Mahārāja, who translated the commentary of Śrīla Bhaktivinoda Ṭhākura into English on Bhaktisiddhānta's behalf and with his authorization. Thus, it was published under their spiritual master's name, also under his authorization. This is recognized in the Preface to Śrīla Bhaktisiddhānta's 1932 edition of the *Brahma-saṁhitā* (but has since been omitted). The booklet *Mahā-mahopadeśaka Śrīla Bhakti Sudhākara*, published in 1940 and edited by Sundarānanda Vidyāvinoda, also reveals this same editorial history of the English edition.

7. See "Preface to *Śrī Kṛṣṇa Karṇāmṛta*," first published in Śrīla Bhaktivinoda Ṭhākura's *Sajjana Toṣaṇī* (1898), Vol. 10, No. 1. English translation by Swami B. V. Giri (https://bhaktivinodainstitute.org/preface-to-sri-krsna-karnamrta/).

8. "Śrī Chaitanya Deva acquired this one *śatakam* of the three *śatakam* from the south of India. He heard it recited at a gathering of Brahmana Vaishnava Pandits on the bank of the river Krishna." See Sambidananda Das, *The History & Literature of the Gaudiya Vaishnavas and Their Relation to other Medieval Vaishnava Schools* (Chennai: Sree Gaudiya Math, 2007, reprint), 50. A *śatakam* is a genre of Sanskrit literature composed of 100 verses, and in total the *Kṛṣṇa-karṇāmṛta* is composed of three of these. Thus, as in the case of the *Brahma-saṁhitā*,

what Mahāprabhu found was only one portion of a larger text—the version of the *Krishna-karṇāmṛta* that He brought back to northern provinces was composed of only 112 verses.

9. Maharashtra is on the western coast of India, but it belongs to Peninsular South India.

10. See S. K. De, ed., *The Kṛṣṇa-karṇāmṛta of Līlāśuka, with Three Sanskrit Commentaries of the Bengal Vaiṣṇava School, the Kṛṣṇa-vallabha of Gopāla Bhaṭṭa, the Subodhanī of Caitanyadāsa, and the Sāraṅga-raṅgadā of Kṛṣṇadāsa Kavirāja* (Bangladesh: University of Dacca, 1938).

11. For more on the *Kṛṣṇa-karṇāmṛta* as historical text, see S. K. De, "A Note on the Text of the *Kṛṣṇa-karṇāmṛta*," *Annals of the Bhandarkar Oriental Research Institute*, Vol. 16, No. 3/4 (1934-35), 173-188. Also see H. G. Narahari, "On the Text of the *Kṛṣṇakarṇāmṛta* of Bilvamaṅgala," *Bulletin of the Deccan College Post-Graduate and Research Institute*, Vol. 17, No. 1 (June 1955), 42-45. Finally, an important academic text on the subject is *The Love of Krishna: The Kṛṣṇakarṇāmṛta of Līlāśuka Bilvamaṅgala*, edited and translated by Frances Wilson (Philadelphia: University of Pennsylvania Press, 1975).]

12. See endnote 7.

13. ibid.

Sixteen

The *Gaura-ganoddeśa-dīpikā*: A Who's Who of Gauḍīya Vaishnavism

IN ADDITION TO THE three standard forms of literature—fictional and non-fictional prose; poetry in its various forms; and drama with its many subgenres, dilated by the addictive wonders of present-day technology—modernity gives us yet another category of composition: "Who's Who" books. These are generally reference publications with concise biographical data about notable personalities in various areas of specialization. (The same phrase is used as an expression to indicate any group of people worth knowing: "You'll soon find out 'who's who' at the temple.")

A text titled simply *Who's Who*, focusing on prominent people in Britain, is perhaps the most well known example of this genre in the West, published annually since the mid-1900s. But there are now literally thousands of unrelated Who's Who titles, elucidating prominent individuals in various religious groups, political parties, musical categories, gender associations, and so on. Such books often offer good summaries of a given tradition or subject through the lives of the people associated with them.

In ancient Indian literature, the notion of Who's Who has an added dimension. It chiefly refers to a given entity's ontological position—who they are in the spiritual realm—and then relates that original identity to who they are in the here and now, or exactly what role they play in Krishna's earthly drama, or that of one of his incarnations.

As far as early texts go, this dual sense of Who's Who can especially be found in the *Mahābhārata*. For example, its first book, the Ādi-Parva, gives a list of partial incarnations, including both demigods and demoniac adversaries, explaining that they take birth as particular individuals to assist in (or to challenge) the Lord's manifested pastimes on Earth (1.61). Similarly, in the Āśramavāsika-parva, the epic's fifteenth book, Vyāsa explains to Gāndhārī that the soldiers who died on the battlefield of Kurukṣetra were all portions of gods and demons in new incarnations (15.39.5–6). He tells her that her own husband Dhṛtarāṣṭra is actually the Gandharva king by the same name from a higher planetary system, while Pāṇḍu is originally a member of the Maruts, a group of storm deities associated with Śiva. Vidura is a portion of the demigod Dharma, as is the new king, Yudhiṣṭhira. She is also told that Duryodhana is an incarnation of Kali, the dark age in which we currently live, and that Duḥśāsana and his crew were all incarnations of *rākṣasas*, or demons (15.39.8–10).

A Vaishnava Who's Who

Moving to more modern (or premodern) times, Śrīla Rūpa Gosvāmī composed a text called the *Rādhā-krishna-gaṇoddeśa-dīpikā* (c. 1550), which takes basic information found in earlier scriptures and elucidates specifics. That is to say, while the *gopīs*, for example, are mentioned as a group in the *Bhāgavata Purāṇa*, and therein remain unnamed, Śrī Rūpa tells us who they are and offers particulars about their life and earthly circumstances. In short, he gives us a Who's Who of Krishna and his associates.

He begins with the Lord's family members, and goes on to outline minutiae about Rādhā, the prominent *gopīs*, and their many loved ones, telling us their names; their age; their bodily complexion; color of clothes, and so on, facilitating meditative practices. He does the same for their male associates, the cowherd boys. In this way, the qualities and characteristics of Rādhā and Krishna are delineated, along with that of those near and dear to them. But it should be noted: Here we find a Who's Who of Krishna-līlā only, without reference to Śrī Chaitanya.

The *Caitanya-caritāmṛta* (completed in 1615), of course, is where we can find a Who's Who of Chaitanya-līlā. This is especially the case in Ādi 7, where we are introduced to the hidden identity of the Pañca Tattva, Lord Chaitanya and his four primary associates: Chaitanya Mahāprabhu is a combined manifestation of Rādhā and Krishna; Nityānanda Prabhu is Balarāma (Krishna's elder brother); Advaita Ācārya is Sadāśiva (or Mahā-Vishnu); Gadādhara Pandita is Rādhārānī (Krishna's eternal consort and Internal Energy); and Śrīvāsa Ṭhākura is an incarnation of Nārada (who represents the ideal devotee). While such Who's Who information is peppered throughout the *Caitanya-caritāmṛta*, it is not rendered systematically, nor is it the main point of the text.

In fact, the notion of the Pañca Tattva predates the *Caitanya-caritāmṛta.* Of course, the concept of Lord Chaitanya in five features is an eternal spiritual principle, but it appears in history in the following way: The earliest reference is said to be in Svarūpa Dāmodara Gosvāmī's no-longer-extant work, *Gaura-tattva-nirūpaṇa,* which was probably written during Śrī Caitanya's manifest pastimes (16th century) or soon thereafter. Although there is scholarly debate about the authenticity of this book, Kavi Karṇapūra's *Gaura-gaṇoddeśa-dīpikā* does indeed credit Svarūpa Dāmodara for systematizing the doctrine of the Pañca Tattva.

It was Kavi Karṇapūra who popularized the doctrine, making it known to the society of Vaishnavas through his own literary projects, first mentioning it in his *Caitanya-caritāmṛta-mahākāvya* (written in 1542) and later in his *Gaura-ganoddeśa-dīpikā* (written in 1576), both predating Kṛṣṇadāsa Kavirāja Gosvāmī's *Caitanya-caritāmṛta.* Still, it is Kavirāja Gosvāmī's work that informs most practitioners today of Pañca Tattva doctrine, and for this we are grateful to Śrīla Prabhupāda, whose literary work and life of devotion have made the Gauḍīya tradition a worldwide phenomenon.

"The Elucidating Lamp"

In many ways, the *Gaura-gaṇoddeśa-dīpikā* ("A lamp elucidating the companions of Śrī Chaitanya") is the ultimate Who's Who of Gauḍīya Vaishnavism, for it correlates the Divine Couple and their loving associates with their counterparts in Chaitanya-līlā.

Kavi Karṇapūra, the author, was born in Kumārahaṭṭa (Halisahar), West Bengal, some forty miles south of Navadvīpa. His birth name was Paramānanda, though he was also called Purī dāsa. The son of Śivānanda Sen, a prominent disciple of Śrī Chaitanya, Paramānanda had two elder brothers, Caitanya dāsa and Rāma dāsa. He was born around 1524, nearly a decade before Mahāprabhu left the planet. Thus, he had the good fortune to encounter the Lord in person.

For example, one day, as a baby, Paramānanda grabbed hold of Mahāprabhu's foot to suck on his toe. Some declare that it was this very act that invested him with his subsequent poetic abilities. Enjoying the sacred interaction, the assembled devotees chanted, "Hari! Hari!" (Antya 12.50)

Then, when Paramānanda was only seven years old, Mahāprabhu himself initiated him into the chanting of the *mahā-mantra*—Hare Krishna, Hare Krishna, Krishna Krishna, Hare Hare/ Hare Rāma, Hare Rāma, Rāma Rāma, Hare Hare. He is therefore understood to be the Lord's initiated disciple (Antya 16, summary). In Śrīla Prabhupāda's translation, this is further confirmed by Svarūpa Dāmodara, one of the Lord's most intimate associates: "My Lord," Svarūpa said, "You have given him initiation into the name of Krishna ..." (Antya 16.71) That said, in Paramānanda's writings, he also mentions Śrīnātha Paṇḍita as his guru. Whatever the actual pedigree of his *dīkṣā*, he later became one of the greatest poets in Vaiṣṇava history, and he is remembered as such to this day. In fact, it was Śrī Chaitanya who bestowed upon him the name *Kavi Karṇapūra* ("the ear-ornament of poets,") in honor of his unique Sanskrit masterpieces, rendered from his earliest years.

The *Gaura-gaṇoddeśa-dīpikā*, one of his later books, is a short and simple work of 215 verses. A summary of the text might run as follows: The very first verse equates Śrī Krishna with Śrī Chaitanya in no uncertain terms. The author then goes on to offer customary respects to Gauḍīya authorities, including his guru, Śrīnātha Paṇḍita. By the fourth verse he offers respects to his father, Śivānanda Sen, and by the fifth he is clear about the book's trajectory: to describe the previous life of the associates of Lord Chaitanya Mahāprabhu.

Verse six introduces the Pañca Tattva and this goes on for some eleven verses—clearly this is one of the book's important teachings. As mentioned, Kavi Karṇapūra attributes the doctrine to one of Mahāprabhu's earliest followers, Svarūpa Dāmodara Gosvāmī.

The text then discusses the various virtues of Navadvīpa, Vṛndāvana, and Purī, and their relation to the subject at hand. Verse 20 outlines the *yuga avatāras*—detailing how the same Lord who assumed a white complexion in Satya-yuga and was called Śukla; a red complexion in Tretā-yuga, under the name Makhabhuk; a black complexion in Dvāpara-yuga and known as Śyāmasundara [Krishna]; has now appeared as Gauracandra [Chaitanya] in the current age of Kali.

After this, we are introduced to the four *sampradāyas*—the Śrī, Brahma, Rudra and Sanaka [Kumara]—which, historically, is an important part of Kavi Karṇapūra's project. He belabors the point for several verses. It can be argued, in fact, that second only to showing the parallel identities of Krishna and Chaitanya's associates, his main purpose in this book is to establish the importance of disciplic succession: To this end, he quotes the famous *Padma Purāṇa* verse saying that if one does not take shelter of one of the four established lineages, the fruits or secrets of spiritual knowledge will remain very far away.[1] Elaboration on these lineages and certain key masters follow next, leading to a description of Mahāprabhu's direct predecessors, such as Madhavendra Purī and the Lord's immediate guru, Īśvara Purī. In this way, Kavi Karṇapūra connects the Gauḍīya Sampradāya to its predecessor lineage, the Brahmā-Madhva tradition.[2]

After discussing a few general points of philosophy, the book's central theme begins with Texts 35 and 36. The initial correlation between Krishna-līlā and Chaitanya-līlā is found in Krishna's grandparents: "He who was previously the cowherd man named Parjanya, the grandfather of Lord Krishna, has now appeared as Upendra Miśra at Śrī Haṭṭa. He had seven sons. She who was previously the respected elderly grandmother of Lord Krishna named Mahāmānyā has now appeared as Kalāvatī, the wife of Upendra Miśra." And so it goes.

An Indispensable Treatise

Kavi Karṇapūra gives some 200 instances of identity equivalence (many verses include more than one correlation). He is careful to indicate that numerous senior devotees have offered diverse opinions, and that these should be respected. At times, he cites the various existing options as authoritative, leaving open the possibility that any of them may be correct—or even, counterintuitively, that they all might be correct. For example, he writes in verse 88: "Some say that Acyutānanda was the incarnation of Kārttikeya, and others learned in transcendental relationships say that he is the incarnation of Acyuta-gopī. Both views are correct (*ubhyam tu samīcīnam*), for both Kārttikeya and Acyuta-gopī were present in the body of Acyutānanda. Aside from this, some devotees say that Śrī Krishna Miśra was also the incarnation of Kārttikeya." We will return to this idea later.

Kavi Karṇapūra humbly uses phrases such as *yathā-mati yathā-śrutam* ("according to my opinion" or "what I have heard"), as found in Text 146. Nonetheless, for practitioners, his opinion is deeply cherished and contemplated—as a direct associate of Śrī Chaitanya, his words carry deep meaning and are invaluable in the study of the Gauḍīya tradition. To be sure, Śrīla Prabhupāda obviously regards Karṇapūra's opinion highly, quoting him as an authority some 78 times in his commentary to the *Caitanya-caritāmṛta*.

Differences of opinion in regard to ontological identity are found throughout the tradition, and we see this crystalized when the great *ācārya* Viśvanātha Chakravartī Ṭhākura publishes his *Gaurāṅga-gaṇa-svarūpa-tattva-candrikā* (early 18th century), a text that, in content, style, and format, closely follows the *Gaura-gaṇoddeśa-dīpikā*. While most of Viśvanātha Chakravartī's identifications are the same, or similar, as those found in Kavi Karṇapūra's work, in some cases Viśvanātha revises the prior reading.

One primary example is that of Rāmānanda Rāya: Whereas Kavi Karṇapūra had said that Rāmānanda was the *gopī* named Lalitā (Text 122), Viśvanātha says that he is Viśākhā (Text 79), which has become the dominant understanding in the Gauḍīya tradition. Of course, with respect to the claim about Rāmānanda Rāya's identity, Kavi

Karṇapūra uses the words "some say" (*āhuḥ*), which allow for uncertainty or equivocation; Viśvanātha, on the other hand, is declarative, especially in this case.

The identity of Rāmānanda with Viśākhā is further confirmed in Dhyānachandra Goswāmī's *Śrī Gaura-Govindārcana-Smaraṇa-Paddhati* (Text 214), as well as in Bhaktivinoda Ṭhākura's commentary on the *Caitanya-caritāmṛta* (Madhya 8.23). Prabhupāda, too, while elsewhere giving credence to the Lalitā option, comments on Madhya 8.23 by directly saying, "Śrīla Rāmānanda Rāya was an incarnation of the *gopī,* Viśākhā." Thus, in some cases, Kavi Karṇapūra is merely opening dialogue about the identities of Mahāprabhu's associates, leaving conclusive statements for future *ācāryas* according to their realization and insight.

One final point. Both in the Rāmānanda Rāya case, cited above, as well as in numerous other *Gaura-gaṇoddeśa-dīpikā and Gaurāṅga-gaṇa-svarūpa-tattva-candrikā* entries —the *ācāryas* tend to attribute multiple personalities from Krishna-līlā to a single entity from Chaitanya-līlā. For example, according to Kavi Karṇapūra, Rāmānanda Rāya is the incarnation of Lalitā-gopī, Arjuniya-gopī, a cowherd boy named Arjuna, and Pāṇḍava Arjuna. (120-124) Such souls were "born together" (*militvā samabhūd*) in one body, as suggested in Text 120.

At first, such proclamations can be jarring. But it is to be remembered that the subject here is spirit-soul, which is part of Krishna—who has unlimited spiritual potency. The laws of spirit need not conform to those of matter. From a material perspective, the notion of one person being several can indicate a form of dissociative identity disorder, or even schizophrenia. But this is not the case on the spiritual platform. Indeed, spiritually potent personalities can accommodate greater dimensions of reality to more effectively facilitate their service to Krishna—all by the Lord's grace.

The example is Śrī Rādhā herself: She so wants to please Krishna that she expands into several personalities just to accommodate his desires in multiple ways. These expansions are technically called *kāya-vyūha*—each one is said to be the same as Rādhā but occupying different space and time for the sake of the Lord's pleasure. Most of the intimate *gopīs* are such expansions of Śrī Rādhā. Great devotees are afforded similar capabilities in their service to the Lord, and we see examples of this in the *Gaura-gaṇoddeśa-dīpikā*.[3]

It would serve us well to avoid thinking in familiar terms when dealing with multi-dimensional or higher realities. In this world, we tend to see in terms of one or the other—"either/or" as opposed to "both/and." But even Quantum Mechanics observes particles that are both this *and* that, that exist simultaneously in more than one place, and that influence other particles instantaneously even at great distances.[4] And if this is so for material objects, how much more might it be true for spiritual phenomena?

The bottom line is this: Greater realities cannot be apprehended by material means. Through the tradition brought to us by great personalities like Kavi Karṇapūra, one can enter into the mysteries of spiritual truth, which includes an understanding of how diverse spiritual beings may incarnate in one personality at the same time, and how one entity can incarnate variously. Indeed, it is only through such a tradition that we can accurately discern Who's Who.

Endnotes

1. "All mantras not received in authorized lineages are to be considered fruitless. In Kali-yuga, there are four legitimate *sampradāyas* inaugurated by Śrī Devī, Lord Brahmā, Lord Rudra, and the Four Kumāras. They are known as the Śrī Sampradāya, the Brahmā Sampradāya, the Rudra Sampradāya, and the Sanakādi Sampradāya, respectively ..." (*sampradāya vihīnā ye mantrāste niṣphalā matāḥ| ataḥ kalau bhaviśyanti catvāraḥ sampradāyinaḥ|| Śrī-brahmā-rudra-sanakā vaiṣṇavā kṣitipāvanāḥ| catvāraste kalau bhāvya hyutkale puruṣottamāt||*) Though this verse cannot be found in current editions of the *Padma Purāṇa*, it was cited (as a verse from that Purāṇa) in Kavi Karṇapūra's *Gaura-gaṇoddeśa-dīpikā* (21), which, again, is an early Gauḍīya text. For this reason alone, it can be assumed that it was gleaned from earlier editions of the Purāṇa. The verse can also be found in the 18th-century *Bhakti-ratnākara* (5.2,111-2), which also quotes it as coming from the *Padma Purāṇa*. A similar verse, almost identical, appears in the *Garga-saṁhitā*, which is a traditional *saṁhitā* in the Vaishnava tradition. (*Garga-saṁhitā*, Aśvamedha-khaṇḍa, 61.24–26) For more on this reference, see Viśvanātha Cakravartī's *Gaura-gaṇa-svarūpa-tattva-candrikā*, trans., Demian Martins (Vrindavan, U.P.: Jiva Institute, 2015), Introduction, *xiii*. The verse is also confirmed by Śrīla Prabhupāda, who attributes it to the *Padma Purāṇa* in his commentary to *Śrīmad Bhāgavatam* 6.8.42.

2. While Kavi Karṇapūra's text may be one of the earliest to cite the disciplic succession from Śrī Krishna to Mahāprabhu, showing its connection to the Mādhva Sampradāya, other early evidence can be attributed to the *Bhakti-ratnākara* (5.2,149–162 and 5.2,169-172) and Baladeva Vidyābhūṣaṇa's *Govinda-bhāṣya* and *Prameya-ratnāvalī*. Viśvanātha Cakravartī also supports the Mādhva affiliation and the general notion of the Gauḍīya disciplic succession in his important work, the *Gaurāṅga-gaṇa-svarūpa-tattva-candrikā*. Additionally, Śrīla Prabhupāda confirms the connection: "Therefore the Gauḍīya Vaiṣṇava-sampradāya is a disciplic succession from Madhvācārya. This fact has been accepted in the authorized books known as *Gaura-gaṇoddeśa-dīpikā* and *Prameya-ratnāvalī*, as well as by Gopāla Guru Gosvāmī." (*Caitanya-caritāmṛta*, Ādi 6.40)

3. There are several possible ways to interpret the "many in one" aspect of the *Gaura-gaṇoddeśa-dīpikā*. For example, one might appeal to the notion of *āveśa*, i.e., that certain verses refer not to literal incarnations as such, but merely to entities who are empowered or infused with the specific characteristics of several individuals. However, this theory begs the following question: Who in Krishna-līlā actually incarnates as an associate in Chaitanya-līlā? Furthermore, in the text itself, literal incarnation seems clear, with few exceptions. The specific word *āveśa* only appears in Texts 71, 73, 74, 76, and 112, and it can be interpreted variously. That said, the notion of mere empowerment as opposed to actual incarnation has certain merits. Most notably, it avoids the potentially unsettling prospect of having to explain how multiple individuals might converge in a single body. Thus, the notion of *āveśa* in this context persists as an alternate and plausible theory.

4. For a layman's explanation of simultaneity and quantum states, see Brian Greene, *The Fabric of the Cosmos* (New York: Knopf, 2004).

Seventeen

Rūpānuga Vaishnavism: An Inner Dimension of Krishna Consciousness

"Unless you become rūpānuga,
you cannot understand Gauḍīya philosophy."
—Śrīla Prabhupāda, *Nectar of Devotion* class.
Vṛndāvana, October 18, 1972

śrī rūpa mañjarī-pada,
sei more sampada,
sei mora bhajana-pūjana

"The lotus feet of Śrī Rūpa Mañjarī
are my dearmost treasure.
They are the topmost object of my worship
and inner devotional practices."

THE WEALTH OF VAISHNAVISM—a rich and expansive monotheistic culture centered on the worship of Vishnu, or Krishna, whether gleaned from sacred texts, passed from lip to ear, or acquired through a combination of the two—descends from teacher to student through several well-established lineages, such as the Brahmā, Śrī, Rudra, and Kumāra Sampradāyas. It is specifically the first of these four, originating with the initial created being, Brahmā, that gives us, by extension, the prestigious Brahmā-Madhva-Gauḍīya tradition, which descends from Śrī Chaitanya Mahāprabhu.

The extension in nomenclature exists because Mādhvācārya (1238–1317), commentator extraordinaire and systematizer of the lineage, played a major role in its development, as did, several centuries later, Śrī Chaitanya, who is both Rādhā and Krishna in the guise of Their own perfect devotee. (Mahāprabhu appeared in the region of Bengal, specifically in the area of Gaudadesh, accounting for the "Gauḍīya" component of the lineage name.) It was He who brought out the inner dimensions of this particular Sampradāya, transforming it into what is arguably the world's most profound philosophical system of knowledge and esoteric approach to divinity.

The superlative quality of this Sampradāya cannot be overstated: While all Vaishnava lineages offer the sweet fruit of love of God (*premā*), manifesting in a variety of relationships (*rasa*), i.e., *śānta* (neutral, peaceful, passive), *dāsya* (helpful, devoted, service-oriented), *sakhya* (friendly, caring, a sense of camaraderie), *vātsalya* (protective, nurturing, parental) and *mādhurya* (intimate, romantic, erotic)—transcendental interactions with the Supreme that are essentially pure, untainted prototypes for all apparently similar relationships in the material world—the Gauḍīya Sampradāya reveals by far the deepest insights into a very particular type of *mādhurya-rasa*.

This esoterica had previously been hinted at by luminous Vaishnava poets such as Jayadeva, Caṇḍīdāsa, and Vidyāpati, embodying revelations that describe the highest attainment of fully blossomed sweetness, and then elaborated upon later by Vaishnava stalwarts. Gauḍīya Vaishnavism's special harvest, then, is a confidential form of divine love in relationship to Śrī Krishna, or God in His highest feature, in which one interacts with Him as a secret lover.

God as secret lover? Hearing this, one may naturally conjure all but the wholesome image of a soul in connection to God. Consequently, it should be made clear from the beginning that what is being referenced is "spiritual" love on the transcendental platform, without any trace of lust. Make no mistake, pure love of God in *mādhurya-rasa* is distinct from any prurient interest whatsoever, just as the precious metal gold is distinct from iron, though both are metals. Whereas gold is incorruptible, iron is just the opposite, and in time it deteriorates, rusts, and disappears. The divine love extolled by Śrī Chaitanya and celebrated in the Brahmā-Mādhva-Gauḍīya Sampradāya is said to be eternal, incorruptible, and wholly pure.

Rūpānuga: Origins and Importance

But even when speaking of pure *mādhurya*, which, again, can also be found in other Sampradāyas, it should be reiterated that the Gauḍīya conception goes further into a more recondite aspect of that love, culminating in Rādhā-dāsyam, wherein one becomes the loving assistant of the Divine Feminine's most immediate servitors. And while the intricacies of this profound love are beyond the scope of this article, it can be noted that in following the methods and practices of Śrīla Rūpa Gosvāmī (1489–1564), one of Śrī Chaitanya's most confidential associates, one is availing oneself of the greatest portion of that love. This, in brief, is what it means to be a Rūpānuga.

The term "Rūpānuga" was originally coined by Gauḍīya poet-saint, Raghunātha Dāsa Gosvāmī in his seminal work, *Manaḥ-śikṣā* (text 12). There he informs us about the glorious result of adhering to three simple procedures: (1) adopting the line of Śrī Rūpa and his followers (*rūpānuga*); (2) taking up residence in Vraja-maṇḍala; and (3) loudly singing his eleven spiritually charged instructions (*Manaḥ-śikṣā*) in a melodious voice with full understanding of their meaning—one who embraces these three items, he says, will certainly obtain the matchless gem of properly worshipping Śrī-Śrī Rādhā-Krishna. In this way, both historically and conceptually, the notion of being a Rūpānuga goes back to the very beginning of the Gauḍīya Sampradāya.

Over 100 years later, Rādhā Krishna Gosvāmī, the 17th-century *mahānta* (chief priest) of the Govindaji temple in Vrindavan, wrote the *Sādhana-dīpika*. In the book's eighth chapter, he lays bare the importance of Rūpa Gosvāmī and what it means to be a Rūpānuga. He opens by saying that Rūpa Mañjarī is topmost among all the dear maidservants of Śrī Rādhā and even stands supreme among Her most intimate servitors, the *mañjarīs*, or youthful *gopis*, like Rati and others. Only in her *ānugatya* ("by following her"), says Rādhā Krishna Gosvāmī, is loving service to the Lord even possible. Rūpa Mañjarī, we will soon learn, is Rūpa Gosvāmī's alter ego in the kingdom of God.

Commenting on a verse from Raghunātha Dāsa Gosvāmī's *Vilāpa-kusumāñjalī* (14), Rādhā Krishna Gosvāmī further states that without following Rūpa (*rūpānugatya*) one simply cannot achieve the unparalleled jewel of Rādhā-Krishna worship (*ata etādṛśānugatyaṁ vinā śrī-nanda-nandanasya tathāvidha-svarūpa-prāptir na bhavati tatrāpi śrī-rūpānugatyaṁ vinā śrī-rādhā-kṛṣṇātula-bhajana-ratnaṁ na labhata iti niṣkarṣārthaḥ*).

He also says that the other Gosvāmīs (except perhaps Sanātana, Śrī Rūpa's guru and elder brother, whom he mentions separately after listing others), are to be considered Rūpānugas, thus indicating Rūpa's supreme position:

gopāla-bhaṭṭo raghunātha-dāsaḥ
śrī-lokanātho raghunātha-bhaṭṭaḥ |
rūpānugās te vṛṣabhānu-putrī-
sevā-parāḥ śrīla-sanātanādyāḥ

"Gopāla Bhaṭṭa, Raghunātha dāsa, Lokanātha, Raghunātha Bhaṭṭa—all of them are Rūpānugas. All of them, headed by Sanātana Gosvāmī, are devoted to the service of Vṛṣabhānu's daughter [Rādhā]."

Elsewhere, even Sanātana—who is again Rūpa's elder—glorifies him as foremost among the Vaishnavas. This can be found in his auto-commentary to *Bṛhad-bhāgavatāmṛta* 1.1.3. In 1.1.11, he even acknowledges that the realizations expressed in his work come from Śrī Rūpa. And in the commentary to the text's last verse (3.7.157), he again says that Rūpa is "best among Vaishnavas," calling him "*bhagavān*," a word usually reserved for God Himself and the greatest of devotees. Clearly, there is no one as esteemed as Rūpa

Gosvāmī, and all Gauḍīya Vaishnavas are thus encouraged to be Rūpānugas.

Some two centuries after Rādhā Krishna Gosvāmī, the great Vaishnava reformer Bhaktivinoda Ṭhākura (1838–1914) augmented our knowledge of Rūpānuga Vaishnavism, beginning with his commentary on *Manaḥ-śikṣā*. Further, in his songbook, *Gītāmālā*, he includes a chapter specifically titled, "Rūpānuga-bhajana-darpaṇa," where he elucidates the concept in several songs. Indeed, in verse two of this work's second song, he says that Rūpa Gosvāmī alone taught the various authentic processes of *bhajan*, and, humbly saying that he has not properly taken advantage of this, suggests that worshiping Krishna is simply not possible without heeding these processes (*bhajana-prakāra jata sakalera sāra mataśikhāilo śrī-rūpa gosāñise bhajana nā jāniyā kṛṣṇa bhajibāre giyātuccha kāje jībana kāṭāi*).

So important is Rūpānuga, both in word and concept, that it is included in the Praṇāma-mantras (reverential prayers) for both Bhaktivinoda Ṭhākura and his son, Bhaktisiddhānta Sarasvatī Ṭhākura (1874–1937), who is the guru of Śrīla Prabhupāda:

Śrīla Bhaktivinoda Praṇati

namo bhaktivinodāya sac-cid-ānanda-nāmine gaura-śakti-svarūpāya rūpānuga-varāya te

"I offer my respectful obeisances unto Saccidānanda Bhaktivinoda, who is transcendental energy of Chaitanya Mahāprabhu. He is a strict follower of the Gosvāmīs, headed by Śrī Rūpa."

Śrīla Bhaktisiddhānta Praṇati

śrī-vārṣabhānavī-devī-dayitāya kṛpābdhaye kṛṣṇa-sambandha-vijñāna-dāyine prabhave namaḥ

"I offer my respectful obeisances to Śrī Vārṣabhānavī-devī-dayita dāsa [another name of Śrīla Bhaktisiddhānta Sarasvatī], who is favored by Śrīmatī Rādhārāṇī and who is the ocean of transcendental mercy and the deliverer of the science of Kṛṣṇa."

mādhuryojjvala-premāḍhya-śrī-rūpānuga-bhaktida śrī-gaura-karuṇā-śakti-vigrahāya namo 'stu te

"I offer my respectful obeisances unto you, the personified energy of Śrī Chaitanya's mercy, who deliver devotional service which is enriched with conjugal love of Rādhā and Kṛṣṇa, coming exactly in the line of revelation of Śrīla Rūpa Gosvāmī."

namas te gaura-vāṇī-śrī-mūrtaye dīna-tāriṇe rūpānuga-viruddhāpasiddhānta-dhvānta-hāriṇe

"I offer my respectful obeisances unto you, who are the personified teachings of Lord Chaitanya. You are the deliverer of the fallen souls. You do not tolerate any statement which is against the teachings of devotional service enunciated by Śrīla Rūpa Gosvāmī."

Perhaps most importantly for members of ISKCON, Śrīla Prabhupāda himself writes as follows in the Preface to *Nectar of Devotion*: "The present Krishna Consciousness movement is based on the authority of Śrīla Rūpa Gosvāmī

Prabhupāda. We are therefore generally known as *rūpānugas*, or followers in the footsteps of Śrīla Rūpa Gosvāmī Prabhupāda."

One might legitimately ask, then, "How can one become a Rūpānuga Vaishnava? What does it mean to be a follower of Rūpa Gosvāmī?"

The first step, obviously, is knowing who Śrī Rūpa is, both in his manifestation during Chaitanya-līlā, for which he is most well known, and also in terms of his internal identity as manifested in Krishna-līlā, where he is in fact a she known as Rūpa Mañjarī.

Who is Rūpa Gosvāmī?

Rūpa Gosvāmī was among the first and most accomplished theologians and poets in the Gauḍīya Vaishnava tradition. He was a direct student of Śrī Chaitanya, who taught him, through word and deed, a methodical approach to *bhakti*, or the science of devotion. Śrī Rūpa shared this methodology through a considerable array of original Sanskrit texts that summarized all he had learned. Specifically, he took the already existing *rasa* theory—so dear to the literati of his time—and adapted its terminology so that it focuses on Krishna and His multifarious relationships.[1] In this way, he elucidated an intricate system of knowledge that could be utilized for uncovering one's now dormant love of God. The details of his adaptation can be found in his classic *Bhakti-rasāmṛta-sindhu*, but he is also renowned for having penned other important devotional works, such as *Ujjvala-nīlamaṇi, Dāna-keli-kaumudī, Haṁsadūta, Uddhava-sandeśa,*

Vidagdha-mādhava, Lalita-mādhava, Padyāvali, Stavamālā and others, thus giving the world a literary current of spiritual knowledge. He had been instructed by Śrī Chaitanya to not only write such books, but to unearth the lost places of Krishna's pastimes in Vrindavan and to show by his own example how to live a life of pure devotion. Overall, he is considered the prototypical devotee-scholar, living as an ascetic for the latter portion of his life.

But Śrī Rūpa has two identities. Kavi Karṇapūra, one of Mahāprabhu's biographers and early associates, reveals in his *Gaura-gaṇoddeśa-dīpikā* (180) that, in the eternal land of Vraja, Śrī Rūpa is Rūpa Mañjarī, chief among all the youthful *gopīs* or cowherd girlfriends of Rādhā, Śrī Krishna's divine consort.[2] Rūpa Mañjarī and her cohorts, due to the purity and innocence associated with their age, are allowed into the most confidential pastimes of Rādhā and Krishna. This is the kind of rarefied information about the spiritual world that one finds in the Vaishnava tradition.

Among all the *mañjarīs*, Śrī Rūpa is the leader, and, at least according to the Gauḍīya Sampradāya, one must follow him/her in both identities as Rūpa Gosvāmī and as *mañjarī* par excellence to achieve the pinnacle of spiritual perfection. In other words, one must follow him both as Rūpa Gosvāmī and Rūpa Mañjarī. This goes back to a fundamental teaching of the tradition found in *Bhakti-rasāmrta-sindhu* (1.2.295) and elsewhere stating that practitioners must, as a matter of course, "follow in the footsteps of those who reside in Vraja, engaging both their practitioner body (*sādhaka-rūpeṇa*) and their spiritual body (*siddha-rūpeṇa*)."

The next question, then, is this: Who are the inhabitants

of Vraja? Without doubt, Nanda, Yaśodā, Rādhikā, and so on—the eternal associates of Krishna—are inhabitants of Vraja, and they are prominent personalities in Krishna's celestial kingdom. But "inhabitants of Vraja" would also include the great souls who reside on the earthly plane, in terrestrial Vraja, i.e., Śrī Rūpa Gosvāmī, Sanātana Gosvāmī, and others. In light of this notion, and to address Śrī Rūpa's statement about following the inhabitants of Vraja *in both practitioner and perfected bodies*, Jīva Gosvāmī and Viśvanātha Chakravartī offer the following explanation—and this is critical for the practice of Rūpānuga Vaishnavism:

> Mental performance with the *siddha-rūpa* [perfected body] is to be done in a manner that follows Śrī Rādhā, Lalitā, Viśākhā, Śrī Rūpa Mañjarī and other *gopīs*. But physical performance, with the *sādhaka-rūpa* [practitioner body], is to be done in a manner that follows Śrī Rūpa, Sanātana, and the other Vrindāvan Gosvāmīs.[3]

Kavirāja Gosvāmī elaborates: "There are both external and internal methods for pursuing the path of Rāgānuga-bhakti. Even when one is self-realized, with one's external body (*sādhaka-dehe*) one follows all scriptural injunctions, especially hearing and chanting. But within one's mind, using one's eternal body (*siddhā-deha*), one serves Krishna in Vrindavan, all day and all night."[4] This is the advanced stage known as *rāgānuga-sādhana*, a form of practice wherein one follows the inhabitants of the spiritual world, at least as a meditative state.

Rāgānuga (not to be confused with Rūpānuga) chiefly involves inner mediation and developing a spiritual identity from within, but the practitioner must cultivate *bhakti* from without as well, adhering to the externals as strictly as the Six Gosvāmīs of Vrindavan. That to say, as taught in ISKCON today, one must scrupulously follow Rūpa Gosvāmī to the best of one's ability, and when one is spiritually advanced, graduating to Rāgānuga-bhakti, one can also inwardly follow the example and moods of Rūpa Mañjarī. It should be understood, parenthetically, that following Rūpa Mañjarī does not necessarily mean *mādhurya-bhāva* as such, although for Gauḍīyas this is the predominant relationship one would have with Krishna.[5]

"Krishna has many types of devotees," says the *Caitanya-caritāmṛta* (Madhya 22.161), "some are servants, some are friends, some are parents, and some are conjugal lovers. Devotees who are situated in one of these attitudes of spontaneous love according to their choice are considered to be on the path of spontaneous loving service (*rāga-mārga*)." Rāgānuga-sādhana, in actuality, points each devotee in his/her own direction, wherein they discover their individual eternal identity in one of the primary *rasas* mentioned above and reach perfection accordingly.

In either case—whether one is in *mādhurya-rasa* or in one of the other relationships—this is an advanced stage of *sādhana*, and one should never imitate advanced practitioners but only allow oneself to gradually progress under the direction of a bona fide spiritual master. In this regard, the tradition emphasizes the distinction between merely "imitating" (*anukāra*) and "following in the footsteps" (*anusāra*). Imitation is often associated with Prākṛta-sahajiyās, a disparate group of practitioners who are said to have taken the tradition cheaply and have consequently been labeled as "Imitationists."

As Śrīla Prabhupāda says, "Don't imitate but try to follow. *Anusaraṇa. Anukaraṇa* is not good. *Anukaraṇa* means false imitation. That is called *anukaraṇa*. And *anusaraṇa* means to follow. Try to follow as far as possible."

Thus, with the background knowledge that one should follow instead of imitate, the example of Rūpa Gosvāmī stands supreme, and, as one advances, one is also called upon to follow Rūpa Mañjarī. But before one can attempt the latter, i.e., following Rūpa Mañjarī, one would do well to excel in the former, following Rūpa Gosvāmī as a dedicated practitioner. Indeed, just as following Rūpa Mañjarī means adhering to one's own *rasa* and not necessarily being in *mādhurya-bhāva*, following Rūpa Gosvāmī does not necessarily mean being a theologian and a renunciant. One can be a simple devotee, even a householder, perhaps, and still follow Śrī Rūpa in terms of his single-minded devotion.

The main thing, especially in the beginning stages, is to follow the rules and regulations of Bhakti-yoga. Therefore, Jīva Gosvāmī writes in *Bhakti-sandarbha*, Anuccheda 275.3: "If one's heart has become pure by surrender, and never abandons hearing and singing the names, forms, attributes and pastimes of the Lord, one can perform *smaraṇam*, or divine remembrance." The simple practices of hearing and chanting are emphasized, because, when properly executed, they can lead to *smaraṇam*, deep meditation and remembrance of Krishna's pastimes, which are the main practice of Rāgānuga-bhakti.

Lalitā Devī and Rūpa Mañjarī

To fully understand Śrī Rūpa, one must have some preliminary understanding of Lalitā Devī, who is a direct expansion and assistant to Śrī Rādhā, Lord Krishna's female counterpart. Rūpa Mañjarī is the chief assistant of this assistant, and together they serve the feminine feature of God, Rādhikā.

We know Lalitā Devī's narrative through Rūpa Gosvāmī and the other Gauḍīya patriarchs. She is one of the principal eight *gopīs* in Vrindavan, we are told, and is often described as "playful and charming," which is a literal translation of her name. Lalitā is the leader of all the *sakhīs* of Rādhikā, and no other friend of Rādhikā is equal to her (*Manaḥ-śikṣā,* verse 9). She is very strict about the service of Rādhā and Krishna, unable to tolerate even the slightest compromise in Their service. In this sense, she is a perfectionist, even hot-tempered. Indeed, sometimes she even takes a position of telling Them what to do, so invested is she in Their service, and so trusted that They sometimes allow her to take the upper hand. However, it is described that she is also merciful to sincere seekers who are junior to her, helping them in their service to Rādhā and Krishna. She brings practitioner devotees to the feet of Rādhikā, allowing them to enter the confidential service of the spiritual world.

The Gosvāmīs are fond of singing her glories and describe her throughout their literature. For example, Rūpa Gosvāmī composed a poem in her honor, "Śrī-Śrī Lalitāṣṭakam," which lovingly and descriptively elucidates her mood of service. His masterwork *Haṁsadūta* ("The Swan Messenger"), too, tells how Lalitā, the confidante of Rādhā, sends a messenger in the form of a swan to Krishna in Dvārakā, to assuage the pain of Their separation. Throughout *Ujjvala-nīlamaṇi*, Śrī Rūpa emphasizes the preeminent position of Lalitā, who he sees as nondifferent from Rādhā (calling her, "Anurādhā"). And he says at the end of Chapter Three: "The *gopīs* whose names are listed here, beginning with Rādhā, proceeding through Viśakhā, Lalitā, Padmā, Śaibya, and others, and ending with Kuṅkumā, are all leaders of groups of *gopīs*. Among them, the eight closest friends of Rādhārāṇī, who are headed by Lalitā, are especially fortunate." The most intimate lovers of Krishna, says Śrī Rūpa, are headed by Lalitā. In this way, various texts inform us of her supreme position as assistant servitor in the kingdom of God.

However, it should be noted that while Lalitā Devī is glorified and described in some detail, her highly confidential interaction with Rūpa Mañjarī is rarely mentioned, thus underlining its esoteric nature.[6]

Lalitā Devī incarnated as Svarūpa Dāmodara Gosvāmī in the pastimes of Śrī Chaitanya, where he acted as intimate confidante and personal secretary. This is confirmed by both Gopāla Guru Gosvāmī's *Śrī Gaura-Govinda-arcana-paddhati* (366) and Dhyānacandra Gosvāmī's *Śrī Gaura-Govinda-arcana-smaraṇa-paddhati* (197). It is interesting that, as Svarūpa Dāmodara, he was protective of Śrī Chaitanya just as, in the form of Lalitā, he is protective of Rādhā and Krishna. The mood is the same. As Kavirāja Gosvāmī writes in the *Caitanya-caritāmṛta* (Madhya 10): "Śrī Svarūpa Dāmodara was the personification of ecstatic love, fully cognizant of the highest transcendental mellows in relationship with Lord Krishna. He directly represented Śrī Gaurāṅga [Chaitanya] Mahāprabhu as His second expansion. In fact, no one could approach or present anything to Gaurāṅga Mahāprabhu without his sanction. If someone wrote a book or composed verses and songs and wanted to recite them before Śrī Chaitanya Mahāprabhu, Svarūpa Dāmodara would first examine them and then correctly present them. Only then would Śrī Chaitanya Mahāprabhu agree to listen."

Still, just as there is precious little on the confidential interaction of Lalitā Devī and Rūpa Mañjarī in the esoteric literature of the Gosvāmīs, so too is this the case with their Chaitanyaite counterparts as Svarūpa Dāmodara and Rūpa Gosvāmī—the two are rarely described in proximity, to underline the confidential nature of their interaction. In the latter case, however, the silence can also largely be traced to a simple geographical consideration: Svarūpa Dāmodara served mainly in Purī, while Śrī Rūpa was in Vrindavan. Nonetheless, one of the few times they are mentioned together is foundational in terms of Rūpānuga philosophy, and this occurred during one of Śrī Rūpa's visits to the land of Lord Jagannātha.

Intimate Revelation at Ratha-yātrā

Every summer, Śrī Caitanya's devotees would journey to Purī and attend the Ratha-yātrā festival, personally relishing the Lord's presence—both as Jagannātha and as the Golden Avatāra. On several occasions, while dancing and singing before the carts, Śrī Caitanya recited a particular verse that, although well known at the time, might have seemed out of context at Ratha-yātrā, or at least unusual, since it originated in literature outside the Gauḍīya community; it was not directly about Lord Krishna, or so it seemed. Only Svarūpa Dāmodara Gosvāmī knew the purpose behind the Lord's recitation. All others were baffled. The verse may be rendered as follows:

> That very personality who stole my youth is now again my master. These are the same moonlit nights of the month of Caitra. The same fragrance of *mālatī* flowers is there, and the same sweet breezes are blowing from the *kadamba* forest. In our intimate relationship, I am also the same lover, yet still my mind is not happy here. I am eager to go back to that place on the bank of the Revā under the Vetasī tree. That is my desire."[7]

The stanza actually has a long history. It is initially attributed to Śīlā Bhaṭṭārikā, a little known Sanskrit poetess from 9th-century India, but it became famous in Mammaṭa Bhaṭṭa's celebrated 11th-century text, *Kāvya-prakāśa*, a technical book on poetics and literary criticism. It was then repeated in Viśvanātha Kavirāja's popular *Sahitya-dārpaṇa*, a masterpiece on aesthetics compiled some three centuries later. The poem also found its way into numerous collections of subsequent Sanskrit poetry, a stray (*muktaka*) verse often cited without context. Finally, it comes to us through Rūpa Gosvāmī's *Padyāvali* (386), and is repeated in both Krishnadāsa Kavirāja Gosvāmī's *Caitanya-caritāmṛta* (Madhya 1.58, 13.121, Antya 1.78) and Jīva Gosvāmī's *Gopāla-campu* (Uttara-campu 36.122), where we are told that the verse was originally uttered by Śrīmatī Rādhārāṇī.[8]

Of course, the verse suggests connections to Krishna that a cultured audience would immediately recognize, especially when uttered by Mahāprabhu. The mood of longing and love-in-separation is characteristic of Gauḍīya theology, and reference to the *kadamba* tree (*Neolamarckia cadamba*) is commonly associated with Krishna throughout India, even today. But who is the beloved evoked in this verse? Is it Lord Jagannātha? And who is the woman, or the pining lover so feelingly brought forth by Mahāprabhu? According to the *Caitanya-caritāmṛta* (Antya 1.69), no one knew.

The inner mystery of this verse, it seems, was known only to Svarūpa Dāmodara, that is, until one particular day, sometime in the second decade of the 16th century, Rūpa Gosvāmī arrived in Purī and attended the festival. Śrī Rūpa showed awareness of Mahāprabhu's intent by composing a parallel verse to bring out its inner meaning:

> "My dear friend," says Śrīmatī Rādhārāṇī, "now I have met My very old and dear friend Krishna on this field of Kurukṣetra. I am the same Rādhārāṇī, and now We are meeting together. It is very pleasant, but I would still like to go to the bank of the Kālindī River beneath the trees of the forest there. I wish to hear the vibration of His sweet flute playing the fifth note within that forest of Vrindavan." (Antya 1.79)[9]

Śrī Rūpa's verse, to be clear, is a *reenactment* and development of *Bhāgavata Purāṇa* 10.82, with additional Gauḍīya nuance. The Bhāgavata discusses Krishna's reunion with Śrī Rādhā and the *gopīs* at Kurukṣetra, but only briefly. Śrī Rūpa ingeniously makes use of this to explain the verse chanted by Śrī Chaitanya, thus revealing His inner intent. According to Rūpa, the personality who is the object of love in the original verse is now revealed to be Krishna, and the woman who speaks the verse, according to Rūpa, is Śrī Rādhā. She is happy to be re-united with Her beloved, but that happiness is minimized because of the specifics of Kurukṣetra, i.e., Krishna is in the mood of a king with royal retinue as opposed to the sweet, endearing cowherd She once knew. Thus, Rūpa's verse tells us that Śrī Rādhā longs to see Krishna in the more intimate, rustic, down-to-earth setting of Vraja, which Rūpa cleverly indicates by mentioning the Kālindī River, found only in Vrindavan. Additionally, Rūpa's reference to the "fifth note" of Krishna's flute further highlights Rādhā's desire for returning Him to Vraja: In Bharata's *Nātya-śāstra*, we learn that the seven musical notes of Indian classical music, *Sa, Ri, Ga, Ma, Pa, Dha,* and *Ni*, are associated with the eight *rasas*, and that the fifth note, *Pa,* is representative of *mādhurya-rasa*.[10]

Ravīndra Svarūpa Dāsa, in an article on Śrī Chaitanya at Ratha-yātrā, elaborates on the principle of love-in-separation, and in so doing sheds further light on Śrī Rūpa's verse:

> The Ratha-yatra festival brought these feelings [of love-in-separation] to their highest pitch. For the festival commemorates the single occasion on which Srimati Radharani again met Krishna. For many years Krishna had ruled as King of Dvaraka exhibiting in the splendor of His capital, the power of His army, the brilliance of His court, and the beauty and refinement of His queens all the opulence of Godhead.
>
> Then, on the occasion of a solar eclipse, Krishna left Dvaraka. Riding with Balarama and Subhadra at the head of endless columns of chariots, elephants, and palanquins, Krishna led His whole royal dynasty to a holy pilgrimage site called Kurukshetra. From all directions, many other royal households converged in state

upon the place of pilgrimage. And finally, a small plodding caravan of bullock carts carried all the residents of the obscure cowherd village of Vrindavan, hoping to see their Krishna, who had left them long ago.

And so Srimati Radharani came once more to behold the lover of Her youth. She first saw Him surrounded by His courtiers, riding in regal splendor. Later, They met in a secluded place. Now, after so many endless years apart. She was together again with the same Krishna of long ago. Her ecstasy was boundless. Yet, strange to say, the joy of meeting did not vanquish the feelings of separation that had possessed Her for years. On the contrary, those feelings became even more intense, even though Krishna—the same Krishna as before—was there. For now He was in royal garb, and all around Them were warriors and their horses, elephants, and the rattling of their chariots.

As She looked at Krishna, She longed to see Him as the simple cowherd boy, carrying His flute, decorated with the forest flowers of Vrindavan. She yearned to see Him in the old places—by the bank of the river there, under the tree where They used to meet. Thus Srimati Radharani merged into the most powerful of ecstatic emotions, paradoxically uniting the ecstasy of union with the ecstasy of separation; the two were felt simultaneously, and they perpetually intensified each other. So although Her joy at having Krishna again knew no bounds, Her heart was breaking in separation. She yearned to take Krishna back to Vrindavan.

Although Srimati Radharani appeared to be suffering in separation, in truth She was neither suffering nor separated from Krishna. In the spiritual realm there is no suffering, for all emotions are varieties of ecstasy. Nor is there any separation as in this world.

> In Her transcendental separation, Radharani was more intimately united with Krishna than ever. In Her transcendental grief, She was actually experiencing the highest bliss.
>
> Separation intensifies love—that is true even in this world. Separate a mother from her child, and see how her material affection blazes up. Pure devotees desire only to increase their love for Krishna, and Krishna satisfies their desire by arranging for them to love Him with strong feelings of separation. Here love of God reaches its peak, and Sri Chaitanya, as the embodiment of Radharani's love, spent His days and nights consumed by this highest and most intense mode of devotional feelings.[11]

These truths are at the heart of Gauḍīya Vaishnava mysticism. But the story of Śrī Rūpa's verse goes on. *Caitanya-caritāmṛta* (Antya 1) informs us that after writing it on a palm leaf, he placed it in the thatched roof of Haridāsa Ṭhākura's hut, where he was staying while in Purī, and went to bathe in the sea. Meanwhile, Śrī Chaitanya discovered the leaf and saw the verse. After reading it, He felt His own ecstatic love reach a new pitch, and just at that moment, Rūpa Gosvāmī returned, having completed his morning bath. Seeing the Lord and offering Him respects, Śrī Rūpa approached Him, and the two of them shared great affection. "My heart is very confidential," said Śrī Chaitanya. "How did you so clearly understand My mind in this way?" After saying this, He firmly embraced Rūpa Gosvāmī with great love.

Thereafter, Śrī Chaitanya took the verse and showed it to Svarūpa Dāmodara, asking him to look it over carefully. The Lord then asked Svarūpa the same question: "How could Rūpa Gosvāmī have understood My heart so well?"

To this, Svarūpa Dāmodara replied, "You must have already bestowed Your causeless mercy upon him. Otherwise, he would not have been able to understand its meaning." Śrī Chaitanya replied, "Yes, I met Rūpa Gosvāmī at Prayāga, and because of his qualification, I naturally bestowed My mercy upon him (*kṛpā ta' ha-ila*) along with My transcendental potency (*śakti sañcāri*). Accordingly, I now ask you, Svarūpa Dāmodara, to give him further instructions. In particular, instruct him in transcendental mellows (*rasera viśeṣa*)." Svarūpa Dāmodara agreed to do so, and thus the transcendental relationship between Svarūpa Dāmodara and Rūpa Gosvāmī—Lalitā and Rūpa Mañjarī—unfolds for all who have the eyes to see it.

Conclusion

By Mahāprabhu's infinite mercy, Rūpa Gosvāmī was able to understand the Lord's inner emotional state—he was able to know the heart of God. And for all who follow in the line of Śrī Rūpa, a similar fate awaits.

To reiterate: On a preliminary level, following Śrī Rūpa means, first of all, becoming a dedicated servant of Guru and Krishna, as Śrī Rūpa was, desiring no identity outside of that. As leader of the *mañjarīs*, Śrī Rupa shows not how to be a direct servant of Rādhā and Krishna, but rather the glory of being a servant of the servant, under Lalitā Devī. The importance of this once-removed devotional position is suggested in Mahāprabhu's famous verse:

nāhaṁ vipro na ca nara-patir nāpi vaiśyo na śūdro
nāhaṁ varṇī na ca gṛha-patir no vanastho yatir vā

> *kintu prodyan-nikhila-paramānanda-pūrnāmṛtābdher*
> *gopī-bhartuḥ pada-kamalayor dāsa-dāsānudāsaḥ*
>
> "I am not a *brāhmaṇa*, a *kṣatriya*, a *vaiśya* or a *śūdra*. Nor am I a *brahmacārī*, a *gṛhastha*, a *vānaprastha* or a *sannyāsī*. I identify Myself only as the servant of the servant of the servant of the lotus feet of Lord Śrī Krishna, the maintainer of the *gopīs*. He is like an ocean of nectar, and He is the cause of universal transcendental bliss. He is always existing with brilliance." (quoted in *Caitanya-caritāmṛta*, 2.13.80, originally in *Padyāvalī*, 74)

In other words, *bhakti*, properly performed, will lead one away from illusory, temporary identification associated with the material body—whether involving social status or even spiritual station in life—and establish one in the Self, whereby one gradually begins to recognize who one is in the spiritual world. While the above verse focuses on *gopī-bhāva*, Śrī Chaitanya's preferred emotion, it should be noted, again, that there are five possible relationships with which one might interact with Krishna, and Rūpānuga Vaishnavism allows this relationship, whatever it may be, to gradually unfold.[12]

To conclude: The phenomenon of Śrī Rūpa knowing Mahāprabhu's heart has a parallel in the pastimes of His Divine Grace A. C. Bhaktivedānta Swami Prabhupāda (1896–1977), the modern-day Rūpānuga par excellence.

In 1936, Prabhupāda wrote a Vyāsa-pūjā offering to his spiritual master, Śrīla Bhaktisiddhānta Sarasvatī Ṭhākura, a poem in which one particular couplet so pleased the Ṭhākura that when guests would come, he would often show it to them, proud of his disciple's insight. Śrīla Bhaktisiddhānta took it as an indication of how well Prabhupāda, then known as Abhay Babu, knew his mind, and Prabhupada was delighted, of course, that the verse so pleased his spiritual master. "One of [Prabhupāda's] Godbrothers" wrote Satsvarūpa Dāsa Goswāmī, "compared this verse by [Prabhupāda] to a verse in which Rūpa Gosvāmī had expressed the inner thinking of Chaitanya Mahāprabhu and had thus moved Him to ecstasy."[13] This refers to the verse discussed in the present article.

Indeed, Prabhupāda himself confirmed the correlation, and also his Guru's pleasure with his own humble endeavor: "We had the opportunity to receive a similar blessing from Śrīla Bhaktisiddhānta Sarasvatī Gosvāmī when we presented an essay at his birthday ceremony. He was so pleased with that essay that he used to call some of his confidential devotees and show it to them. How could we have understood the intentions of Śrīla [Bhaktisiddhānta Sarasvatī] Prabhupāda? (2.1.71, purport)

As Rūpa Gosvāmī was able to understand Śrī Chaitanya Mahāprabhu's mind, so Śrīla Prabhupāda was able to understand Rūpa Gosvāmī's mind and was thus empowered to fulfill his mission by spreading it throughout the world. "Śrīla Rūpa Gosvāmī and Sanātana Gosvāmī had no fixed residence," writes Śrīla Prabhupāda. "They stayed beneath a tree for one day only and wrote huge volumes of transcendental literature. They not only wrote books but chanted, danced, discussed Krishna and remembered Śrī Chaitanya Mahāprabhu's pastimes. Thus they executed devotional service. In Vrindavan, there are *prākṛta-sahajiyās* who say that writing books or even touching books is taboo. For them, devotional service means being relieved from these activities. Whenever they are asked to hear a recitation of Vedic literature, they refuse, saying, 'What business do we have reading or hearing transcendental literatures? They are meant for neophytes.' They pose themselves as too elevated to exert energy for reading, writing and hearing.

"However," Prabhupāda continues "pure devotees under the guidance of Śrīla Rūpa Gosvāmī reject this *sahajiyā* philosophy. It is certainly not good to write literature for money or reputation, but to write books and publish them for the enlightenment of the general populace is real service to the Lord. That was Śrīla Bhaktisiddhānta Sarasvatī's opinion, and he specifically told his disciples to write books. He actually preferred to publish books rather than establish temples. Temple construction is meant for the general populace and neophyte devotees, but the business of advanced and empowered devotees is to write books, publish them and distribute them widely. According to Śrīla Bhaktisiddhānta Sarasvatī Ṭhākura, distributing literature is like playing on a great *mṛdaṅga*. Consequently we always request members of the International Society for Krishna Consciousness to publish as many books as possible and distribute them widely throughout the world. By thus following in the footsteps of Śrīla Rūpa Gosvāmī, one can become a *rūpānuga* devotee." (*Caitanya-caritāmṛta,* 2.19.132, purport)

Prabhupāda further writes, "In the Ādi Purāṇa the Supreme Personality of Godhead Himself says: 'Lord Brahmā, Lord Śiva, the goddess of fortune and even My own self are not as dear to Me as the *gopīs*.' Of all the *gopīs*, Śrīmatī Rādhārāṇī is the topmost. Rūpa Gosvāmī and Sanātana Gosvāmī are the most exalted servitors of Śrīmatī

Rādhārāṇī and Lord Śrī Caitanya Mahāprabhu. Those who adhere to their service are known as *rūpānuga* devotees." (2.8.246, purport)

These two comments, taken together, reveal what a Rūpānuga Vaishnava truly is. First and foremost, it means following in the footsteps of Rūpa Gosvāmī, which essentially means embracing the path of *bhakti* in one's own life and distributing it to others. However, if one does this to perfection, one will also follow Śrī Rūpa internally, which implies a sophisticated practice of meditation on one's spiritual form in service to Śrīmatī Rādhikā, regardless of one's specific relationship. But make no mistake, this is a very advanced practice, and it must be precipitated by perfectly following the example of Rūpa Gosvāmī as manifested some 500 years ago. Nonetheless, it is this multifaceted process of self-realization, involving one's outer and inner world, that is at the heart of true Rūpānuga Vaishnavism.

Endnotes

1. *Rasa* theory is an ancient system of Indian aesthetics attempting to describe any visual, literary, or musical work that evokes an ineffable emotion or feeling in the reader or audience. It is originally associated with Bharata's *Nāṭya Śāstra*, and was later developed by Abhinavagupta (c. 950–1016 CE) and King Bhoja (circa, 11th century), among others, but its full theological dimensions were not explicated until the work of Śrīla Rūpa Gosvāmī.

2. There are other traditional texts (besides the *Gaura-gaṇoddeśa-dīpikā*) that affirm the identification of Rūpa Gosvāmī with Rūpa Mañjarī. For example, Dhyānacandra Gosvāmī's *Śrī Gaura-Govindārcana-Smaraṇa-Paddhatiḥ* (verses 294-297) would be considered an early source as well. Viśvanātha Cakravartī's *Gaura-gaṇa-svarūpa-tattva-candrikā*, verse 80, also makes the identification, but this is a somewhat later text.

3. See the specific verses in Viśvanātha Chakravartī Ṭhākura, *Rāga Vartma Candrikā: A Moonbeam to Illuminate the Path of Spontaneous Devotion,* trans., Bhaktivedanta Narayana Maharaja (Mathura: Gaudiya Vedanta Publications, 2001), pp. 42-51. Also, Viśvanātha Chakravartī Ṭhākura, *Śrī Bhakti-rasāmṛta-sindhu-bindu: A Drop of the Nectarine Ocean of Bhakti-rasa,* trans., with commentary by Bhaktivedanta Narayana Maharaja (Mathura: Gaudiya Vedanta Publications, 1996), pp. 121-122.

4. See *Caitanya-caritāmṛta,* Madhya 22.156-157 (*bāhya, antara--ihāra dui ta' sādhana'bāhye' sādhaka-dehe kare śravaṇa-kīrtana'mane' nija-siddha-deha kariyā bhāvanarātri-dine kare vraje kṛṣṇera sevana*).

5. Of course, in a very technical sense, being a follower of Rūpa Mañjarī *does* necessitate embracing *mādhurya-bhāva* as a *mañjarī.* As stated, in Vraja-bhakti, one aspires for any of the four main *rasas,* i.e., *dāsya, sakhya, vātsalya,* or *mādhurya.* Pursuing the first three of these *rasas,* one would follow the leader of a group who is accomplished in those relationships, e.g., Raktak (*dāsya*), Subala (*sakhya*), and so on. If one is not in *mādhurya-rasa,* one would not specifically follow Rūpa Mañjarī as such. But in this article I am speaking in a more generic sense: that following Rūpa Mañjarī simply means to follow Rāga-marga. Rūpa Mañjarī is highlighted because in Gauḍīya Vaishnavism her *ānugatya* is the highest ideal.

Ultimately, there are both exoteric and esoteric dimensions of what it means to be a Rūpānuga. Certainly, the most immediate dimension is to be a follower of Rūpa Gosvāmī, heeding the practices and conclusions epitomized in his Gosvāmī literature. But there are elements of his literature that point to the exclusivity of Rādhā-dāsyam, and thus, while acknowledging exceptions whereby adherents of the lineage may embody other *rasas,* which is certainly acceptable, the emphasis is clearly on *mādhurya* in the mood of Rūpa Mañjarī. Indeed, Bhaktivinoda Ṭhākura writes in his *Śrī Rūpānuga-bhajana-darpaṇa* (Song 8, verse 3), "Those who are devoted to *bhajana* that follows in the footsteps of Śrī Rūpa become situated *only* in *mādhurya-rasa.*" (*śrī rūpera anugata, bhajane je haya rata, sthiti tāra kevale mādhure*) The word *kevale* means "only" or "exclusively." He further says (in Song 14, verse 4), "The Rūpānugas know no other treasure than Śrī Rādhikā's divine lotus feet." (*śrī-rūpānuga jana, śrī rādhikā-śrī-caraṇa, binā nāhi jāne anya dhāna*). This is the emphasis of the Gauḍīya Sampradāya, even if it is willing to acknowledge the other *rasas*.

Still, in the end, we must accommodate a three-tiered definition of Rūpānuga: (1) Follower of Rūpa Gosvāmī; (2) follower of both Rūpa Gosvāmī and Rūpa Mañjarī, specifically according to her own *bhāva* in *mādhurya-rasa*; and finally, (3) follower of both Rūpa Gosvāmī and Rūpa Mañjarī, though not necessarily with regard to *mañjarī-bhāva* but according to one's own *rāga* (passion), which can manifest in any of the established relationships of the spiritual world.

6. One of the few such instances occurs in Krishnadāsa Kavirāja Gosvāmī's *Govinda-līlāmrta*, Chapter 10. A short passage tells us of an incident wherein Krishna's flute is playfully passed around from one *gopī* to another and ends up in Rūpa Mañjarī's possession. When Krishna approached her to get His flute back, she passes it to Lalitā, her eternal protector. In this way, the *gopīs* enjoyed playful pastimes with Krishna.

7. *yaḥ kaumāra-haraḥ sa eva hi varas tā eva caitra-kṣapās/ te con-mīlita-mālatī-surabhayaḥ prauḍhāḥ kadambānilāḥ// sā caivāsmi tathāpi tatra surata-vyāpāra-līlā-vidhau/ revā-rodhasi vetasī-taru-tale cetaḥ samutkaṇṭhate//*

8. Special thanks to Brijbasi Dāsa, Prem Prayojan Dāsa, David Buchta, Simon Haas, Bhanu Swami, and Kiyokazu Okita for their assistance in uncovering the history of this verse and for their translation and research work in general. They were forthcoming and accommodating in their scholarly correspondence, making this article more thorough. Also see Okita's article from 2014, "Devotion and Poetry in Early Modern South Asia: A Gauḍīya Vaiṣṇava Interpretation of a Muktaka Verse Attributed to Śīlābhaṭṭārikā" *Journal of Indological Studies*, 24, 187-201.

9. *priyaḥ so 'yaṁ kṛṣṇaḥ saha-cari kuru-kṣetra-militas/ tathāhaṁ sā rādhā tad idam ubhayoḥ saṅgama-sukham// tathāpy antaḥ-khelan-madhura-muralī-pañcama-juṣe/ mano me kālindī-pulina-vipināya spṛhayati//* Rūpa Gosvāmī included this important stanza in his book *Padyāvalī* (387) as a penultimate verse.

10. I am indebted to Kiyokazu Okita for the information in this paragraph. See especially "Devotion and Poetry in Early Modern South

Asia: A Gauḍīya Vaiṣṇava Interpretation of a Muktaka Verse Attributed to Śīlābhaṭṭārikā," *ibid.* The eight *rasas* according to *Nāṭya-Śāstra*: *Śriṅgāra* or *mādhurya* (erotic), *hāsya* (comic), *karuṇā* (compassion), *raudra* (terror), *vīra* (heroic), *bhayānaka* (fear), *bibhatsā* (disgust), and *adbhuta* (wonder). *Nāṭya-Śāstra* 19.38-40 correlates the eight *rasas* with the seven individual notes of the musical scale (Sa, Ri, Ga, Ma, Pa, Dha, Ni) in the following order: erotic – Pa (fifth), comic – Ma (fourth), compassion – Ga (third) and Ni (seventh), disgust and fear – Dha (sixth), heroic, terror, and wonder – Sa (tonic) and Ri (second). In other words, several of the *rasas* are doubled up, thus accounting for seven notes correlating with eight *rasas*: *bhayānaka* (fear) and *bibhatsā* (disgust) are represented by Dha; *karuṇā* (compassion) doubles as Ga and Ni, and the three *rasas* of *raudra* (terror), *vīra* (heroic) and *adbhuta* (wonder) represent both Sa and Re. See Guy L. Beck, "Bhakti Sangit: The Art of Music in Vaishnava Tradition," *Journal of Vaishnava Studies*, 21.2, Spring 2013, 149-150.

11. See Ravīndra Svarūpa Dāsa, "Lord Chaitanya at Ratha-yātrā" (http://www.krishna.com/lord-chaitanya-ratha-yatra).

12. Technically speaking, of course, *śānta-rasa* is not usually an option for those on the path of Rāgānuga-bhakti, since there is no passionate path (*rāga*) to follow (*anuga*). In *Bhakti-rasāmṛta-sindhu*, Rūpa Gosvāmī describes *śānta-rasa* mostly in terms of impersonal realization or Vaikuṇṭha *rasas*. He does not specify any Vraja *rasas* as *śānta*, although Śrīla Prabhupāda and Śrīla Bhaktisiddhānta Sarasvatī sometimes did. They both identified the cows, trees, animals, etc., as being in *śānta-rasa*.

13. Satsvarūpa Dāsa Gosvāmī, *"A Lifetime in Preparation," Śrīla Prabhupāda-līlāmṛta*, Vol. 1 (Los Angeles: Bhaktivedanta Book Trust, 1980), 86.

Eighteen

Prema-Vilāsa-Vivarta-Mūrti: Śrī Chaitanya as the Embodiment of the Highest Love

"Those who say 'I love you' know nothing about *prema*, for in *prema* there is no other."

— Swami B.V. Tripurari[1]

Introduction

THE PRIMACY OF LOVE is appreciated by many, both as a concept and as a way of life. Most people, in fact, would say that it is love, first and foremost, that gives life meaning. This same truth is fundamental to the world's major world religions, regardless of the particular tradition. For example, the Bible says, "Beloved, let us love one another, for love is from God, and whoever loves has been born of God and knows God. Anyone who does not love does not know God, because God is love." (See 1 John 4:7-8) Jesus goes further, quoting the tradition of Leviticus: "You must love the Lord your God with all your heart, all your soul, and all your mind.' This is the first and greatest commandment. A second is equally important: 'Love your neighbor as you love yourself.'" (See Matthew 22:37-39)

Yet what, exactly, is meant by love?[2] Religious traditions often acknowledge that love exists with both a lowercase "l" and a capital "L," referring to our relationships with man and God, respectively. And both are important, the Vaishnava sages tell us, even if love of God is considered particularly indispensable. A traditional analogy might serve to clarify: God is like the root of the tree of life, while all other living beings are compared to twigs and branches. If we water any of the tree's appendages separately, the tree will quickly die, but if we water her roots, perhaps spraying the twigs and branches as well, life-giving sustenance is enjoyed by all.

Regarding love of both man and God, there is also a second category of lower and upper: One can love individual beings of this world with selfish motivation, merely trying to satisfy personal urges, or one can love more fully, selflessly, more in tune with the beloved's desires than one's own, though such love is said to be rare. Similarly, in terms of love of God, one can love God minimally, with one's own wants and desires taking a prominent role, or one can love "with heart, mind, and soul," considering God before oneself.

Gauḍīya Vaishnavism teaches adherents how to love in this more holistic way, both in interpersonal relationships and in terms of loving the Supreme. Indeed, it teaches how to be a *sāragrāhin*, that is, one who reaches for the essence, looking into the heart of love, as opposed to a *bhāravāhin*, wherein one settles for superficials, allowing surface affections to predominate.

All of this may serve as background to the kind of love witnessed in the person and teachings of Śrī Chaitanya Mahāprabhu (1486–1534), seen by his followers as Krishna himself in the mood of his divine counterpart, Rādhā. Chaitanya promulgated a love that is "unmotivated and uninterrupted," and thus completely pure. (See *Śrīmad-Bhāgavatam* 1.2.6-7) Gauḍīya tradition teaches that he brought to this world an ultimate form of love (*prema*) illuminated as a detailed science (*tattva*), with methodical approach and procedure (*sādhana*), and concrete, analytical ways of gauging progress and accomplishment (*pragati-māpinī viśleṣaṇātmaka-praṇāli*).

Although Śrī Chaitanya left only eight devotional verses in writing, he instructed his chief followers to compile literature that would thoroughly explain the Vaishnava tradition, with special attention to the philosophy and theology of love. Śrī Rūpa Gosvāmī's *Bhakti-rasāmṛta-sindhu* and its appended text *Ujjvala-nīlamaṇi*, for example, stand supreme in this realm of devotional writing, detailing specifics of divine love as never before. The *Bhakti-rasāmṛta-sindhu* (1.3.1) compares love of God to the rays of the sun, whose warmth softens the devotee's heart without limit. Such a devotional heart, the tradition teaches, lies far beyond the best that this world has to offer. Indeed, it is a transcendental phenomenon, understood only by those who receive Krishna's grace.

In Śrī Rūpa's work, he articulates both a vocabulary and method for understanding divine love in all its forms. For example, he outlines bhakti-rasa theory, through which his readers can explore the various kinds of relationships one may have with God (*mukhya-bhakti-rasa-nirūpaṇa*).[3] Such relationships manifest in either neutrality (*śānta-rasa*); the mood of a loving servant (*dāsya-rasa*); fraternity (*sakhya-rasa*); parenthood or a similar, nurturing love (*vātsalya-rasa*); and, finally, conjugal affection (*mādhurya-rasa*), according to one's interaction with Krishna in the spiritual realm.[4] It is *mādhurya*, the last and highest form of love, that concerns us here, with its numerous levels of intimacy leading to a stage called *prema-vilāsa-vivarta*, which we will define below.

It should be noted, too, that *mādhurya* accommodates the qualities of all the rest. To clarify, *Caitanya-caritāmṛta* (Madhya 8.86) tells us: "As the qualities increase, so the taste also increases in each and every relationship. Therefore, the qualities found in *śānta-rasa, dāsya-rasa, sakhya-rasa* and *vātsalya-rasa* are all manifested in conjugal love (*mādhurya-rasa*)." In the words of Tony K. Stewart: "While *dāsya* may include elements of *śānta, sakhya* will embrace both, and *vātsalya* all four. Only *śṛṅgāra* [*mādhurya*] can range through the full permutation of forms, for lovers variously experience the feelings of friendship, of being a parent or a child, of being a servant, and even being overawed by the mate."[5] In fact, a brief look at the lexicon found in Rūpa Gosvāmī's *Ujjvala-nīlamaṇi* (chapters 14 and 15) should lay bare the depth and profundity of Śrī Chaitanya's approach to love of God. It will show how such love develops in the heart of the spiritual adept—particularly in the hearts of Rādhā and the *gopīs*, its ultimate exemplars.

Although exploring the minutiae of this love may seem a circuitous way to discuss the central theme of our essay, *prema-vilāsa-vivarta*—particularly in relation to Śrī Chaitanya—it will later be seen that perusing this knowledge can heighten one's understanding and appreciation of this love as markedly distinct from love in the material sphere. For this reason, among others, Gauḍīya *ācāryas* enriched their literature with these elaborate details to facilitate deeper entry into the topic at hand.

Part I: Divine Love in the Gauḍīya Tradition

We begin with the Sanskrit *rati*, which means "attraction" or "pleasure," but which culminates in the concept of the purest love. "When *rati* is firm, it becomes *prema*," says Śrī Rūpa in his *Ujjvala-nīlamaṇi* (UN). "This then morphs into *sneha*, followed by *māna, praṇaya, rāga, anurāga*, and *mahābhāva*." (UN 14.59)

He defines these terms at length.

In summary, *sneha* is fully developed *prema*, when love is at its peak—it is a level of love that fully illuminates its central object of adoration, melting the hearts of both lover and beloved. (UN 14.79)

But this is just the beginning. Recognizing the intricacies of love—including the apparent reverses that ultimately deepen our emotional response—the tradition tells us that *māna*, or righteous indignation, comes next. When overcome by feelings of *māna*, one may exhibit a form of non-cooperation (*vāmyam*), even feigning disinterest, just to get the beloved's attention; by doing this, one increases the thrill of the exchange. (UN 14.96)

Through these methods, one gradually achieves *praṇaya*, the deepest of intimate feelings, unattainable through the kind of mutual respect and polite consideration one finds in more formal relationships. *Praṇaya* engenders a type of closeness known only by the most intimate of lovers, even if, externally, they might seem as if they are taking each other for granted. In fact, they simply feel that they are one and the same person, i.e., closer than humanly possible, and thus can take unspeakable liberties with each other. (UN 14.108)[6] As we will see, this has a certain resonance with the *prema-vilāsa-vivarta* concept, to be explained in due course.[7]

Praṇaya gives birth to *rāga*, the level of love where any tinge of discontent is eclipsed by inner happiness, creating a deep level of passion and leading to union. (UN 14.126) One becomes intensely determined or even "greedy" (*lobha*) to achieve the beloved, with a deep and insurmountable hankering for consummation. Such intensity leads to a type of ingenuity, in which one conceives ever-fresh ways of pleasing their beloved; at this point, one has reached *anurāga*. (UN 14.146) While in this state, one has an intense desire to be controlled by their lover, fearing their absence even while in their presence (*prema-vaicittya*); and, sometimes, the reverse is true: one sees them as present even during separation. (UN 14.149). Here too one finds intimations of *prema-vilāsa-vivarta*, even if one is still far away from that highest level.

As our mood deepens, we approach the dawn of the highest love, described as *bhāva* and *mahābhāva*. To begin, *bhāva* is achieved when *anurāga* reaches its most mature state, which is difficult for the body to contain. That is, one is forced to exhibit *sāttvika-bhāvas*, or uncontrollable, overt bodily symptoms of love, such as profuse weeping or cold shivers. (UN 14.154)[8]

Mahābhāva, which comes next, is described as being the essence of love's nectar, totally absorbing the mind and soul, with its "victims" unable to focus on anything else. In its higher stages, *prema-vilāsa-vivarta* begins to manifest. Indeed, *mahābhāva* appears in two forms: *rūḍha* and *adhirūḍha* (UN 14.157-158), and the distinction should be understood.

Briefly, *rūḍha mahābhāva* can be called love's high-point, which is free from any sense of awe and reverence and expectation of return. One simply wants to please the beloved. One's love becomes like a blazing, uncontrollable fire. If one finds that their desired object of affection is gone for even a zeptosecond, they become mad with the mood of separation. For example, the *gopīs* bemoaned the nature of the eye—which blinks—for this necessitates losing sight of Krishna, if even for a brief moment.[9]

As for *adhirūḍha mahābhāva*, it may be understood as an amplified version of *rūḍha-bhāva*, and it is only found in the hearts of the *gopīs*. (UN 14.170) Here there is inconceivable and simultaneous happiness and suffering caused by both union and separation, the merger of which is said to cause incomparable joy—with separation enhancing eventual union. (see UN 14.171, along with commentary of Viśvanātha Cakravartī) Indeed, this level of love is characterized by the feeling that each moment of being separated from the beloved is like an eternity, and each moment in his or her presence is conversely far too swift or short.

Adhirūḍha mahābhāva exists in two varieties: *modana* and *mādana*. (UN 14.172) Madness, indescribable bliss, and emotional trembling are the chief characteristics of both, catapulting one into the highest state of divine intoxication. (UN 14.173, with the commentary of Jīva Gosvāmī) The *modana* variety appears only among Rādhā's group of *gopīs*, as opposed to the other groups who express their love for Krishna in a more mild way. *Modana* is the ultimate expression of *hlādinī-śakti*, Krishna's internal energy. (UN 14.176) But it goes on from there.

Modana transforms into *mohana*, a yet higher stage, wherein one experiences intense moods of separation, intolerable for the soul. (UN 14.179) In such a state, Krishna's happiness becomes one's foremost concern, and to this end, his lover is willing to accept untold suffering for the sake of the Lord's pleasure. For such a *gopī*, *divyonmāda*, or divine madness, is never far away, often engulfing both lover and beloved in a river of ecstasy. (UN 14.181-183) Still greater is *mādana-bhāva*, also referred to as *mādanākhya-mahābhāva*. This is an experience that occurs at the time of perfect union, where love in separation finds its ultimate repose. Indeed, this highly esoteric dimension of love is associated only with Śrī Rādhā, who loves Krishna like no other.[10] It is from these higher platforms that we gain our first true glimpse of *prema-vilāsa-vivarta*.

The Vraja *gopīs,* being portions of Śrī Rādhā, are therefore portions of *mahābhāva*. Nevertheless, because they lack the essential characteristic called *mādana,* a quality found only in Rādhikā, they are never identified with *mahābhāva* in its fullness. It is Rādhā, and she alone, who is known as Mahābhāva-svarūpiṇī—the personification of the highest love. Indeed, rivers, streams, and ponds are bodies of water, yet they are distinct from the ocean, whose magnitude can effortlessly accommodate not only these tributary rivulets, but so much more. This analogy attempts to shed light on the *gopīs' mahābhāva* in relation to Rādhā's.

With these love-specific categories to inform our understanding, we may proceed to explore the subject at hand, which is exceedingly esoteric. To my knowledge, the phrase "*prema-vilāsa-vivarta*" is only mentioned in the *Caitanya-caritāmṛta*, at least as far as premodern Gauḍīya texts go, and that only in a single verse (Madhya 8.192). This is saying quite a bit, since Rūpa Gosvāmī, Jīva Gosvāmī, and others provide an incalculably rich literature on the various levels of mystical love, as summarized above.[11]

As a side note, it may be mentioned that there are several 17th-century Gauḍīya Vaishnava classics, roughly contemporaneous with the *Caitanya-caritāmṛta*, that have names such as the *Prema-vilāsa* (Nityānanda Dāsa) *Prema-vivarta* (Jagadānanda Paṇḍita), and *Vilāsa-vivarta* (Akiñcana Dāsa).[12] These texts, profound though they are, tend to circumvent the full phrase "*prema-vilāsa-vivarta*," both in book title and in terms of the subjects explored in their pages. But *prema-vilāsa-vivarta*, as a specific book, is conspicuous by its absence. The one reference we have to a volume with all three words in the title is mentioned by Śrīla A. C. Bhaktivedanta Swami Prabhupāda (*Caitanya-caritāmṛta* 2.8.193, purport), and ascribed to Rāmānanda Rāya himself, but this might merely refer to the brief verse that Rāmānanda sings in the Madhya-līlā, soon to be discussed. That said, an entire book by that name, at least today, seems no longer extant.

Part II: My Introduction to the Subject

In 1984, while I was in India, noted Gauḍīya Vaishnava scholar O. B. L. Kapoor (1909–2001) expressed a desire to meet with me. He had become aware of a soon-to-be-published book that I was writing on the life and times of Śrī

Chaitanya, and he wanted to advise me in a specific way. I was surprised, though, when I discovered exactly what he wanted to say: he asked me to include in my book a section on *prema-vilāsa-vivarta*. Although I was of course familiar with the *Caitanya-caritāmṛta* and the tradition surrounding it, the topic he raised was one I knew nothing about.

Then he explained. *Prema-vilāsa-vivarta*, he told me, was the highest stage of divine love, and its inner dimensions were tasted by Mahāprabhu himself. Indeed, Kapoor was emphatic that *prema-vilāsa-vivarta* comprised the summit of Mahāprabhu's blissful experience of divine love. How could I not be intrigued? And as he spoke, my fascination increased more and more.

Here's how he introduced the subject: "In the *Caitanya-caritāmṛta*, Rāmānanda Rāya responds to Śrī Chaitanya's request: 'Recite a verse from the revealed scriptures to elucidate the ultimate goal of life.' Rāma Rāya began by quoting a text in support of Varnāśrama-dharma, but Mahāprabhu asked him to go further. Accordingly, he moved on, quoting verses that espoused the virtues of karma; the rejection of karma; knowledge mixed with devotion (*bhakti*); *bhakti* that was not diluted by knowledge; *prema-bhakti*; and *Rādhā-prema*. In this section of the *Caitanya-caritāmṛta*, called 'Rāmānanda Samvāda,' we also find profound details about Krishna-tattva, Rādhā-tattva, Rādhā-Krishna-prema-tattva, and finally *prema-vilāsa-vivarta*." And Kapoor concluded that there is nothing beyond *prema-vilāsa-vivarta*. *This, he said, is the last word in love of God.*

Dr. Kapoor's conclusion that *prema-vilāsa-vivarta* is the highest level of love is confirmed by scholarly stalwarts in the tradition.[13] The first and most significant evidence, of course, is in the *Caitanya-caritāmṛta* itself (2.8.196), where Mahāprabhu says, "This is the topmost limit, or the ultimate goal of human life (*prabhu kahe—'sādhya-vastura avadhi' ei haya*).

The build-up to this is also fascinating: In 2.8.192, Rāmānanda suggests that the subject is so esoteric that Mahāprabhu may not want to hear it. And, sure enough, in the next verse, Chaitanya physically covers Rāmānanda's mouth (*mukha ācchādila*), stopping him from uttering more than he already has. The tradition avers that the reasoning for this physical action is twofold, with one exoteric explanation and the other esoteric: (1) *prema-vilāsa-vivarta* is a highly confidential subject—the pinnacle of divine love—and the tradition forbids non-devotees and neophytes from prematurely availing themselves of such advanced topics. Covering Rāma Rāya's mouth, therefore, is almost a symbolic gesture, meant to remind those who have not qualified themselves that they should instead focus on more rudimentary subjects; and, on a more confidential level, (2) the truth of *prema-vilāsa-vivarta* hints at Mahāprabhu's distinct *avatāra*—he is Rādhā and Krishna combined—and, though we will define it more thoroughly below, *prema-vilāsa-vivarta* basically refers to the paradoxical oneness that the Divine Couple experience due to their profound love. Mahāprabhu wanted to keep his identity as Krishna a secret (for his mission was to experience the *bhāva* of a devotee, self-consciously underplaying his manifestation as God). To be sure, the revelation of Rādhā and Krishna's oneness, as espoused in the doctrine of *prema-vilāsa-vivarta,* would point in the direction of Mahāprabhu's purposely undisclosed identity; he was thus naturally resistant to its being articulated.[14] Nonetheless, Rāmānanda sang the truth of *prema-vilāsa-vivarta* for posterity, as preserved in the *Caitanya-caritāmṛta*, and he eventually revealed himself as the combined form of Rādhā and Krishna, specifically to Śrī Rāmānanda.

"How could I write about this?" I asked Dr. Kapoor. "The subject is light-years beyond my pay grade."

Beaming with compassion, he laughed as he assured me that I would be guided by Krishna. But then his face turned grave, and he added that I should thoroughly read the texts passed down in the tradition. Moreover, he emphasized that I should also make good use of the *ācāryas'* writing. They have analyzed the subject in great depth, he mused, and expressed its complexities in a way that makes this otherwise abstruse knowledge completely accessible. He went further, advising me to consult peers and experts, both devotees and scholars, whose realization and command of the subject would surely help me to write about it in a lucid way.[15]

Over the years, I followed those instructions as best I could, studying the *Caitanya-caritāmṛta* and related texts by Gauḍīya *ācāryas*, tracking down obscure literature on the subject, and consulting with experts. Apropos of this, I sincerely hope that what I write here contains some measure of accuracy, capturing both the content and spirit of the subject under discussion.

All of this said, it must be remembered that this level of divine love is extremely nuanced, making its full comprehension somewhat evasive. In Viśvanātha Cakravartī's *Śrī Prema-sampuṭa* (51), Rādhikā herself tells us that people who talk about *prema*, or intellectualize about it, will likely miss the point. And in Bhaktivinoda Ṭhākura's *Jaiva Dharma*, toward the end of Chapter Two, we again read that words themselves are insufficient when it comes to *prema*. Rather, one must have the *adhikāra* (qualification) to understand it, and this comes from practice (*sādhana*) and grace (*kṛpā*). Still, it must also be noted that we study it as part of that practice, and we read about it to attain that grace.

Part III: Prema-Vilāsa-Vivarta Defined

Before defining *prema-vilāsa-vivarta*, there is one other highly esoteric term that will prove useful to our study: *sva-saṁvedya-daśā*. *Sva* means "one's self," *samvedya* means, "capable of being realized," and *daśā* means "a state of consciousness." In our present context, it is a type of all-encompassing self-awareness that subsists within the highest reaches of love. When Rādhikā serves Śrī Krishna, for example, she is fully in this *sva-saṁvedya* state, i.e., aware of every facet of her loving service. Thus, she loses herself in serving Krishna, without ever focusing on her own desires—her only interest is in pleasing him. Because of this unique level of intensity, the Divine Couple begin to feel that their minds and bodies are one, to the point where they lose awareness of their individuality. Since love itself has captured their full attention, it effectively becomes yet another self-aware experience (*sva-saṁvedya daśā*), as if taking on a life of its own—and gaining complete control of the Divine Couple themselves.[16]

To be sure, the primary *gopīs* and even Krishna himself are not devoid of this *sva-saṁvedya-daśā*, though they experience it to different degrees and in different ways. That said, Rādhikā's sense of *sva-saṁvedya-daśā* is supreme, even if the foremost *gopīs* may approximate this level due to their being her direct expansions, and Śrī Krishna, God himself, also has a means of experiencing it: he appears as Śrī Chaitanya Mahāprabhu and tastes this highest level of *sva-samvedya-daśā*, usually reserved only for Rādhā (for he fully adopts her *bhāva*). We will address this more fully below, but for now, we turn to defining the phrase at the heart of this essay.

In its most simple expression, *prema-vilāsa* means "playful, divine pastimes that are generated by love," and *vivarta*, which is a bit more complicated, refers to "changing from one state to another, modification, alteration, transformation, altered form or condition" and even "mistaking one thing for something else"[17]—we will soon see how these cryptic meanings play into the pastimes of Rādhā and Krishna.

The term *prema-vilāsa-vivarta*—considering all that has been written about it—could more meaningfully be understood as follows: "the topmost evolution (*paripāka*) of Krishna's divine play (*vilāsa*), which arises from a form of spiritual love (*prema*) that is so intense, it causes 'identity inversion' (*viparīta*), a form of spiritual alchemy that leads to transformation (*vivarta*) or even a type of confusion (*bhrānti*), where lover and beloved are merged as one (*paraikya*)." How one arrives at this longer definition involves an in-depth study of *Caitanya-caritāmṛta* commentaries, along with the exegesis of Kavi Karṇapūra, Jīva Gosvāmī and Viśvanātha Cakravartī, in particular.

The latter two *ācāryas* tell us that *prema-vilāsa* means

"loving pastimes," as is commonly understood.[18] But *vivarta*, they say, is the telling word, for in this context it includes a sense of *paripāka* (fully mature), *bhrama* or *bhrānti* (bewilderment), and *viparīta* (reversal), along with its usual sense of transformation. As we will see, this same terminology informs the explanation of modern-day Gauḍīya writers as well, who trace these definitions to the *ācāryas*, and depending on how one defines the word *vivarta*, a given instance of *prema-vilāsa-vivarta* will have specific meaning or a more general one, as we will see.

To begin, then, let us look at the primary definition of the phrase: in the full maturity of their love, Rādhā and Krishna cannot distinguish between themselves; their sense of individuality is effectively obliterated, for their love has made them one. From Rādhā's point of view, in particular, her love is so total that she sees the two of them as fundamentally nondifferent. In other words, there is a type of role reversal (*viparīta*), or, in the extreme, a complete merger of identities (*paraikya*), brought on by a transcendental form of confusion (*bhrānti*).[19] This is the essence of *prema-vilāsa-vivarta*. That is to say, there is a certain oneness that exists between the Divine Couple, and in the height of their supreme love, this truth becomes prominent, eclipsing the fact that they are two distinct entities.

The "oneness" of Rādhā and Krishna, as referenced in *prema-vilāsa-vivarta*, should be clearly understood: As Dr. Rādhāgovinda Nāth (1879–1970), the much lauded contemporary writer on Gauḍīya Vaishnavism, reminds us, "Here the *bheda-rāhitya* ('absence of distinction') is not the *bheda-rāhitya* of *jñāna-mārga* practitioners, who are seeking the impersonal Brahman."[20] Rādhā-govinda Nāth goes on for some pages in his *Caitanya-caritāmṛta* commentary to explain that Rādhā and Krishna are forever two beings, who subsist in eternity in loving relationship. It is their minds and hearts, if you will, that meld into one, and that only in the sense that their love is so complete that they can no longer see distinction, even if said distinction is prerequisite for that very same love. (This distinction between the oneness propounded by Advaitins and that found in the doctrine of *prema-vilāsa-vivarta* is so important that we will return to it throughout this essay, particularly in our conclusion.)

Rādhāgovinda Nāth further explains that "neither Rādhā nor Krishna are *nirviśeṣa-brahma* covered by *ajñāna*, as Māyāvādīs or followers of Śaṅkara would argue. Rather, they are *anāvṛta* ('non-covered') *saviśeṣa-brahma*. They are eternal, and their *vilāsa* is also eternal. Compelled by *prema's* supremely ripened state, their minds and hearts have achieved *ekātmatā*, 'one-soul-ness,' and because of this absorption and sense of oneness, they are deprived of proper awareness of '*ke ramaṇa, āre ke ramaṇī*—i.e., who is the lover, and who is the beloved.' Neither *ramaṇa* nor *ramaṇī* disappear; only the awareness or mental comprehension of who is who disappears. This is the fruit of the ultimate ripeness of love."[21] He continues:

> Śrī Śrī Rādhā-Krishna's bodies are separate, the minds within their bodies are also separate; only the moods of their minds become one. The *jñāna-mārga sādhakas*, or the Advaitins, desire no individual existence in their perfected state. They do not have any sense of experience, because in their perfection, there is no knower, nothing to be known, and no knowledge. All

> is one. However, in *prema-vilāsa-vivarta*, Śrī Śrī Rādhā-Krishna have individual existences, and they have an awareness or experience of being keen on the joy of *vilāsa*. Their efforts for *vilāsa* endure, as does the *vilāsa* itself.[22]

In fact, Rādhāgovinda Nāth takes great care to fully explain the mysteries of *prema-vilāsa-vivarta*, specifically in his gloss of Madhya 8, *payāra* 150 (which corresponds to text 192 in the Bhaktivedanta Book Trust edition), where he quotes both Jīva and Viśvanātha to good effect. This is found in the third volume (Madhya, Part 1) of his six-volume series. He also begins his massive commentary with a 450-page *Bhūmika*, an introductory volume, in which he further illuminates the subject.

His initial point is that *prema-vilāsa-vivarta* focuses on the highest stage of love, *adhirūḍha-mahābhāva*. He also notes that although other levels of *prema* may share some of the same characteristics as those found in *prema-vilāsa-vivarta*—and so, too, might mundane love—*prema-vilāsa-vivarta* stands countless miles above either of them. He reminds us that *prema-vilāsa-vivarta* is not the sort of *vilāsa* that is inspired by desires for one's own happiness; that sort of *vilāsa* is called *kāma-vilāsa*, he says, or the pastimes of material enjoyment. As he points out, the tradition draws a considerable distinction between the two.

After this, he explains that the word *vivarta* is highly mysterious (*rahasyamaya*) and filled with the utmost significance (*viśeṣa-gurutva-pūrṇa*). This is where he gives us Viśvanātha Cakravartī's gloss that the word means *viparīta*, i.e., "inverted" or "reversed," as stated above. So, too, does he refer to Jīva Gosvāmī's commentary on *Ujjavala-nīlamaṇi*, *Uddīpana-vibhāva-prakaraṇa*, verse 37, where we learn that the word *vivarta* is also understood to mean *paripākaḥ*, or "fully ripened," "completely evolved," or "uniquely transformed," also indicated above. And still again he informs us that the word *vivarta* can refer to *bhrama*, "perplexity," or *bhrānti,* "confusion," although, in this context, it refers only to a perplexity and confusion that is steeped in the topmost spiritual love. With these meanings as our starting point, Rādhāgovinda Nāth now directs us to the two statements of the Rāmānanda-samvāda, which is the main source for understanding *prema-vilāsa-vivarta* in the Chaitanya tradition.

At the height of his conversation with Mahāprabhu, Rāmānanda explains *prema-vilāsa-vivarta* with two examples: (1) a poem that he composed in the Bengali vernacular, using the voice of Rādhā (*Caitanya-caritāmṛta* 2.8.194); and (2) a Sanskrit verse originally penned by Rūpa Gosvāmī in his *Ujjvala-nīlamaṇi* 14.155. (*Caitanya-caritāmṛta* 2.8.195) Here are those two verses in full:

> "Alas, before We met there was an initial attachment between Us brought about by an exchange of glances. In this way attachment evolved. That attachment has gradually grown, and there is no limit to it. Now that attachment has become a natural sequence between Ourselves. It is not that it is due to Kṛṣṇa, the enjoyer, nor is it due to Me, for I am the enjoyed. It is not like that. This attachment was made possible by mutual meeting. This mutual exchange of attraction is known as *manobhava*, or Cupid. Kṛṣṇa's mind and My mind have merged together. Now, during this time of separation, it

is very difficult to explain these loving affairs. My dear friend, though Kṛṣṇa might have forgotten all these things, you can understand and bring this message to Him. But during Our first meeting there was no messenger between Us, nor did I request anyone to see Him. Indeed, Cupid's five arrows were Our via media. Now, during this separation, that attraction has increased to another ecstatic state. My dear friend, please act as a messenger on My behalf, because if one is in love with a beautiful person, this is the consequence."[23]

And then:

"O my Lord, You live in the forest of Govardhana Hill, and, like the king of elephants, You are expert in the art of conjugal love. O master of the universe, Your heart and Śrīmatī Rādhārāṇī's heart are just like shellac and are now melted in Your spiritual perspiration. Therefore one can no longer distinguish between You and Śrīmatī Rādhārāṇī. Now You have mixed Your newly invoked affection, which is like vermilion, with Your melted hearts, and for the benefit of the whole world You have painted both Your hearts red within this great palace of the universe."[24]

References to "Cupid" are common in Vaishnava literature, and it is often used as a catchword to indicate a number of love-inflected deities, according to context.[25] It is especially interesting in the above verse. In his commentary, Bhaktivinoda Ṭhākura suggests that during those moments that Rādhā and Krishna actually come together, in union, the resultant attachment and depth of love might be compared to the work of Cupid. So, too, is this the case during the period of separation, when Cupid becomes a messenger of an even higher order. Accordingly, Śrī Rādhikā addresses this messenger as a friend, indicating that she relishes separation as much as union, if in a different way. As Śrī Rūpa informs us elsewhere (*Padyāvali* 240), Rādhā's perspective on separation is as follows: "[In certain respects] I prefer separation to union, because in union I see Krishna only in one place, whereas in separation, I see him everywhere." In *prema-vilāsa-vivarta*, she has gone even further, becoming one with him.

The tradition refers to this oneness as "*paraikya,*" a word that conveys total harmony or uniformity—fundamental unity.[26] Although we have dealt with this subject elsewhere (when discussing the difference between this kind of oneness and that promulgated by the Advaitins), it should be understood in the current context as well. In fact, this oneness is artfully elaborated upon in 2.8.195 by the shellac or wax (*lākṣa*) analogy, above. As stated in this verse, under the influence of *prema*, both Rādhā and Krishna's minds melt and mix (*miśiyā*), and have thus become indistinguishable. That is to say, they have attained the state of "*nirdhūta-bheda-bhramam*—a sort of spiritual confusion wherein all sense of separateness is washed away." They are described as being like two pieces of wax that have melted and become one under intense heat (*tīvra-tāpa*). And yet they remain two individuals.

Commenting on these verses, Vaishnava scholar and guru, Gour Govinda Swami Mahārāja (1929–1996), shares his insights:

> This is *prema-vilāsa-vivarta*. There is no difference between *ramaṇa*, the enjoyer, and *ramaṇī* the enjoyed. *Ramaṇa* is Krishna. *Ramaṇī* is Rādhā. In

> *prema-vilāsa-vivarta* there is oneness. *Nā so ramaṇa, nā hāma ramaṇī*—"It is not that He is the enjoyer and I am the enjoyed." *Duṅhu-mana manobhava peṣala*—"His mind and My mind have became one." This is the last stage known as *mādanākhya-mahābhāva. Mādanākhya-mahābhāva* is Rādhārāṇī's attitude. There is no difference between the lover and the beloved. The minds of these two, Krishna and Rādhā, are crushed together. *Peṣala* means crushing. Then it is transformed into a form known as *praṇaya*. This is the explanation. *Mano dadhāno viśrambhaṁ praṇayaḥ procayate budhaiḥ*. That means, when *māna* becomes more condensed it becomes *praṇaya*, the stage of *viśrambha. Viśrambha* means a feeling of oneness between *kānta*, the lover, and the *kāntā*, the beloved. They are crushed together, "His mind and My mind became one." *Nā so ramaṇa, nā hāma ramaṇī duṅhu-mana manobhava peṣala jāni*. This is the activity of *hlādini-śakti*. There is a difference between *śakti*, the energy, and *śaktiman*, the energetic source. But in *praṇaya-vikṛtir*, there is oneness between the *āsvādika*, the enjoyer, and the *āsvādita*, the enjoyed. ... Rādhā and Lord Krishna are one, yet They have taken two forms to enjoy the mellows of pastimes.[27]

To make it clearer still, O. B. L. Kapoor offers the following analogy:

> It is, as Jīva Gosvāmī explains, like the union between fire and a piece of iron. A piece of iron, when put for a long time in fire, becomes red-hot like the fire. Every part of it is animated by fire and acquires the characteristics of fire. Still, iron remains iron and fire remains fire. Similarly, both Krishna and Rādhā retain their identity. They are so absorbed in each other's love and lost in each other's thoughts that there is hardly any room in their hearts for the thought of anything else.[28]

In summary, then, *prema-vilāsa-vivarta* in its highest form is understood as an inversion of sorts that is created by the most acute form of love. Along these lines, in Vaishnavism's most esoteric literature, particularly in the poetry of the Vrindavan Gosvāmīs, we see Rādhā and Krishna lose their sense of individuality and mistake one for the other. He thinks he is her, and she thinks she is him, resulting in a sort of merging of the two, where their two hearts, again, melt into one. Ultimately, *prema-vilāsa-vivarta*, at least according to its primary definition, means "the culmination of loving pastimes in which the hero and heroine exchange roles," a phenomenon also known as *viparīta-kāma-krīḍā*.

Perhaps the best summation of the subject as a whole, at least in regard to the special oneness that Rādhā and Krishna feel in relation to each other, can be found in Viśvanātha Cakravartī's *Śrī Prema-sampuṭa*, although the phrase *prema-vilāsa-vivarta* does not appear in this text:

> *anyonya-citta-viduṣau nu parasparātma-*
> *nitya-sthiter iti nṛṣu prathitau yad āvām*
> *tac-caupacārikam aho dvitayatvam eva*
> *naikasya sambhavati karhicid ātmano nau (107)*

> Śrī Rādhikā then spoke: "Common people say, 'Rādhā and Kṛṣṇa are eternally present in each others' hearts, and that is why They know each others' minds.' Factually, the real truth is this: We are one soul. It is not possible for one soul to become two.

> *ekātmanīha rasa-pūrṇatame 'tyagādhe*
> *ekā susaṅgrathitam eva tanu-dvayaṁ nau*

kasyiṁścid eka-sarasīva cakāsad eka-
nālottham abja-yugalaṁ khalu nīla-pītam (108)

"In a lake, two lotuses—one blue and one yellow—may bloom from a single stem. In the same way, Our two bodies, one blue and one yellow, are connected as one life. They are one supremely profound soul composed of topmost *rasa*. As bodies, We are separate, but by nature, We are one. Kṛṣṇa is by nature blissful (*ānanda*) and I by nature am joyful (*hlādinī*). Just as fire and its burning potency are one, there is no difference between the potency (*śakti*) and the possessor of the potency (*śaktimān*). We cannot be distinguished from each other when seen as a person and the person's potency, but for the sake of *rasa*, We manifest in separate forms as Rādhā and Kṛṣṇa. Without pastimes, We cannot relish each other; and without form, We cannot perform pastimes."

Part IV: The Black Tamāla Tree and the Switching of Clothes

A related phenomenon, which we will now discuss, addresses how this transcendental merger might be seen externally, resulting in action that has resonance with *prema-vilasa-vivarta*. Indeed, some may even call it a second-tiered instance of *prema-vilasa-vivarta*. In other words, there are other forms of divine bewilderment that attest to *prema-vilāsa-vivarta* as well.

For example, when Rādhārāṇī sees a black *tamāla* tree, thinking it to be Krishna, and she embraces it with heart and soul—her spiritual delirium has reached a pitch that involves mistaken identity, even if she is not personally identifying with the tree. Such pastimes echo the truth of *prema-vilāsa-vivarta* and so, in this section, we will briefly explore them.

Given our essential definition—that *prema-vilāsa-vivarta* is a product of the topmost love (*adhirūḍha-mahābhāva*); that it manifests as a type of confusion (*bhrānti*); and that it includes a sense of mistaken identity (*viparīta*)—let us consider Rādhārāṇī misconstruing a black *tamāla* tree for Krishna and whether it has any relation to what we now know about the subject.

The story is told throughout the Purāṇas and Gosvāmī literature. We find a prominent version of it in Śrīla Viśvanātha Cakravartī Ṭhākura's *Śrī Krishna-Bhāvanāmṛta Mahākāvya.*[29] In this text, during the Divine Couple's evening pastimes, we meet Rādhā as she enters the magical forest of Vraja. There, she notes that everything she sees, hears, smells, and feels reminds her of Krishna, i.e., every sound is his flute, every scent is his fragrance, every tree his form, and so on. The text then focuses on a particular *tamāla* tree: Its blackish form gives her shivers, and she is not able to contain herself in its presence. She embraces the tree with a heart full of love. "Thus, Krishna became just like the *tamāla* tree and Rādhikā like the golden vine who embraced him."[30]

Another example of the *tamāla* tree "illusion" is found in Rūpa Gosvāmī's *Vidagdha-mādhava.* Although this distinct arboreal lookalike appears throughout the play, with numerous poetic comparisons between the tree and Krishna's form, it relates to our subject most effectively in

Act Six, where Lalitā says in a matter-of-fact tone: "This girl sees a *tamāla* tree and thinks it is Krishna."[31] Donna Wulff comments on the incident as a whole:

> The intense preoccupation of Rādhā and Kṛṣṇa with one another is indicated by another set of parallel passages with similar metaphysical overtones. So obsessed with Kṛṣṇa does Rādhā become that she sees him everywhere; when she mistakes a black *tamāla* tree for her dark lover, Viśakhā asks her how it is that the three worlds have become Kṛṣṇa for her. Kṛṣṇa poses the corresponding question for himself as he eagerly awaits Rādhā at their point of rendezvous: "Rādhā appears before me on every side; how is it that for me the three worlds have become Rādhā?" (V.18). Rūpa seems to have been especially taken with this mode of indicating Kṛṣṇa's infatuation, for on two additional occasions he has other characters make virtually the same observation about Kṛṣṇa's "delusion" (III.18; VI.23. 20-21). Moreover, it is not only Rādhā in her obsession with Kṛṣṇa who is explicitly termed "mad," but also Kṛṣṇa in his unbridled passion for her. At one point, as Kṛṣṇa is rushing headlong to meet her, Madhumaṅgala, steadying him, asserts that he has been "driven mad (*unmādita*) by an evil spell [uttered] by the wicked *gopīs*." (VI.14.3-4)."[32]

Acknowledging Śrī Rādhā's love-mad misapprehensions, Bhaktivinoda Ṭhākura singles out the black *tamāla* tree incident as a form of *prema-vilāsa-vivarta*. In his *Amṛta-pravāha-bhāṣya* to *Caitanya-caritāmṛta* (2.8.194), he writes: "In seeing the *tamāla* tree as Krishna, Rādhikā is subject to a type of *sambhoga* [union] in *vipralambha* [separation], particularly in the form of *vivarta-bhāvāpanna adhirūḍha-mahābhāva* [i.e., *prema-vilāsa-vivarta*]."[33]

Further, drawing on Bhaktivinoda's insights, Śrīla A. C. Bhaktivedanta Swami Prabhupāda says it even more directly: "When Śrīmatī Rādhārāṇī was fully absorbed in love of Kṛṣṇa, She mistook a black *tamāla* tree for Kṛṣṇa and embraced it. Such a mistake is called *prema-vilāsa-vivarta*."[34] Thus, we have identified what might be considered a secondary tier of *prema-vilāsa-vivarta,* without *viparīta* in the sense of complete identity inversion or *paraikya* in the form of an identity merger between Rādhā and Krishna. Yet there is, in this instance, still a case of mistaken identity based on the topmost love. And one must always ask, since Krishna is ultimately everything: Is this indeed a case of mistaken identity, or is Rādhā merely seeing things as they truly are?

Another example—as ubiquitous as the black *tamāla* tree narrative—would be when Rādhikā mistakenly adorns herself with Krishna's yellow cloth, or he, her blue *sari.* This almost comical state of affairs points to the same kind of misidentification or confusion (*bhrānti*) we see in other examples of *prema-vilāsa-vivarta*, for it too takes place as a result of the highest love. We even see here a case of mistaken identity (*viparīta*), though it is not exactly a merging of hearts, at least not in the same way.

Indeed, this pastime might be regarded, again, as suggestive of *prema-vilāsa-vivarta.* As Shrivatsa Goswami, head priest and eminent scholar at Vrindavan's famous Radharamana temple, eloquently writes, "She wears his peacock feather, he dons her lovely, delicate crown; she sports his yellow garment, he wraps himself in her beautiful *sari.* How charming the very sight of it . . . The daughter of Vṛṣabhānu [Rādhā] turns [into] Nanda's son [Krishna], and Nanda's son, into Vṛṣabhānu's girl."[35]

These truths are conspicuous in the switching of clothes: On one occasion, the *gopīs*, seeing that Krishna is wearing Rādhikā's blue cloth and not his usual yellow *dhoti*—and not wanting his mother to find out that he and Rādhā had slept together—make excuses for him; they point out to Mother Yaśodā that on this day Krishna seems to have chosen Balarāma's clothes (for the latter, too, wears blue, like Rādhikā). In this way, they had hoped to deceive Mother Yaśodā, distracting her from the truth that her son had spent the evening with Rādhā.[36] This "unconscious" switching of clothes is indicative of an "identity switch," and is thus suggestive of *prema-vilāsa-vivarta*.

We see a similar scene, too, in Śrī Raghunātha Dāsa Gosvāmī's *Prārthanā* (from *Śrī Stavāvalī*), specifically in a song called "*Prātaḥ pīta-paṭe kucopari*." Therein, he tells us that one day, in early morning, Jaṭilā-devī, Śrī Rādhā's mother-in-law, met Rādhā and her friend Lalitā on the road. Jaṭilā noticed that Rādhā was wearing a yellow garment on her upper chest, which was unusual, and that she seemed overly sleepy as well. Jaṭilā thus made innuendos that Rādhā had perhaps spent the night with Krishna. Although frightened that she had been found out, Rādhā externally assumed a confident pose, as Lalitā composed a network of believable lies to help her transcendental friend. When it was over, Rādhikā glorified Lalitā for her skillful help.

Or consider Krishnadāsa Kavirāja Gosvāmī's *Govinda-līlāmṛta* 1.79-80: "Krishna, seeing that Rādhārāṇī's restless eyes were accosted by fear, nervously donned her fine blue cloth, quickly arising from bed. Wearing each other's clothes, Rādhā and Krishna held each other's hands and emerged from the *kuñja*." We find much the same, and perhaps a summation of all that precedes this, in Jīva Gosvāmī's *Gopāla-campū* (*Pūrva* 15.9):

imau gaurī-śyāmau manasi viparīrtau bahir api
sphurat tad tad vastrāv iti budha-janair niścitam idam
sa ko 'py accha-premā vilasad ubhayoḥ sphūrtikatayā
dadhan mūrttī-bhāva-pṛthag-apṛthag apy āvirudabhūt

These two, Rādhā and Krishna, are *gaura-varṇa* (gold complexion) and *śyāma-varṇa* (blue complexion), respectively. But in their minds, it is the opposite. In other words, Śrī Rādhikā's mind fully reflects Śrī Krishna, and so it is *śyāma-varṇa*, whereas Śrī Krishna's mind has likewise mirrored Śrī Rādhikā and is *gaura-varṇa*. Additionally, their minds are manifesting outwardly, too, which is why their garments are gold and blue. In other words, Śrī Krishna's *pītāmbara* is reflecting his own mind, which is *vibhāvita*, or overwhelmed, by Śrī Rādhā's *varṇa*. And Śrī Rādhikā's blue *sari* is providing a *sphūrti*, or glimpse, of her mind, as it is absorbed in Śrī Krishna's complexion. Wise persons have determined the nature of this matter accordingly. Because that indescribable, pristine *prema* manifests in two different forms to perform enchanting pastimes, it is understood that these forms are both different and nondifferent (*pṛthag-apṛthag*).

Part V: Śrī Chaitanya as Prema-Vilāsa-Vivarta-Mūrti

When those familiar with Gauḍīya Vaishnavism hear the words *gaura-varṇa*, as in the above verse, their minds naturally turn to Śrī Chaitanya Mahāprabhu, who is famously the same golden color as Śrī Rādhikā. Indeed, the truth of Śrī Chaitanya's person, identity, and reason for appearance is the very essence of *prema-vilāsa-vivarta*, for he is the ultimate manifestation of Rādhā and Krishna becoming one. As the *Caitanya-caritāmṛta* (Ādi 1.5) reminds us:

rādhā kṛṣṇa-praṇaya-vikṛtir hlādinī śaktir asmād
ekātmānāv api bhuvi purā deha-bhedaṁ gatau tau
caitanyākhyaṁ prakaṭam adhunā tad-dvayaṁ caikyam āptaṁ
rādhā-bhāva-dyuti-suvalitaṁ naumi kṛṣṇa-svarūpam

> "The loving exchanges between Rādhā and Krishna are completely spiritual, a product of the Lord's *hlādinī-śakti*. Indeed, although Rādhā and Krishna are one, they exist as separate entities. Now, in the form of Śrī Chaitanya, these two divine entities have again become one. I offer obeisance to him [Śrī Chaitanya], who manifests [in the world] with the sentiment and complexion of Śrī Rādhā, although he is Krishna himself."

The implicit message of this verse is that Rādhā and Krishna unify in the person of Śrī Chaitanya, and yet, inconceivably, they never lose their "two-ness." The verse begins by affirming their oneness (*ekātmānāv*), and then moves on to their obvious duality (*deha-bhedaṁ*)—and then returns to inevitable unity (*aikyam āptaṁ*) in the form of Śrī Chaitanya. And Chaitanya himself, as has been well recorded, spent his entire lifetime longing for Krishna, thus reaffirming a sense of duality yet again. Indeed, the cycle goes ever on, for as soon as one affirms one side (*bheda*), one must immediately acknowledge the other (*abheda*), a truth confirmed by Chaitanya and his followers in various ways.[37]

Moreover, the notion of *prema-vilāsa-vivarta* is indirectly mentioned in this verse: *Praṇaya* (love) is a synonym for *prema*, and *vikṛtiḥ* (transformation) is another way of saying *vivarta*. Accordingly, when the verse tells us that Rādhā and Krishna are in fact one, even if they exist as two separate entities—and that they unite once again in the form of Śrī Chaitanya—it is inadvertantly expressing the truth of *prema-vilāsa-vivarta*. Thus, according to this verse, Mahāprabhu is the ultimate manifestation or culmination of Rādhā and Krishna's union, and thus, extrapolating freely, may be seen as the very "embodiment" of *prema-vilāsa-vivarta*, i.e., the Prema-Vilāsa-Vivarta-Mūrti, a phrase to which we will return in a few moments.

In the context of our present subject, the ontological position of Śrī Chaitanya, in which he partakes of the moods and intensity of Śrī Rādhā, must be clear. Along these lines, the Vaishnava poet-saint, Śrīla B. R. Śrīdhara Dev-Goswāmī Mahārāja (1895–1988), famously referred to Chaitanya as a "golden volcano of divine love," making explicit Mahāprabhu's divine connection to Rādhā-bhāva:

> Diving deep into the reality of His own beauty and sweetness, Krishna stole the mood of Rādhāraṇī and, garbing Himself in Her brilliant luster, appeared as Śrī Chaitanya Mahāprabhu. . . . He was deeply absorbed in the mood of union and separation and shared His heart's inner feelings with His most confidential devotees. In the agony of separation from Krishna, volcanic eruptions of ecstasy flowed from His heart, and His teachings, known as *Śikṣāṣṭakam*, appeared from His lips like streams of golden lava. I fall at the feet of Śrī Chaitanya Mahāprabhu, the Golden Volcano of Divine Love.[38]

The overarching and complete correlation between Śrī Rādhā and Śrī Chaitanya is thus critical for understanding Mahāprabhu as the very epitome of *prema-vilāsa-vivarta*. This is because the "misapprehension" or "illusion" that is so much a part of *prema-vilāsa-vivarta* must take place as a result of *adhirūḍha-mahābhāva*, and, at its peak, *mādanākhya-mahābhāva*, a level of love known only to Śrī Rādhā. As we will see, Mahāprabhu exhibits such misapprehension in abundance, and for the same reasons as Rādhā does.

The tradition takes great pains to show that Mahāprabhu experiences the depth of Rādhā's love, since he is said to be Krishna himself specifically incarnating to realize that purpose—to feel the love that his devotees feel for him, especially that of Śrī Rādha, the topmost devoteē.[39] And, as the tradition makes clear, he is successful in his purpose.

With that much as a backdrop, one can understand Śrī Chaitanya as the very form of *prema-vilāsa-vivarta*, i.e., the Prema-Vilāsa-Vivarta-Mūrti.

I initially discovered this phrase in an article by Vaishnava scholar Śrī Prem Prayojan Prabhu.[40] Of course, as I looked more carefully, I could see that numerous variations were to be found in most any thorough book on Śrī Chaitanya. Indeed, in the first volume of Rādhāgovinda Nāth's 450-page *Bhūmika*—the introductory volume for his commentary on the *Caitanya-caritāmṛta*—he writes, "For all these reasons, it has been said that Śrī Śrī Gaurasundara [Chaitanya] is the *mūrta-rūpa* (personified form) of *prema-vilāsa-vivarta*."[41] Or, as O. B. L. Kapoor articulates it, "Śrī Caitanya is the substantial or personalized form of this union."[42]

And why not? If we look into many of Śrī Chaitanya's later life narratives, we can identify at least certain elements of *prema-vilāsa-vivarta*, especially if we consider that his inner identity was more and more ensconced in Rādhā-bhāva—and the texts indeed tell us that it was. For example, the whole 14th chapter of *Caitanya-caritāmṛta*'s Antya-līlā, which culminates in Mahāprabhu running like a madman to "Govardhana," seems dependent on him being so focused on Krishna that he forgets himself, identifying instead with Rādhā, overtaken with her *adhiruḍha-mahābhāva*. Thus, he finds himself in a state of divine madness (*divyonmāda*) or bewilderment (*mohana-bhāva*), clearly reminiscent of Krishna's divine consort.

When Mahāprabhu finally sees Caṭaka-parvata, the sand dune he "mistakes" (*bhrānti, vivarta*) for Govardhana Hill, it acts as an *uddīpana* to stimulate his remembrance of the actual mountainous region of Krishna's pastimes, triggering his transition from external consciousness to a more internal or transcendent realm. Halfway through the transition, he sees Govardhana in his mind's eye while his outer senses still act out on the physical plane, resulting in incoherent behavior. While Krishnadāsa Kavirāja Gosvāmī does not term this *prema-vilāsa-vivarta*, it has enough of its pertinent elements to be seen as at least a pointer in that direction.

In fact, there are numerous examples in Chaitanya-līlā of "a type of love-filled madness, wherein the Lord found it difficult to distinguish one thing from another, overtaken, as he was, by various cases of mistaken identity" (*viparīta*). These cases are not unlike the incident of Śrī

Rādhā mistaking the black *tamāla* tree for Krishna, and so could indeed play a role in our understanding of *prema-vilāsa-vivarta*. Moreover, we see examples of this phenomenon engaging each of Mahāprabhu's five senses:

> Antya 17 — "Hearing": Śrī Chaitanya heard and followed the sound of Krishna's flute in the night (which no one else heard), as well as the tinkling of Rādhā and Krishna's foot ornaments. He also heard the sound of Krishna and the *gopīs* joking, with their laughter, until he arrived at the sound's source and found nothing more than a group of cows. He was later found in the shape of a turtle (*kūrmera ākāra*), and then that of a pumpkin (*kuṣmāṇḍa-phala*), next to the Jagannātha temple.
>
> Antya 14 — "Seeing": He looked upon the Deity of Jagannātha, but instead saw the threefold humanlike figure of Krishna in Vrindavan. After his divine reverie was broken, he saw Jagannātha of Purī/Kurukṣetra and lamented for having lost his vision of Vrindavan Krishna. In the same chapter, Śrī Chaitanya saw the sand dune that he mistook for Govardhana Hill.
>
> Antya 18 — "Touching": He saw the ocean at Purī and mistook it for the Yamunā, where he saw Rādhā-Krishna and the *gopīs* engaged in mock fighting, playfully expressing their love for each other. He watched as they "splashed water on one another. Then they fought hand to hand, then face to face, then chest to chest, teeth to teeth and finally nail to nail."
>
> Antya 19 — "Smelling": He saw Krishna standing beneath an Ashoka Tree in the Jagannātha Vallabha gardens at Purī, and when he ran to embrace him, he was disappointed that Krishna had disappeared—even if the fragrance of Krishna's body lingered. Śrī Chaitanya lost consciousness due to its otherworldly aroma.

> Antya 16 — "Tasting": He tasted the flavor of Krishna's lips when he honored Jagannātha *prasāda*.[43]

Although it can be argued that these examples are not technically direct instances of *prema-vilāsa-vivarta*—that is to say, they are not described as such in the text itself—we see here clear examples of divine bewilderment, all based on Śrī Chaitanya's overflowing love in the mood of Rādhā.[44] Whether they are direct instances or just pointers to the larger ideal is a matter for experts in *rasa*. But since Mahāprabhu is universally viewed by such experts as Prema-Vilāsa-Vivarta-Mūrti, we feel justified in bringing these examples to our readers' attention. At the very least, they can serve as indicators of his pure, otherworldly love, which foisted upon him a type of divine intoxication (*pramattatā*) that is wholly reminiscent of Krishna's divine lover, Śrī Rādhā.

The notion of Rādhā and Krishna becoming one in the form of Śrī Chaitanya is the capstone of *prema-vilāsa-vivarta*, whose central quality involves an inner perception of mystical unity (*paraikya*). Indeed, it is this unity, forged through the overpowering mood of Śrī Rādhikā, outstripping the heart of Śrī Krishna himself, that allows Mahāprabhu to experience the mystical illusions (*bhrānti*) depicted in Antya-līlā, wherein perceived transformations (*vivarta*) seem to occur in natural phenomenon due to the presence of an overpowering love.

Conclusion

Śrī Chaitanya's very existence is the ultimate expression of *prema-vilāsa-vivarta*, for just as the Lord originally manifests as two beings—Rādhā and Krishna—to taste *rasa*, or loving relationship, that same love intensifies to the point of making them one again. This, the tradition teaches, is the inner position of Śrī Chaitanya, and it is from this fact that we derive the term "Prema-Vilāsa-Vivarta-Mūrti."

Dr. Rādhāgovinda Nāth again offers insight along these lines, and I paraphrase: He tells us that generally, the enamored *nāyaka* (hero) embraces the enamored *nāyikā* (heroine), and he leads her in a dance of love. But in *prema-vilāsa-vivarta*, the *nāyikā* takes the lead and embraces the *nāyaka*. In other words, Rādhā is in charge, taking the first step, and in doing so, she makes the *nāyaka* dance like a puppet.[45]

When Krishna adopts the form of Śrī Chaitanya, we see that Nāyikā Śrī Rādhā has eternally and uninterruptedly embraced Nāyaka Śrī Krishna and caused him to become absorbed in her moods, thereby enacting various forms of uncontrollable *līlā*, a new dance, as it were, wherein reality itself is turned on its head. By the influence of her moods, Śrī Krishna, God, has forgotten his own identity, his *svarūpa-jñāna*. This leads to *vaiparītya* (a reversal of behavior), and *bhrānti* (illusion), which are considered the pinnacle of this level of love, and the very stuff of *prema-vilāsa-vivarta*.[46]

But the unprecedented characteristic of this higher level, Rādhāgovinda Nāth continues, is that while there is a deep appreciation of being united with one's beloved, because such union is the supreme, ultimate perfection and maturation of *prema*, one finds that there is also deep appreciation of *viraha* (separation) as well—on a par with the thrill of being together (*milana*)—for the Divine Couple herein realize how it is actually both states, separation and union, that lead to the ultimate achievement in divine love. In a word, Union has greater meaning after separation.[47]

"This truth," Rādhāgovinda Nāth continues, "is fundamental to the manifestation of Śrī Chaitanya, and it exists in him in its most radiant and radical configuration, for he is none other than the full amalgamation of Rādhā and Krishna in one form. More, even within this eternal, uninterrupted union (*sambhoga*), which is his very essence, the supreme manifestation of separation (*viraha*) is manifest, too, and to an overwhelming degree, as seen in his Gambhirā-līlā, the pinnacle of his confidential pastimes of pining for the Lord. For all these reasons, it has been said that Śrī Chaitanya is the personified form of *prema-vilāsa-vivarta*."[48]

We conclude and sum up with the words of Professor Abhishek Ghosh, noted scholar of Gauḍīya Vaishnavism: "Reversals in love that enhance passion are known as *prema-vivarta*. For example, when Śrī Chaitanya Mahāprabhu, from far away in Puri, was experiencing his deepest love for Śrī Krishna and his hamlet Vrindavan, he would mistake a rock to be a Govardhana-śilā, or ordinary forests to be the forests of Vraja. We witness here God making mistakes. How is it possible? It is a 'mistake' born of the highest love, which he allows himself to enhance the flavors of transcendental enjoyment. In this experience, Mahāprabhu functions at a highly liminal stage of existence, completely spiritual, where he feels not only separation from Krishna, but also simultaneous union with him. Similarly, in Krishna-līlā, Śrīmatī Rādhārāṇī is sometimes in distress, even while in Krishna's presence, knowing that no matter how prolonged those moments of their togetherness may be, by the wish of Yoga-māyā, these moments will not last, and thus she starts feeling separation from Krishna even while gazing at his moon-like face. Such is the pain of real love, which can only be found, at its highest pitch, in the exchanges of the Divine Couple, Rādhā and Krishna.

"It is a great mystery," concludes Dr. Ghosh, "and it is hinted at in the *Bhagavad-gītā*, which teaches us in its fifteenth chapter that this world is like a warped reflection, an inverted reality—Krishna gives the example of a banyan tree, whose roots point upward and branches face down. When next to a pond, such a tree looks upside down. Yet, we know, we are observing only its reflection. So it is in this world. We are further told that the leaves of this mystical tree are the verses of the Vedas, and thus, stretching that most appropriate metaphor to its limit, *prema-vilāsa-vivarta* is the pinnacle of *līlā*, for it is the ultimate fruit of the "Vedic tree." It is, so to speak, the culmination of Vedānta, and therefore what Vedānta is to the Vedas—its very essence—so, too, is *prema-vilāsa-vivarta* the essence of esoteric Gauḍīya *siddhānta*. It is the Vedānta within Vedānta. In the same way, Gauḍīya *rasikas* know that Chaitanya Mahāprabhu is the Prema-Vilāsa-Vivarta-Mūrti, for he is the inner portion of Krishna himself in the mood of Rādhā. He is Krishna within Krishna. Thus, the Akhila-Rasāmṛta-Mūrti known as Śrī Krishna manifests as the Prema-Vilāsa-Vivarta-Mūrti: Chaitanya Mahāprabhu, the representative of the highest love."[49]

Endnotes

1. From personal correspondence with Swami B.V. Tripurari (4-24-23). The notion of oneness in regard to lovers—how they both crave and experience it—is found throughout Western literature and philosophy as well, especially in the work of the poets. But it is nowhere as developed as in the narratives of Rādhā and Krishna. For Western examples we may look to E. E. Cummings' "i carry your heart with me (i carry it in my heart)" and Emily Brontë's *Wuthering Heights*, specifically Catherine's expression of love for Heathcliff. As Aaron Ben-Zeév Ph.D. writes, ". . . Plato claimed that love is essentially the process of seeking our missing half. In the same vein, the psychoanalyst Eric Fromm argued that erotic love 'is the craving for complete fusion, for union with one other person. It is by its very nature exclusive and not universal.' Likewise, the philosopher Robert Nozick said that in romantic love, 'it feels to the two people that they have united to form and constitute a new entity in the world, what might be called a we.'" See Aaron Ben-Zeév "Are Lovers Two Faces of the Same Coin?" *Psychology Today* (https://www.psychologytoday.com/ca/blog/in-the-name-of-love/200901/are-lovers-two-faces-of-the-same-coin).

2. In Jagadānanda Paṇḍita's 16th-century work *Śrī Śrī Prema-vivarta*, Chapter Sixteen, the Gauḍīya tradition highlights this important question: "What is Love?" The query comes from the lips of Gauḍīya Vaishnavism's quintessential mystic, Raghunātha Dāsa Gosvāmī, who asks the question of Svarūpa Dāmodara, one of Chaitanya Mahāprabhu's most intimate associates. The answer is initiated in Text 21: "Those who are intoxicated by the vulgar pleasures of this world do not attain the essence of love of Krishna, and the divine flute player never becomes the object of their love. ..." This, of course, only tells us what love is not. The author elaborates on a more positive definition as well, revealing in no uncertain terms that, in its ultimate form, real love is found in the writings of great Vaishnava poets, such as Jayadeva, Vidyāpati, and Caṇḍīdāsa—that is, real love is nothing more or less than the sweet love of Krishna. Although such love may externally appear nondifferent from lust, it is nonetheless something far more refined, like the difference between iron and gold. Briefly, love is summed up in the *Bhakti-rasāmṛta-sindhu* (1.1.11) as follows: "One should render devotional service to Lord Krishna favorably and

without desire for material profit or gain, whether gross or subtle. That is called pure bhakti, or devotional love." (*anyābhilāṣitā-śūnyaṁ jñāna-karmādy-anāvṛtam ānukūlyena kṛṣṇānu-śīlanaṁ bhaktir uttamā*)

3. *Rasa* theory is an ancient system of Indian aesthetics that describes audience reaction to any visual, literary, or musical work, specifically one that evokes an ineffable emotion or feeling. The concept is originally associated with Bharata's *Nāṭya Śāstra*, and was later developed by Abhinavagupta (c. 950–1016 CE) and King Bhoja (circa, 11th century), among others. But according to the Gauḍīya perspective, its full theological dimensions were not revealed until the work of Śrīla Rūpa Gosvāmī.

4. Interestingly, Greek philosophers identified six forms of love, though not exactly in line with Rūpa's Sanskrit categories: love of family (*storge*), friendly love (*philia*), amorous love (*eros*), narcissistic love (*philautia*), love of strangers (*xenia*), and divine love (*agape*).

5. See Tony K. Stewart, *The Final Word: The Caitanya-caritāmṛta and the Grammar of Religious Tradition* (New York: Oxford University Press, 2010), 211.

6. See also Viśvanātha Cakravartī's commentary on this verse. Interestingly, the tradition teaches that the earlier stages of love, like *praṇaya*, find themselves in the higher stages as well, if in a more developed form. It is a phenomenon that we also see in the five primary *rasas*, whose characteristics all appear in some form in *mādhurya*, the highest stage, as mentioned above. In other words, each iteration of love contains elements of the former iteration, as suggested in UN 14.60: "[In this way, the progressive stages of love] may be compared to a seed, the sugar cane plant, sugar cane juice, molasses, solidified molasses, granulated sugar, refined sugar and rock candy." Commenting on this verse, Viśvanātha Cakravartī illuminates the analogy: "One object, by changing its previous state, takes on a new name according to its more developed level of excellence. This is shown with the example of a seed, which becomes a sprout and, soon, a stalk. Similarly, *rati* becomes *prema*. This produces juice, which is analogous to *sneha*. Juice produces molasses, *māna*, which eventually becomes solid, i.e., *praṇaya*. After this, it becomes sugar, or *rāga*, and then refined sugar, or *anurāga*. Finally, it becomes rock candy, which is comparable to *mahābhāva*." See also UN 14.219 (along with the commentaries of Jīva and Viśvanātha):

"*Mādana*, the essence of *hlādinī-śakti*, is superior to *mohana*, and it makes all prior *bhāvas* blossom as never before; these qualities are fully present in Rādhā."

7. Of course, one can say that *praṇaya* is a more fundamental level than *prema-vilāsa-vivarta*. But it should be remembered, too, that there is necessarily a form of *praṇaya* in the higher stages as well, as per endnote 6. According to the saint-scholar Ananta Dāsa Bābājī (1925–2018), "When *praṇaya* becomes intense, then mind and intelligence become one, and a sweet meeting takes place. *Praṇaya* is an essential ingredient in *prema-vilāsa-vivarta*. If there was no loving intimacy and a feeling of union devoid of awe and reverence under all circumstances, how could such pastimes exist?" (https://gaudiyadiscussions.gaudiya.com/topic_23.html)

8. The standard *sāttvika-bhāvas*, or the outward manifestation of spiritual emotion, are usually delineated as follows: *stambha* (paralysis), *sveda* (perspiration), *romāñca* (horripilation, or hair standing on end), *svarabheda* (voice change), *vepathu* (trembling), *vaivarṇya* (bodily color change), *aśru* (weeping), and *pralaya* (fainting).

9. See *Śrīmad Bhāgavatam* 10.31.15. Also see Śrīla Bhaktivinoda Ṭhākura, *Jaiva Dharma*, *Our Eternal Nature*, Bhaktivedānta Nārāyaṇa Mahārāja, Araṇya Mahārāja, et. al., translation (Mathura: Gauḍīya Vedānta Publications, 2002), Chapter 36.

10. Although most of these higher levels of love are within the provenance of *mādhurya-rasa*, they sometimes manifest in other *rasas* as well. For example, Krishna's intimate cowherd playmates, such as the *priya-narma-sakhās*, are known to experience a similar mood in relation to Krishna. Specifically, Subāla and others in his camp are privy to (*rūḍha*) *mahābhāva*, a level often said to be unique to the *gopīs*. (14.233, see also *Jaiva Dharma*, Chapter 36) Still, *mādanākhya-mahābhāva*, the highest level of love, is found only in the heart of Rādhikā, though it expands into the hearts of her personal *sakhīs* as well, for they are her *kāya-vyūha*, or immediate expansions and assistants—they are said to be alternate versions of her very self. Thus, like Rādhā, they relish an inconceivably high form of *mahābhāva*. And under their guidance, the *mañjaris*, too, experience such divine affection to the fullest. In fact, the tradition teaches that because of their relation to Rādhā, the *sakhīs* and *mañjaris* can experience even more than Krishna, as suggested in the

Caitanya-caritāmṛta (Madhya 8.210): "When the nectar of Krishna's pastimes is sprinkled on that creeper, the happiness derived by the twigs, flowers and leaves is ten million times greater than that derived by the creeper itself." Consequently, in Gaura-līlā, Krishna himself falls at their feet and even takes *śikṣā* from them. Parenthetically, the tradition avers that Śrī Chaitanya Mahāprabhu, who partakes of Rādhā's nature, also naturally experiences the highest levels of *mahābhāva*; this will be the subject of our paper's latter portion.

11. Śrī Rūpa makes it clear in *Ujjvala-nīlamaṇi* (15.182) that, in this work, he abbreviated the various levels of divine love, hoping that the finished volume would not be too unwieldy: "The states of love described herein are ordinary for the different types of *prema*. The extraordinary states have not been described for fear of making the volume too large." (*etās tu prema-bhedānām anubhāvatayā daśāḥ | sādhāraṇyaḥ samastānāṁ prāyaśaḥ sambhavanty api*) This may be a partial explanation of why *prema-vilāsa-vivarta* is not directly mentioned in the UN. That said, it is clearly alluded to in various texts, such as 14.155 (the one quoted by Rāmānanda Rāya), where we may especially note Viśvanātha Cakravartī's commentary: "Their hearts are like lac, melted by the heat of *prema*, or have become liquid by the heat of fire. This indicates *sneha* ... The hearts merge (*yunjan*)."

12. Of the three, Jagadānanda's work comes closest to discussing the subject at hand, though in a somewhat disguised format. The first three introductory sequences of *Śrī Śrī Prema-vivarta* evoke the "*rādhā-kṛṣṇa-praṇaya-vikṛtir* . . ." verse (*Caitanya-caritāmṛta*: Ādi-līlā, 1.5), wherein we learn about the oneness of Rādhā and Krishna, how they become two, and then become one again in Śrī Chaitanya. I have elaborated on this verse elsewhere in this article. The second verse again tells us, "The Absolute is sometimes two, as Rādhā and Krishna, and sometimes one, as Śrī Chaitanya, the Supreme Being." (*sei tattva kabhu dui rādhā-kṛṣṇa-rūpe kabhu eka parātpara chaitanya-svarūpe*) This articulation hints at *prema-vilāsa-vivarta*. Chapter Five is called "*Vivarta-vilāsa-sevā*," and Chapter Fourteen, "*Viparīta Vivarta*"—thus we see quite a bit of the same terminology one finds in discourses on *prema-vilāsa-vivarta*. In this way, Jagadānanda introduces his readers to the concept in a nutshell. Even so, conceptually, one has to read between the lines to find it in this particular text, and the phrase itself is never mentioned.

13. Here are but a few examples: Sudhindra Chandra Chakravarti, *Philosophical Foundations of Bengal Vaiṣṇavism* (Calcutta: Academic Publishers, 1969), 352, writes: "While closing his account of the highest stage of *Mādhurya-bhakti* with a song composed by him, Rāmānanda designates this experience as *Prema-vilāsa-vivarta* (maturing of the display of love)." Similarly Bhaktivinoda Ṭhākura writes in his *Amṛta-pravāha-bhāṣya* (commentary) to *Caitanya-caritāmṛta* 2.8.194: "This highest platform of divine love is the messenger of *prema-vilāsa-vivarta*, in which there is an experience of union even during separation." Finally, Śrīla A. C. Bhaktivedanta Swami Prabhupāda, in his book, *Śrī Rāmānanda Samvāda: In Search of the Ultimate Goal of Life* (California: Mandala Publishing, 2004), 70, writes: "This sort of feeling during separation of the lover and the beloved is called *prema-vilāsa-vivarta*, which is the topmost sentiment in loving affairs." And also, p. 72: "In concluding this explanation of *prema-vilāsa-vivarta*, the highest stage of transcendental relationships, Lord Caitanya said ... 'Now I understand the topmost limit of the ultimate goal of life. This has been possible by your grace. The goal cannot be reached without the endeavor of the devotee and the mercy of a pure devotee. Please therefore let me now know the means of reaching this topmost goal.'"

14. The exoteric reason for Mahāprabhu covering Rāmānanda Rāya's mouth is found in the *Caitanya-caritāmṛta* (2.8.193), particularly in Prabhupāda's commentary. The esoteric reason is related in Śrī Śrīmad Bhaktivedānta Nārāyaṇa Gosvāmī Mahārāja, *Śrī Rāya Rāmānanda Samvāda* (Vrindavan: Gaudiya Vedanta Publications, 2009), 177: "Śrī Gaurahari wished to conceal His nature as being Śrī Kṛṣṇa internally, covered by a golden complexion. He did not want Śrī Rāmānanda Rāya to reveal His identity, so He covered Rāmānanda's mouth before he could utter this fact." This view is also suggested in the writings of Śrīla B. R. Śrīdhar Mahārāja. See Swami B. R. Śrīdhar, *Encounters with Divinity: The Path of Dedication, Vol. II* (Bangalore: Gosai Publishers, 2005), 199.

15. In addition to the traditional texts on the subject and the commentaries of the *ācāryas*, what follows is a partial list of devotees, friends, and scholars that I consulted as well: Śrīla B. V. Nārāyaṇa Mahārāja, Prem Prayojan Prabhu, Bhanu Swami, Tripurāri Mahārāja, Rasikānanda Swami, Dhanurdhara Swami, Śrīvāsa Prabhu, Revatī Dāsī, Uttamaśloka Prabhu, Mukunda Prabhu, Jan Brzezinski

(Jagadānanda), Abhishek Ghosh, Śyāmarāṇī Dāsī, Satyanārāyaṇa Dāsa Bābājī, Navadvīpa Prabhu, Advaita Prabhu, Reverend David Carter, H. D. Resnick, Joshua Greene, and others.

16. The tradition asserts that Rādhā and Krishna are actually embodied forms of this omnipotent love—the energies of *hlādinī* (blissful experience) and *saṁvit* (cognition) combined. Accordingly, they allow their love to actually exert control over them (*prema-vaśyaḥ*). Indeed, according to the *Bhakti-rasāmṛta-sindhu* (1.1.41), "Having made Hari [Krishna] the vessel of love, along with his dear ones, this *prema-bhakti* is called *śrī-kṛṣṇākarṣiṇī* [the attractor of Krishna]—verily, it brings him under its complete control." (*śrī-kṛṣṇākarṣiṇī—kṛtvā hariṃ prema-bhājaṃ priya-varga-samanvitam | bhaktir vaśīkarotīti śrī-kṛṣṇākarṣiṇī matā*) That is to say, in the Gauḍīya tradition, divine love (*prema*) is supreme. What does that mean in the present context? Following Viśvanātha Cakravartī's commentary on *Ujjvala-nīlamaṇi* 14.154 (see full verse below), we learn that the word "*sva*" in the compound phrase *sva-saṁvedya-daśā* refers to *anurāga* as it expands into *mahābhāva*, thus becoming "self-aware." To say that the Divine Couple's love becomes self-aware is to say that they lose their sense of individuality and instead identify with that love, almost as an entity unto itself. And as they become fully absorbed in that experience, it is as if they are becoming a third person. In other words, love itself becomes the dominant force, overtaking both Rādhā and Krishna according to their implicit desire.

All of this is based on Śrīla Rūpa Gosvāmī's *Ujjvala-nīlamaṇi*, with particular attention to 14.154, cited here with the incorporated commentaries of Jīva and Viśvanātha: "When *anurāga* reaches a special state of intensity, it is known as *bhāva*. This state of intensity has three characteristics: (1) *anurāga* reaches the state of *sva-saṁvedya*, *which means that it becomes the object of its own experience* (italics added), (2) it becomes *prakāśita*, radiantly manifest, which means that all eight *sāttvika-bhāvas* become prominently displayed, and (3) it attains *yāvad-āśraya-vṛtti*, in which the previous stages of *praṇaya* and *rāga*—especially the oneness of body and mind felt in *praṇaya*—come to their crescendo, catapulting *anurāga* into *bhāva*. It then spreads its influence to all devotees who are ready to embrace it."

The significance of this verse in terms of *prema-vilāsa-vivarta* is as follows: It immediately precedes the verse quoted in the

Caitanya-caritāmṛta (from the same *Ujjvala-nīlamaṇi*) by Rāmānanda Rāya, wherein he succinctly utters the truth of *prema-vilāsa-vivarta* and establishes its conceptual framework for the tradition. That is to say, Text 154 cites the essential characteristics of the highest love, including its ever-growing transformations, while 155, cites an example of this love in terms of Rādhā and Krishna, thus offering a complete overview of the subject.

17. In Indian philosophy, one typically encounters the notion of *vivarta*, or "transformation," within a Śaṅkarite or Advaitin context. That particular school of thought, known as Vivartavāda, centers on the idea that the visible world is nothing more than an illusion, an unreal manifestation or transformation of Brahman (spiritual substance). This understanding is fostered by the traditional "rope-snake analogy," which runs as follows. Imagine, if you will, that a person enters a dark room and suddenly sees a snake. He draws back in fear, but then, upon turning on the lights, he sees that the "snake" is actually just a large curled up piece of twined rope. In this analogy, the snake represents the material world, which is illusory, while the rope represents the overarching truth of Brahman. The light that helps us distinguish truth from illusion comes from spiritual aids, such as scripture, or the guru, which allow us to see the truth as it is, to distinguish the snake from the rope. Extrapolating from this example, Vivartavādīs say that the varieties we see around us, which are part of our darkened world, are false, just as the snake in the analogy is false. When we are enlightened, they say, we see that all varieties are just illusions, that they are simply unreal. Vaishnava philosophers, however, point out that while the rope is certainly not a snake, snakes as such are not false. That is, in reality, both snakes and ropes exist, and the illusion is merely when we mistake one for the other. Similarly, this world, which is full of varieties, is not a mere illusion, as the Vivartavādīs say; instead, it is a reflection of the reality in the Vaikuṇṭha world, the spiritual world, which is also full of variety. The *Śrīmad Bhāgavatam*, in fact, includes numerous examples that use the analogy in a Vaishnava way (see, for instance, 4.22.38, 6.9.37, and 10.6.8). While the above is a summary of the standard rope-snake analogy as expressed in various schools of Indian thought, Bhaktivinoda Ṭhākura, in his commentary on the *Caitanya-caritāmṛta*, Madhya 8.194 (*Amṛta-pravāha*), goes further, fully reclaiming the analogy for Vaishnavas by using it to describe

the profound illusion produced by the highest levels of love, specifically *prema-vilāsa-vivarta,* wherein Rādhā and Krishna lose their sense of self-identity, thinking each is the other. It is to be noted that while the usual snake-rope analogy focuses on *jaḍa-vivarta* (mundane delusion), *prema-vilāsa-vivarta* focuses on *divya-vivarta* (divine delusion).

18. The words *vilāsa* and *līlā* are interrelated, although likely derived from completely different roots (√las & √lī respectively). Some argue that the root of the word *līlā* remains unknown. That said, vi+√lās, like *līlā*, means "to play, sport, dally, and to be amused or delighted." Thus, *vilāsa* can, by way of a general, initial definition, be interchangeable with *līlā*, but the latter more suggests play, imitation, etc., while *vilāsa* moves more towards sensuality, erotic dance, and even lovemaking. To summarize: In common parlance, *līlā* refers to play or sport, and *vilāsa* is the enjoyment of that play.

19. It may be questioned how a divinity like Rādhā or Krishna can fall into "illusion." This is a complex subject, and many Vaishnava writers attempt to explain it to practitioners' satisfaction. Suffice it to say, God's illusion is unlike ours. When we fall into illusion, it takes us away from reality. This is known as *mahā-māyā*. But God's "illusion," and that of his close associates, bring them closer to each other, closer to ultimate reality. It is the opposite of illusion as we know it. This is called *yoga-māyā*. Expressed another way, the word *tattva* represents hard fact, or "truth," *līlā* means "the Lord's play," and *rasa* means "relationship" (through which he plays). From the Gauḍīya perspective, *līlā* and *rasa* are higher than *tattva*, for the former allows practitioners to partake of a yet higher truth. For more on this subject, see Viśvanātha Cakravartī Ṭhākura, *Rāga-vartma-cāṇḍrikā*, Second Illumination, Text 6, where this is elucidated with graphic examples. Starting in verse 1 of that section we learn that Krishna can simultaneously be both bewildered and omniscient, for he is unlimited and inconceivable, and thus need not adhere to our laws of logic. For the sake of his pastimes, in which he interacts with his close associates, he is both *mugdhatā* (innocently unaware) and *sarvajñatā* (all-knowing), and in this way he relishes exchange with his devotees. Otherwise, it would not be possible for an unlimited being to function in a world of three dimensions. Again, one must keep in mind the distinction between *jaḍa-vivarta* and *divya-vivarta*.

20. See Krishnadāsa Kavirāja, *Caitanya-caritāmṛta*, edited with the commentary *Gaura-kṛpā-taraṅgiṇī-ṭīkā* by Rādhāgovinda Nātha, 4th ed., 6 vols. (Kalikātā: Sādhanā Prakāṣanī, 1952), Vol 1, pp. 231-232.

21. *ibid.*

22. *ibid.*

23. I am here using the translation of His Divine Grace A. C. Bhaktivedanta Swami Prabhupāda, translation, and commentary, Krishnadāsa Kavirāja Goswāmī's *Śrī Caitanya-caritāmṛta*, 9-volume set (Los Angeles, California, 1996, reprint), 2.8.194.

24. *ibid.*, 2.8.195.

25. Cupid (from the Latin *cupido*, meaning "desire") is the god of erotic love, traceable to Roman and Greek mythology. In the Indic tradition, he is sometimes identified with the demigod Kāmadeva, though the name is also periodically used for Krishna's son, Pradyumna. It is also used as a name for Krishna himself, and sometimes, as in the *Caitanya-caritāmṛta*, as a divine messenger who instigates loving emotions.

26. For the significance of the word "*paraikya,*" or "supreme oneness," see Kavi Karṇapūra, *Kṛṣṇa-Caitanya Caritāmṛtam Mahākāvyam,* edited with an introduction and Bengali translation by Prāṇa-kiśora Gosvāmī (Kolkata: Śrī Gaurāṅga Maṇḍira, n.d.), Verse 13.45. See also Śrī Kavi Karṇapūra, *Caitanya-candrodaya-nāṭaka* (7.83 and 87), for the oneness of Rādhā and Krishna. Although he doesn't use the term *prema-vilāsa-vivarta*, he describes its essence: "Śrī Rādhā says: 'I no longer think in terms of, 'I am your beloved and you are my lover.' For us, the conception of 'I' and 'you' has been macerated. I no longer sense any distinction between us. It seems like Cupid has ground our hearts together in the most intense way, dusting them with the nectar of perfect love."

27. See Śrī Śrīmad Gour Govinda Swami Mahārāja, *Mathura Meets Vrindavan* (Bhubaneswar, Orissa, Gopal Jiu Publications, 2003), 111-112.

28. O. B. L. Kapoor, *Śrī Chaitanya and Rāgānuga Bhakti* (Vrindavan U.P.: The Vaishnava Book Trust, 1995), 3-4.

29. See Viśvanātha Cakravartī Ṭhākura, *Śrī Kṛṣṇa-Bhāvanāmṛta*, translated by Advaita Dāsa (Vrindavan U.P: Ras Bihari Lal and Sons, 2000), Chapter 18, Texts 37, and 45-57.

30. *ibid.*

31. Wulff, Donna M., *Drama as a Mode of Religious Realization: the Vidagdhamādhava of Rūpa Gosvāmī*, American Academy of Religion, Academy Series (Chico, CA: Scholars Press, 1984), Act Six: See especially Text 7.

32. *ibid.*, 123-124.

33. See Bhaktivinoda Ṭhākura, *Amṛta-pravāha-bhāṣya* to *Caitanya-caritāmṛta* (2.8.194).

34. See His Divine Grace A. C. Bhaktivedanta Swami Prabhupāda, *Caitanya-caritāmṛta*, Madhya 8.194, purport.

35. See Shrivasta Goswami, "Rādhā: The Play and Perfection of Rasa," in John Stratton Hawley and Donna Marie Wulff (eds.), *The Divine Consort: Rādhā and the Goddesses of India* (Berkeley religious studies series, 1982), 87.

36. See Viśvanātha Cakravartī Ṭhākura, *Śrī Kṛṣṇa-Bhāvanāmṛta*, *op. cit.*, Chapter Three, Texts 14, 38-64. It starts in chapter 1, when the Divine Couple initially wake up, and then again when they get caught in chapter 2, exposed for wearing each other's clothes.

37. Of course, the subject of *bhedābheda* is vast, spanning the entire gamut of Indian philosophy, but it exists in a distinct form in the Gauḍīya tradition, as conceived by Jīva Goswāmī in his auto-commentary to *Paramātmā Sandarbha* (Anuccheda 77, 78). For an in-depth view of the notion of *acintya-bhedābheda*—Śrī Jīva's particular version of "inconceivable and simultaneous oneness and difference"—as an explanation for all reality, with special attention to the interrelation of Krishna and his various energies, see Steven J. Rosen, "Deferring to Difference: The Essence of Śrī Chaitanya's Acintya-Bhedābheda Vedānta," *Journal of Vaishnava Studies*, Volume 25, No. 1 (fall 2016), 223-248.

38. B. R. Śrīdhara Swami, *The Golden Volcano of Divine Love* (Nadiya, West Bengal: Sri Chaitanya Saraswat Math, 1996, reprint), 10.

39. In addition to *Caitanya-caritāmṛta* Ādi 1.5, already quoted, see Ādi 4.230: "Desiring to (1) understand the depth of Rādhā's love, (2) the incomparable sweetness of Krishna's nature through her eyes, and (3) the bliss that Rādhā feels due to that sweetness, the Supreme Lord Hari, draping himself in her emotions, appeared from Śacī-devī's womb [as Chaitanya] just as the moon appears from the ocean." Also see Madhya 2.80: "During his previous incarnation in Vṛndāvana, Lord

Krishna wanted to enjoy these three forms of ecstasy, but despite his best efforts, they evaded him, for they are solely tasted by Śrī Rādhā. Therefore, Śrī Krishna accepted her mood of love in the form of Śrī Chaitanya." There are numerous verses to this effect.

40. "On the one hand," writes Vaishnava scholar Prem Prayojan Prabhu, "Kṛṣṇa is consumed with greed to taste the highest love, in which Rādhā loses awareness of her individuality. And on the other, Rādhā ardently dreams of fulfilling all of Kṛṣṇa's desires. Inevitably, their mutual emotions arising from *samvit* and *hlādinī*, find the support of *sandhinī* (being), resulting in the coming into being of a combined form of Rādhā and Kṛṣṇa, in which Kṛṣṇa takes on the golden complexion of Rādhā and experiences her otherwise inaccessible sentiments. This *prema-vilāsa vivarta mūrti*, the extraordinary form in which Kṛṣṇa finally fulfills his desire to experience *prema-vilāsa vivarta*, is Śrī Chaitanya Mahāprabhu." See Prem Prayojan Dāsa, "The Ontology of a Tīrtha: Śrī Navadvīpa Dhāma in Gauḍīya Vaiṣṇavism," in *Journal of Vaishnava Studies*, Volume 27, No. 1 (Fall 2018), 120.

41. See Krishnadāsa Kavirāja, *Caitanya-caritāmṛta*, edited with the commentary *Gaura-kṛpā-taraṅgiṇī-ṭīkā* by Rādhāgovinda Nātha, op. cit., Volume 1 (*Bhūmika*), 239.

42. See O. B. L. Kapoor, *Śrī Chaitanya and Rāgānuga Bhakti* (Vrindavan U.P.: The Vaishnava Book Trust, 1995), 4.

43. I am indebted to Śrī Prahlāda (Ace Simpson) for the specifics in this list. (personal correspondence, 3-8-23)

44. It is our thesis that *prema-vilāsa-vivarta* can exist in various iterations, as we have seen in the example of Rādhārāṇī mistaking the black *tamāla* tree for Krishna. In other words, certain qualities normally associated with this highest stage of love, such as inversion (*viparīta*), or the absence of distinction (*bheda-rāhitya*), might be unavailable in a given pastime, but that need not disqualify it from being an instance of *prema-vilāsa-vivarta*. To wit: Regarding the black *tamāla* tree incident, we may note the following. While Śrī Rādhā saw the tree as Krishna, she did not personally identify with it, nor did she become one with it. Yet the pastime is still cited by Gauḍīya authorities as an example of *prema-vilāsa-vivarta*. With this in mind, let us consider that Mahāprabhu is known to have experienced all aspects of Rādhā-bhāva. In general, it is said that these higher moods of love are peculiar to Rādhā, but in as much as the *gopīs* and Mahāprabhu take part in Śrī

Rādhā's inner moods, they too can partake of *prema-vilāsa-vivarta*, if not to the same degree or in the same way that Rādhā does.

It might be argued that I am being too liberal with my extension of *prema-vilāsa-vivarta*, and that it should solely be used in ways that align with its primary definition as per the *Caitanya-caritāmṛta*. To be sure, Kavirāja Gosvāmī uses the term in a specific way, but there are more general ways that the term can be used, too, as when Bhaktivinoda and Śrīla Prabhupāda apply it to the black *tamāla* tree. One further example may be cited as well: Śrīla Nārāyaṇa Mahārāja writes: "When Madhu-maṅgala says, 'O Rādhā, Madhusūdana has gone away,' Śrī Rādhā begins to lament in separation from Him, even though Śrī Kṛṣṇa is right next to Her. This is *prema-vilāsa-vivarta*." He further writes, "*Prema-vilāsa* means 'loving pastimes,' and *vivarta* indicates '*prema-vaicittya*.'" Of course, *prema-vaicittya* constitutes a separate area of *prema* altogether, as defined in the *Ujjvala-nīlamaṇi* (see 15.4, 15.147, 150, 151). But Nārāyaṇa Mahārāja finds enough resonance to acknowledge its kinship to *prema-vilāsa-vivarta*, indicating that there are both primary and secondary definitions of the term. See Śrī Śrīmad Bhaktivedānta Nārāyaṇa Gosvāmī Mahārāja, *Śrī Rāya Rāmānanda Samvāda* (Vrindavan: Gaudiya Vedanta Publications, 2009), 173. Incidentally, Nārāyaṇa Mahārāja is here following Śrīla Bhaktisiddhānta Sarasvatī, who aligns the two in the following way in his *Caitanya-caritāmṛta* commentary (*Anubhāṣya* on Madhya 8.191): "The *vilāsa-vaicitrya* and *vilāsa-vivarta* of *mohana-mādanādi adhirūḍha-mahābhāva* that exists within *prema-vaicittya* [that is *antargata* to *prema-vaicittya*] is expressed in Śrī Rāmānanda Rāya's song."

45. See Krishnadāsa Kavirāja, *Caitanya-caritāmṛta*, edited with the commentary *Gaura-kṛpā-taraṅgiṇī-ṭīkā* by Rādhāgovinda Nātha, *op. cit.*, Volume 1 (Bhūmika), 238-239.

46. *ibid.*

47. *ibid.*

48. *ibid.*

49. Personal correspondence with Abhishek Ghosh (June 14, 2023). For *prema-vilāsa-vivarta*'s connection to Vedānta, also see Also Haridāsa Dāsa, *Gauḍīya Vaiṣṇava Abhidhāna* (Navadvīpa: Haribola Kuṭīra, 1957, reprint, Kolkata, Sanskrit Pustak Bhandar, 2014), especially Vol. 1, p. 506.

Afterword

SO WHAT IS ONE TO MAKE of Śrī Chaitanya? Encyclopedias, Hindu scholars, practitioners, and authorities on Indian religion view him variously, calling him "saint," "*avatāra*," and everything in between. As should by now be clear, he could neatly fit into all these categories, and yet he was, according to those who seriously study him, so much more. Naturally, any such labels can hardly do him justice.

Indeed, the scholar/saint Bhaktivinoda Ṭhākura suggests that how one views him, in this sense, really doesn't matter—what matters is that we consider his teachings deeply, taking full advantage of the process he brought to this world for human edification:

> We leave it to our readers to decide how to deal with Mahaprabhu. The Vaishnavas have accepted Him as the great Lord, Shri Krishna Himself . . . . Those who are not prepared to accept this perspective may think of Lord Chaitanya as a noble and holy teacher. That is all we want our readers to believe . . . . We make no objection if the reader does not believe His miracles, as miracles alone never demonstrate Godhead. Demons like Ravana and others have also worked miracles and these do not prove that they were gods. It is unlimited love and its overwhelming influence that would be seen in God Himself.[1]

In light of this liberal perspective, we leave our readers

with the insights of a Christian scholar whose religious sensibility stands far outside the formal Vaishnava tradition. Although these insights may not accurately reflect the full Gauḍīya Vaishnava view of who Mahāprabhu is, at least in terms of his complete ontological identity and unique spirituality, it does capture certain essential traits, or aspects of his personality, and a wide range of emotional components that his life and mission bring into sharp focus:

> If I were asked to choose one man in Indian religious history who best represents the pure spirit of devotional self-giving, I would choose the Vaishnavite saint Chaitanya, whose full name in religion was Krishna-Chaitanya, or "Krishna consciousness." Of all the saints in recorded history, East or West, he seems to me the supreme example of a soul carried away on a tide of ecstatic love of God. This extraordinary man, who belongs to the rich period beginning with the end of the fourteenth century, represents the culmination of the devotional schools that grew up around Krishna . . . . Chaitanya delighted intensely in nature. It is said that, like St. Francis of Assisi, he had a miraculous power over wild beasts. His life in the holy town of Puri is the story of a man in a state of almost continuous spiritual intoxication. Illuminating discourses, deep contemplation, moods of loving communion with God, were daily occurrences.[2]

What more needs to be said? Oh, yes: Chant and be happy.

Endnotes

1. Bhaktivinode Ṭhākura, *Shri Chaitanya Mahaprabhu: His Life and Precepts* (Madras: Sree Gaudiya Math, 1896; reprint, 1984), 60–61.

2. John Moffitt, *Journey to Gorakhpur: An Encounter with Christ Beyond Christianity* (New York, N.Y.: Holt, Rinehart, and Winston, 1972), 129, 135–136.

STEVEN J. ROSEN (Satyaraja Dasa) is a biographer, scholar and author in the fields of philosophy, Indic religion, and comparative spirituality. He is the founding editor of the *Journal of Vaishnava Studies* and associate editor of *Back to Godhead* magazine. A disciple of His Divine Grace A.C. Bhaktivedanta Swami, his thirty-plus books include *Essential Hinduism* (Rowman & Littlefield); *Yoga of Kirtan: Conversations on the Sacred Art of Chanting* (FOLK Books); *Krishna's Other Song: A New Look at the Uddhava Gita* (Praeger-Greenwood); and *Sri Chaitanya's Life and Teachings: The Golden Avatara of Divine Love* (Lexington Books).

www.ingramcontent.com/pod-product-compliance
Lightning Source LLC
Chambersburg PA
CBHW031603110426
42742CB00037B/822
9781880404591